D0986500

To our daughter Ingrid

赵琳

Shifting Tides

Culture in Contemporary China

AN INTERMEDIATE CHINESE COURSE

SIMPLIFIED CHARACTER EDITION

HONG GANG JIN
靳洪刚

DE BAO XU
许德宝

WITH

SONGREN CUI
崔颂人

YEA-FEN CHEN
陈雅芬

YIN ZHANG
章吟

Photography by
Laurie A. Wittlinger

Cheng & Tsui Company
Boston • Worcester

Copyright © 2003
Hong Gang Jin, De Bao Xu
with Songren Cui, Yea-fen Chen, and Yin Zhang

All rights reserved. No part of this publication may be reproduced or transmitted in any form or
by any means, electronic or mechanical, including photocopying, recording, scanning, or any information
storage or retrieval system, without written permission from the publisher.

Published by

Cheng & Tsui Company
25 West Street
Boston, MA 02111-1213 USA
Fax (617) 426-3669
www.cheng-tsui.com
"Bringing Asia to the World"™

Printed in the U.S.A.

09 08 07 06   10 9 8 7 6 5 4 3 2

Library of Congress Control Number: 2002115108

(Simplified Character Edition)

Book and 2 Audio CDs, ISBN 0-88727-372-6

目 录

课文
(Texts)

附录
(Appendixes)

Acknowledgments

We would like to express our heartfelt thanks to those people who have been most instrumental to this project. Among them are our special student, Laurie Wittlinger, who took spectacular photographs for the book while she was a project assistant at Hamilton College, Qunhu Li who worked very hard to help acquire permission from Tianjin TV Station to use their TV segments, and the students of the Associated Colleges in China (Hamilton College's China Program) who appear in the photographs. Without these visually valuable pictures, the book would not be as effective and attractive as it is.

We also deeply appreciate the professors, instructors, and students of Associated Colleges in China (ACC) for their valuable comments and suggestions at the various stages of the project. Among them are Professor Hsin-hsin Liang who offered many valuable suggestions based on her own first-hand teaching experiences and ACC instructors Yin Zhang, Chunxue Yang, Wenzheng Liu, Fei Wang, Chen Wang, and many others who proof-read early drafts and made comments. Our special thanks also go to our four-year student assistant, Megan Manchester, for her English editing at the initial stage, and our Chinese students Joshua Jenkins and Benjamin Zoll for their time and efforts on this project.

We would also like to acknowledge the people who have assisted us throughout the six years of the project development. Among them are Pei Pei who has been a hard working assistant in collecting authentic materials for us, Dana Hubbard for her kind assistance in picture scanning and editing, and Amy James for her assistance in selecting pictures.

We are especially grateful for Vivian Ling who has done a superb job editing the book and providing the most valuable comments and suggestions.

We would like to thank Jill Cheng for her support for this project and her faith in us, and Sandra Korinchak, Production Manager at Cheng & Tsui, who worked patiently with us to ensure the quality of the book. Finally, our special thanks go to Tianjin TV Station and Beijing TV Station for their generosity to allow us to use their TV segments.

前言

　　《中国之路》是为学过三至四个学期以上中文学生设计的一套语言文化教科书。这套教材旨在通过一系列中国的社会文化主题让学生了解和掌握表达、讨论、以及分析问题时所需要的一系列语言结构和交流方式。

　　自1997年开始，《中国之路》就在美国部分大学、美国政府机关、北京的ACC汉语中心和其他语言项目进行试用，至今已经修改了五版，实验使用了近五年。《中国之路》主要由课本和配合课本的光盘组成。

一、教学目的与教学设计

　　多年的教学实践和理论研究告诉我们，中级汉语教学的目标应集中在以下三个方面：第一、培养学生在目标语国家进行生活和思想文化交流的基本能力；第二、培养学生有目的地、有效地使用整句或段落来表达思想、进行交流，以作好向篇章过渡的准备；第三，训练学生利用已知信息和已经掌握的语言结构对新的语言信息进行科学推理、猜测的能力，以便在真实语境下进行语言文化交流。除了以上三个方面，我们还认为中级汉语的学习是进入目标语社会、与当地人进行思想文化交流的一个十分关键的阶段，中级汉语的教学目标也应放在真情实景的教学上，不但应该为学生去目标语国家留学或在目标语国家生活和学习作好充分的准备，而且应该让学生能最大限度地利用语言环境进行语言文化方面的学习和交流。基于以上几个目的，我们设计了《中国之路》一书。下面是我们在设计全书时遵循的一些原则：

　　（一）在教材选择上，尽量选择来自不同媒体的中国社会、文化、经济、科学技术、以及文学艺术的有关报道，做到每一课的题目都具有一定的思想性、代表性、讨论性和扩展性，让学生感觉到语言学习是一种在真实语境下、有社会背景的、自发的、有思想和有目的的实际交流。

　　（二）在文体选择上，尽量采用叙述、描述、介绍、对话和采访等形式，先以短文介绍社会文化背景，然后用真实媒体引出和展开讨论的主题。

　　（三）在教学重点的设计上，打破以前语法重点就是教学重点的旧框框，将教学重点放在以交流为中心的多个语言层次上。每一课的语言重点不局限于较复杂的语法结构，而是从词汇、语法、语义、语用等多个层次出发决定每课的重点。此外，我们还将课文中出现的语言结构分为两大类：一类是交际价值较高的重点结构，另一类为语法或语义较复杂、容易成为理解障碍的基本结构。第一类是每课练习的重点，要通过不同类型和不同形式的解释与练习让学生掌握并使用自如；第二类是帮助学生预习课文、进行课堂有效交流的必要知识，大都以参考阅读和课文脚注的形式出现。

（四）在教学安排上，坚持以句型串词汇的教学法，即句型领先、词汇辅助的原则。首先帮助学生理解和巩固句型在交流中的作用以及在整句中的基本位置和使用限制，然后帮助学生建立词汇和句型的联系以正确运用词汇。使用这种方法可以避免以词汇为中心的教材常见弊端（例如，学生往往出现语言表达零散、简单，交际不连贯问题等）。

（五）在练习设计上，采用以语言结构为中心和以语言功能为中心的两种练习。首先让学生有重点地练习在交际中必须用到的一些结构和词汇，在此基础上，学生再将所学结构和词汇运用到与之相应的语言功能上。语言功能的练习突出真实语境下的交流以及对学习策略的培养，如猜测能力，推理能力等等。

（六）在教材媒体的选择和版面设计上，尽量采用多种媒体形式，如电视报道、报纸杂志，公益广告以及图象信息等以加强语料的真实性和视觉效果。

二、课文内容及设计

　　《中国之路》共有课文十二篇，题目包括：慈母之爱、独生子女、人际关系、个体与赚钱、家庭结构、下岗女工、婚姻问题、科技发展、隐私讨论、摇滚歌星、住房问题、城市污染等。围绕每一个主题，课文均介绍一系列与之相关的语言交际功能，例如：举例、说明、定义、描述、叙述、对比、分析、理解因果关系等等。另外，这十二个话题在介绍中国文化的同时，突出强调中国改革开放以后的变化。每课的素材均来自当代中国媒体的报道，包括电视、书籍、报纸、杂志、因特网及公益广告等，以充分反映当代中国的风貌。比如"文化比较"一课即以一个真实的电视公益广告为背景，抓住隐私这个对中国人来说的新概念，让学生充分讨论和比较中西文化的不同。在讨论的过程中，也使学生认识到语言学习不单纯是一个语言形式的学习，也是一种联系个人、充分分析和比较、讨论和认识，乃至批判研究的过程。

　　每篇课文一般由三个主要部分组成：课文、语言重点和练习。
　　（一）课文部分分为三个分项：课文、生词以及课文注释。课文一般由两个部分组成，采用各种不同文体：第一部分是围绕主题的介绍短文；第二部分是与主题相关的电视报道、报纸选读、文章改编等。语体形式多样，有第一人称叙述，如第一、四、七课；有对话采访等，如第二、三、六、十课；也有较为正式的新闻文体，如第十一、十二课等。

每课生词的编纂按出现顺序编号，书后附有全书生词索引，以便于查找和使用。课文注释部分将一些语法较为复杂、容易混淆的词汇以及文化知识进行详细解释、辨析。在排版上，课文注释部分与之有关的词条都有数字编号，并与有关的课文呈现在同一页上以方便学生查找。

（二）语言重点着重解释有交际价值的句型，一般每课有八到十二个。每一个重点句型下都附有课文原句，以示出处便于查找学习。句型附有详细的英文解释以说明句型使用的规则及限制。在英文解释之下，列举两个以上运用目标句型的例句以进一步说明句型使用的上下文及词汇搭配规则等。

（三）练习部分包括两种类型的活动：语言形式练习和语言功能练习。语言形式练习旨在加强学生对语言结构和词汇的掌握，通过回答问题、完成对话、听力练习、翻译和阅读短文等形式让学生在课下有重点地练习和复习课上所学的语言结构及其使用规则。在语言形式练习的基础上，学生进而转入语言功能练习。语言功能练习一般有以下几种形式：

1、段落练习：段落练习提供一个中心话题，同时明确指导学生按照所列出的语言功能使用与之相关的语法结构以及词汇讨论有关题目，使学生不但能紧紧围绕中心主题进行讨论，而且能按提供的语法结构和词汇进行有控制有难度要求的段落以上的表达。例如：在"下岗女工"一课，段落练习要求学生介绍美国的蓝领人和白领人。这种练习并不是随意性的讨论，而是要求学生通过定义和对比分析等方法，用所给的结构和词汇分三段完成讨论。

2、讨论：讨论通过不同方面的问题和话题为学生提供自由延伸和扩展语言功能和知识的机会，同时也提供学生与学生、学生与老师之间的进一步交流的机会。

3、作文：通过写作练习来进一步强化本课所学的语言功能与结构。

4、语言实践：通过课外的一系列有目的的活动来进一步加强和巩固课上所学的知识。

我们希望通过教材的新尝试来推动中级汉语教学，使之更上一层楼。

靳洪刚、许德宝
纽约克灵顿小镇
2002年10月

To Students

Welcome to *Shifting Tides: Culture in Contemporary China*. This set of textbooks uses authentic and multimedia materials to help you acquire the basic communication skills required in daily interaction with Chinese speaking people. Whether you are planning to go to China or you are in China, *Shifting Tides: Culture in Contemporary China* will help you establish a solid foundation for interaction and communication with Chinese people and to help you move on to the advanced level of language proficiency.

The topics and settings of the lessons in this text all come from the real experiences of hundreds of students who studied abroad in China and from professors who taught and lived with students in China. These topics have been rated as the most important and useful ones for living and learning in China.

In *Shifting Tides: Culture in Contemporary China*, each lesson consists of three important parts: the text, key sentence structures, and exercises. In order to help you use this textbook effectively and master as much material in the lesson as possible, we would like to make the following suggestions:

Text

We suggest that you start your class preparation with the text rather than vocabulary. Before going to your daily Chinese class, read through the text carefully at least two or three times. The first time, read along with the audio CD and try to get the gist of the story, for example, the topic sentence, the main ideas, the characters involved, the setting, etc. The second time, read for more detailed information, for example, the factual information supporting the main topic and the relationship of the setting and characters to the main idea. At the same time, you should mark down unfamiliar words and sentences and check them against the vocabulary list and grammar notes. Each time you read the text, try to comprehend the text by asking yourself questions and answering them according to the text. The questions listed in Item I of Tasks on Language Forms can be used for this purpose. After you have finished reading the text twice, write down any questions you have about the text. It is vitally important that you are familiar with the story before going to class.

Vocabulary

We suggest that you study the vocabulary list in the lesson along with the text. You can take the following three steps to learn the new words. First, while reading the text, highlight unfamiliar words and check them against the vocabulary list for Pinyin and English meaning. Second, read the sentence containing the new word(s) and try to comprehend the meaning of the entire sentence. Finally, go over the text in its entirety with the CD. In this way, you will learn new words in context rather than in isolation.

Notes

In each lesson, notes on the text are provided at the bottom of the text page. You should read them either during or after the second round of text reading. The numbers of the notes correspond to the numbers marked in the text; these numbers will help you understand the context of each note. The notes are not meant to be key structures for you to master and practice during class time. They are, however, very helpful for comprehending the text, reviewing the learnt grammar, distinguishing similar words and structures, and understanding the cultural context.

Key Sentence Patterns

Key sentence patterns are listed after the text in each lesson. Each pattern is accompanied by an original sentence from the text, a detailed grammar and usage explanation in English, and two sentences in Chinese exemplifying the usage of the structures. While studying the sentence patterns, you should pay special attention to the following three elements: (a) the communicative context of the structure; (b) the rules and constraints of the structure; and (c) the examples on the usage of the structure. It is important that you go over the sentence patterns before coming to class so that you can be ready to use the structures to engage in interaction with your instructor and your classmates. We believe conscious use of the patterns in your conversation will help increase the level of sophistication, efficiency, and accuracy in your communication.

Exercises

1. Form-oriented Tasks

A variety of form-oriented tasks are provided at the end of each lesson to help you master the key structures and vocabulary of the lesson and to help improve your ability to listen, read, and discuss in Chinese. The tasks include question-answer, dialogue completion, listening comprehension, reading comprehension, and English to Chinese translation exercises. We suggest that, while working on these exercises, you remind yourself of the new sentence patterns and new vocabulary learned in that lesson and in previous lessons. It is important to make a conscious effort to use these newly acquired structures to express your thoughts and feelings.

2. Function-oriented Tasks

After you are familiar with language forms, you must learn to apply your linguistic and cultural knowledge to real life situations. A variety of function-oriented tasks are provided in the exercises of each lesson to help you use language forms to achieve communicative functions effectively. These tasks include: (a) activities involving authentic situations; (b) discussions of various aspects of the theme of the lesson, such as "birthday celebration in different countries", "traffic and transportation in large cities", "the single-child generation", etc.; (c) language practica, which center on the same theme but are conducted outside of the classroom with Chinese speaking people. These exercises help extend your learning beyond the classroom; (d) essay writing on given topics; and (e) pictocomp, which uses picture sets and your own imagination to encourage creativity with newly acquired language forms and functions.

You should keep in mind that we purposely selected materials that are unedited and authentic for you to read and comprehend, for example, real advertisements, newspaper segments, brochures, and photographs. Because of the nature of these materials, you should expect to encounter unknown words and new structures. While you are working on performance tasks, we suggest that you keep an open mind and try to use your language knowledge, context, and cultural information to make an educated guess about the materials. Ultimately these "risk-taking" activities will prove to be helpful in developing language-learning strategies, such as tolerance of ambiguity and the ability to infer meaning by guessing and using contextual clues.

An Intermediate Chinese Course

第一课　中国人谈自己的母亲

人们对母亲的爱和感情是一样的

课文

一、简介 ⚓

虽然世界上有很多人种，也有各种文化，但是人们对母亲的爱和感情是一样的。一个人无论从哪儿来，都会讲出很多关于母亲的故事。下面就请你听听普通的中国人讲述自己母亲的故事，从他们的故事里，你可以看到中国母亲的爱和无私。你也可以看看这种母爱有没有中国文化的特色。

------ ◆❖◆ 生词 ◆❖◆ ------

1. 简介	jiǎn jiè	N.	a brief introduction
2. 谈	tán	V.	to talk about
3. 人种	rén zhǒng	N.	racial or ethnic group
4. 感情	gǎn qíng	N.	feelings, emotion
5. 无论	wú lùn	Conj.	no matter (what)
6. 关于	guān yú	Prep.	regarding
7. 故事	gù shi	N.	story
8. 下面	xià mian	Loc.	the following
9. 普通	pǔ tōng	Adj.	common, ordinary
10. 讲述	jiǎng shù	V.	to tell about, to give an account of
11. 无私	wú sī	Adj.	selfless, unselfish
12. 母爱	mǔ ài	NP.	motherly love
13. 特色	tè sè	N.	characteristics, distinguishing features

你会用下面的词吗？
简介、谈、人种、感情、无论、关于、故事、下面、普通、讲述、无私、母爱、特色

我永远不会忘记我的妈妈

二、电视节选 ■

中国母亲

每天讲述一个母亲的故事……

采访（一）：小学生付荃荃

我妈妈非常关心我。我呢，有一项爱好就是画画。我妈妈在（我）放假的时候呢，为了培养我画画这门爱好，就带我去少年宫去学习。不管刮风下雨，我妈妈都是按时让我去上课。有一次下着大雨，而且地面非常地滑。为了不让我把裤子、衣服都弄[1]湿了着凉，我妈妈就推着车，带我到车站，然后在车站看着我上（了）车才放心地回家。我上完课，妈妈还到车站去接我，然后跟我一起回家。

——— 生词 ———

14. 节选	jié xuǎn	*N/V.*	excerpt; to take an excerpt
15. 采访	cǎi fǎng	*V.*	to interview
16. 付荃荃	fù quán quán	*Personal N.*	Fu Quanquan
17. 项	xiàng	*Classifier.*	item
18. 爱好	ài hào	*N.*	interest, hobby
19. 画画	huà huà	*VO.*	to paint, to draw a picture
20. 培养	péi yǎng	*V.*	to cultivate, to nurture

Notes [1]弄 is mostly used in colloquial Chinese and is similar to 搞 or 做. It also carries a causative sense, followed by an Adjective or Verb as its complement, meaning "to make...", "to cause...". For example,

弄湿	make/get wet	弄滑	make smooth/slippery
弄好	make nice	弄坏	cause damage, to break
弄干净	make clean	弄清楚	make clear

4

21. 门	mén	*Classifier.*	item, subject
22. 少年宫	shào nián gōng	*NP.*	youth palace
23. 不管	bù guǎn	*Prep.*	regardless of
24. 刮风	guā fēng	*VO.*	(wind) blows, windy
25. 下雨	xià yǔ	*VO.*	to rain
26. 按时	àn shí	*PrepP.*	on time, on schedule
27. 地面	dì miàn	*N.*	ground
28. 滑	huá	*Adj.*	slippery
29. 裤子	kù zi	*N.*	trousers, pants
30. 弄湿	nòng shī	*VP.*	to get wet
31. 着凉	zháo liáng	*VO.*	to catch a cold
32. 推	tuī	*V.*	to push
33. 车站	chē zhàn	*N.*	bus station, bus stop, train station
34. 放心	fàng xīn	*V/Adj.*	to be at ease; feel relieved

你会用下面的词吗？
节选、采访、项、爱好、画画、培养、门、不管、刮风、下雨、按时、滑、裤子、弄湿、着凉、推、车站、放心

采访（二）：高级编辑陈明

　　我记得最清楚的就是我去上大学的那一天。我没出过远门[2]，我母亲把我的东西准备好了以后就送（我）到车站，突然间（她）就想起来还少一样东西。她赶快跑了去买。我回来一看，她给我买了很多梨。另外呢，上车以后，因为我第一次出远门，没经验，母亲就跟同

Notes [2]出远门 means 离开家到别（远）的地方去 but not in the literal sense of "going out (door)". Although we may say 页鲈睹庞, there is no 出近门 as its counterpart.

车厢的一位女同志打个招呼，说这是我的孩子，没出过远门，路上给照顾一下。这样呢，我母亲也挺会⁽³⁾说话的，那个阿姨就在路上对我照顾很多，这样，我顺利地到了学校。这件事我印象一直很深。我现在做了节目主持人，我知道做一个人应该怎么样去对待别人，别人就会怎么对待你。

生词

35. 高级	gāo jí	*Adj.*	senior, high-ranking, high class
36. 编辑	biān jí	*N./V.*	editor; to edit
37. 陈明	chén míng	*Personal N.*	Chen Ming
38. 出远门	chū yuǎn mén	*VP.*	to go far away from home
39. 突然间	tū rán jiān	*Adv.*	suddenly, unexpectedly
40. 梨	lí	*N.*	pear
41. 经验	jīng yàn	*N.*	experience
42. 车厢	chē xiāng	*N.*	train car
43. 同志	tóng zhì	*N.*	comrade
44. 打招呼	dǎ zhāo hu	*VO.*	to greet, to let (someone) know, to touch base (with someone)
45. 路上	lù shang	*PrepP.*	on the way, during the journey
46. 照顾	zhào gù	*V.*	to take care of
47. 挺	tǐng	*Adv.*	very, rather, quite
48. 会说话	huì shuō huà	*VP.*	to be a good talker
49. 阿姨	ā yí	*N.*	auntie
50. 顺利	shùn lì	*Adv/Adj.*	smoothly; smooth
51. 印象	yìn xiàng	*N.*	impression

✏️ **Notes** ⁽³⁾会 here means "good at" and is usually followed by a Verb Phrase. 我母亲也挺会说话的 (My mom was rather persuasive.) More examples:

他很会开玩笑。　　He is good at joking.
小白很会唱歌。　　Little Bai is good at singing.

52.	**一直**	yì zhí	*Adv.*	all along, continuously
53.	**深**	shēn	*Adj.*	deep
54.	**节目**	jié mù	*N.*	program
55.	**主持人**	zhǔ chí rén	*N.*	(program) host/hostess, moderator
56.	**对待**	duì dài	*V.*	to treat (people)

你会用下面的词吗？
高级、编辑、出远门、突然、梨、经验、车厢、同志、
打招呼、路上、照顾、挺、会说话、阿姨、顺利、印
象、一直、深、节目、主持人、对待

我妈妈非常关心我

句型

一、无论……都／也…… (no matter what/who/where/when)

> ✍ This pattern indicates that the result or conclusion remains the same regardless of what the circumstances are or what happens. Following 无论 is an Interrogative structure - either a choice-type question ("是不是" or "A 还是 B") or a question using an interrogative pronoun (谁、什么、哪儿、怎么, etc.). The second clause of the "无论" structure usually contains 都 or 也.

☞ 一个人无论从哪儿来，都会讲出很多关于母亲的故事。

1、周玲来北京以后，无论什么时候都说汉语，所以进步很快。

Since Zhou Ling came to Beijing, she has spoken Chinese at all times. Therefore, her Chinese has improved quickly.

2、这个字太难写了，无论我怎么写也写不好。

This character is too hard to write. No matter how I write it, I always write it wrong.

3、无论下不下雨，我都要去长城。

No matter if it rains or not, I will go visit the Great Wall.

二、为了…… (in order to, for the purpose of)

> ✍ 为了 meaning "in order to", usually goes before a Verb Phrase to indicate the purpose of the action stated in the following clause.

☞ 为了培养我画画的这门爱好，妈妈就带我去少年宫去学习。

1、为了早点到学校，他叫了一辆出租汽车，没有坐机场大巴。

In order to reach the campus a little earlier, he took a cab instead of taking the airport shuttle.

2、为了学好中文，周玲计划到中国去留学一年。

In order to learn Chinese well, Zhou Ling plans to go to China and study for a year.

三、关于……(with regard to, about, concerning)

> ✍ 关于 is used in two different ways. 1) As part of a prepositional phrase that modifies a noun (as in the sentence from the lesson text and example 1). 2) As a coverb that introduces a dependent clause that precedes the main clause in a two-clause sentence (as in example 2). 关于 has various English equivalents depending on its context.

☞ 每个人都有讲不完的关于母亲的故事。

1、这个星期，我看了两本关于中国文化的书。
This week, I read two books about Chinese cultural history.

2、关于怎样打国际长途电话，你可以去问小刘。
You can ask Xiao Liu (about) how to make an international phone call.

四、不管……都……(regardless of)

> ✍ 不管 is a less formal synonym of 无论. While 无论 is mostly used in written Chinese, 不管 is used in both colloquial and written Chinese.

☞ 不管刮风下雨，我妈妈都是按时让我去上课。

1、不管白天还是晚上，留学生宿舍都有热水供应。
Whether it's day or night, the foreign students' dormitory always provides hot water.

2、她不管多忙，每个星期都会给父母打电话。
Regardless of how busy she is, every week she calls her parents.

五、按时+V (on time, on schedule)

> ✍ 按时 normally goes before a Verb to mean "to V on time", "to V on schedule". Notice the different word order between Chinese and English: "我们要按时上课，按时下课"。 (We should start class on time, and finish class on time).

☞ 每天妈妈都按时去车站接小荃回家。

1、因为下大雨，飞机不能按时起飞。

Because it is raining hard, the airplane can't take off on time.

2、我们按时上课，可是老师不按时下课，怎么办？

We start class on time, but the teacher dismisses class late. What are we going to do?

六、想（／记）起来…… (to recall, to remember)

> ✍ This is a verb+complement structure that means "to recall", "to remember". As with many words that function as verb complements, 起来 in this context has a meaning different from its original meaning of "to get up". The negative form for 想起来 is either 没想起来 (didn't remember/haven't remembered), or 想不起来 (couldn't/can't remember). 不想起来 is not a verb+complement structure and therefore is unrelated to any of the above. Rather, it is 不想+起来, which means "don't want to get up".

☞ 突然间，她想起来还少了一样东西。

1、那个故事叫什么名字，我已经想不起来了。

I can't remember what the name of that story is.

2、我记起来了，您就是去首都机场接我和高明的陈老师。

I remember, you're the Professor Chen who picked up Gao Ming and me at the Capital Airport.

七、跟（／给）……打招呼 (to greet, to touch base with)

> ✍ In addition to the meaning of "to greet", "to say hello to (somebody)" as in example 1, 打招呼 can also mean "to tell", "to instruct", "to touch base with", as in the text and in example 2. Sometime, we may add "（一）个" before 招呼 in spoken Chinese.

☞ 母亲跟同车厢的一位女同志打了个招呼，说这是我的孩子，没出过远门，没经验，路上给照顾一下。

1、他才学了几天中文，只会用中文跟人简单地打个招呼。

He's only been studying Chinese a few days and can use Chinese only to make simple greetings.

2、我已经跟前台值班的服务员打过招呼了，你一到就可以办理登记手续。

I've already spoken with the on-duty service person at the front desk. As soon as you arrive you can go through the registration procedures.

练习

一、读课文回答问题 (Answer questions based on the text)

1、小学生付荃荃有什么爱好？
2、她的爱好是怎样培养起来的？
3、她妈妈是怎样关心她的？
4、陈明记得最清楚的是什么事情？
5、陈明的妈妈突然想起了什么？她马上做了什么？
6、陈妈妈为什么叫同车厢的一位女同志照顾陈明？
7、这件事对陈明有什么影响？

二、听录音回答问题 (Answer questions while listening to the audio CD)

1、周采现在的工作是什么？
2、为什么周采从小由阿姨照顾？
3、阿姨以前的工作是什么？
4、阿姨是怎么对待周采的？
5、阿姨为什么不到美国来住？
6、周采怎样跟他的阿姨联系？他为什么要这样做？

三、完成对话 (Complete the dialogs)

1、A: 中国母亲爱自己的孩子，美国母亲呢？
　　B: （无论……都……）

2、A: 这个电影是讲什么的？
　　B: （关于……）

3、A: 现在下大雨，你过一会儿再去接你妈妈吧。

    B: （不管……都……）

4、A: 那个人是谁？你为什么跟他说话？

    B: （为了……；跟……打招呼）

四、阅读短文回答问题 (Answer questions based on the reading passage)

胡适和他的母亲

胡适是中国有名的文学家，他不到四岁的时候，父亲就去世了，那年他的母亲只有二十三岁。胡适是在母亲无私的关心和照顾下长大的，他对母亲的爱和感情也就非常深。

胡适刚三岁多的时候，母亲就要他去学校念书、认字。那个时候，家里并不宽裕，但是无论家里有多困难，胡适的母亲给老师的学费一直是最高的。别的学生家给老师一年两块钱，可是胡适的母亲第一年就给六块钱，以后每年还多给两块钱。因为她知道胡适从小就喜欢看书，为了培养他的这个爱好，母亲总是请老师把课给胡适讲清楚，让胡适把书上每个字、每个句子的意思都弄明白，所以胡适越来越爱看书，从来都不觉得读书很苦。

除了读书以外，胡适的母亲也教会了胡适怎么做人。家里没有父亲，母亲对胡适的要求非常严格，在这一点上，她既是母亲，也是父亲。每天早上，母亲都按时跟胡适谈话，告诉他前一天他做错了什么事，说错了什么话。母亲生活在大家庭里，她对待别人最客气，从来都不说伤别人感情的话。

胡适十四岁的时候就离开了母亲，出去念书。在母亲身边生活的这九年中，胡适受到了母亲极大极深的影响，他永远都感谢他的母亲。

问题:

1、胡适的母亲是怎么培养胡适对读书的爱好和兴趣的？

2、从什么方面可以看出胡适的母亲对胡适的要求非常严格？

3、胡适在什么方面受到了母亲的影响？

4、在你看来，胡适的母亲是一个什么样的人？

五、翻译  (Translation)

1. I think that no matter where you are, your love and feelings for your mother will always remain the same.

2. In order to understand his passion for his work, I decided to follow (跟随 gēn suí) him to his job at the train station in Beijing.

3. We all understand that this lesson not only taught us about life, but also about how a person should properly treat others.

4. While he was in the hospital, his professor took very good care of him. For a long time, this left a deep impression on him.

六、段落练习  (Paragraph practice)

一件印象最深的事情

第一段: 事情的时间、地点和人物
我记得很清楚的是……; 那一天, ……; ……为了……, ……

第二段: 事情的前前后后
因为……所以……; 后来……; 特别是……; 不但……而且……; 另外呢, ……; 这样, ……

第三段: 最后留下的印象
由于……; ……给我留下了很深的印象; 无论……都……; 所以……

七、作文 (Composition)

《我的母亲》
《世界上的母亲都一样吗》

八、讨论 (Discussion)

1、你有什么爱好？你母亲对你的爱好有什么看法？
2、你第一次出远门的经验是怎样的？
3、请你说一件你印象最深的、关于你妈妈的事情。

九、语言实践 (Language practicum)

采访两个中国人和两个美国同学，请他们给你讲一个印象最深的关于父亲的故事。比较一下他们的故事，看看从故事中你能找到中美文化的哪些相同点和不同点。

父亲教我应该怎么样去对待别人

An Intermediate Chinese Course

第二课 中国的独生子女都是
"小皇帝"吗？

我们也有很多压力和烦恼，请您帮帮忙！

课文

一、简介

> 独生子女是中国的一种特殊的文化现象。很多人说中国的独生子女是"小皇帝"，因为他们都是在一种优越的环境下长大的，常常受到爷爷、奶奶、爸爸、妈妈的溺爱。这一种说法其实只反映了问题的一个方面。说这种话的人并不知道独生子女的生活也不完全是"小皇帝"式⁽¹⁾的，他们也有很多的压力和烦恼。这是因为现在的家庭都只有一个孩子，父母把他们所有的希望都放在孩子身上，为他们的孩子花了很多时间和钱。他们都希望孩子按照父母的期望发展，甚至让孩子去实现自己没有实现的理想。这种作法当然对孩子的成长有影响，籁籁的故事就是一个很好的例子⁽²⁾。

生词

1. 小皇帝	xiǎo huáng dì	*NP.*	Little Emperor
2. 特殊	tè shū	*Adj.*	special
3. 现象	xiàn xiàng	*N.*	phenomenon

Notes (1)式, a "bound form" meaning "...style" or "type", is always preceded by a noun or adjective, and often modifies a noun which follows it. For example, 中式点心 (Chinese-style pastry), 美式足球 (American football), 小皇帝式的生活 (the life style of a little emperor), 旧式钢琴 (old-fashioned piano).

(2)例子 is a rather formal word for "example", especially when we say "This is an example of ..." （这是一个……的例子） or "Please give me an example" （请给我一个例子）; neither 比方 nor 比如 is used in such expressions. However, when we give a specific example in informal speech, we would simply say 比方说／比如 "for example", and launch into the example, rather than say something like "我现在来给你一个例子……" (Now I'm going to give you an example...).

4. 优越	yōu yuè	*Adj.*	superior, advantageous
5. 环境	huán jìng	*N.*	environment
6. 长大	zhǎng dà	*VP.*	to grow up
7. 受到	shòu dào	*VP.*	to receive
8. 爷爷	yé ye	*N.*	(paternal) grandfather
9. 奶奶	nǎi nai	*N.*	(paternal) grandmother
10. 溺爱	nì ài	*V.*	to spoil (a child)
11. 说法	shuō fǎ	*N.*	way of saying something, explanation, view
12. 反映	fǎn yìng	*V.*	to reflect
13. 方面	fāng miàn	*N.*	aspect
14. 完全	wán quán	*Adj/Adv.*	complete; completely
15. 式	shì	*N.*	type, style
16. 压力	yā lì	*N.*	pressure
17. 烦恼	fán nǎo	*N.*	worry, vexation
18. 希望	xī wàng	*N/V.*	hope; to hope
19. 花	huā	*V.*	to spend
20. 按照	àn zhào	*Prep.*	according to, in accordance with
21. 期望	qī wàng	*N/V.*	expectation; to expect
22. 发展	fā zhǎn	*V/N.*	to develop; development
23. 实现	shí xiàn	*V.*	to realize, to become reality
24. 理想	lǐ xiǎng	*N.*	ideal
25. 作法	zuò fǎ	*N.*	way of doing something
26. 成长	chéng zhǎng	*N.*	growth, maturation
27. 影响	yǐng xiǎng	*N/V.*	influence; to influence
28. 籁籁	lài lai	*Personal N.*	Lailai
29. 例子	lì zi	*N.*	example

你会用下面的词吗?

小皇帝、特殊、现象、优越、环境、长大、受到、爷爷、奶奶、溺爱、说法、反映、方面、完全、式、压力、烦恼、希望、花、按照、期望、发展、实现、作法、成长、影响、例子

二、电视节选

教子不可强按头

根据电视原文改编

（爸爸坐在沙发上用手弹什么，女儿正在往墙上贴自己画的画，妈妈过来了）

妈妈：籁籁，籁籁，该练琴了。

籁籁：又是练琴，我不想练琴。一练就是两个钟头，爸爸又这么厉害(3)，我不想练。

妈妈：好孩子，爸爸从小就喜欢钢琴，那时候家里穷啊，买不起。他没有成为钢琴家，现在，他可希望你能成为钢琴家呢。

籁籁：他想当钢琴家，又不是我想当。好妈妈，咱把钢琴卖了不行吗？我喜欢画画，我想当画家。

妈妈：小声点儿，别让你爸爸听见，啊。爸爸妈妈省吃俭用给你买钢琴容易吗？好孩子，就顺着爸爸吧，啊。

爸爸：叫你练琴，你怎么就是不听。你知道邻居听到你的钢琴声有多羡慕(4)，你还不知足。走，跟我练琴去。

籁籁：爸，能不能再画一会儿？

爸爸：走，走，走，跟我练琴去。

✏ **Notes** (3)厉害 has a variety of meanings in different contexts, and may be translated as "serious", "fierce", "terrifying", or even "awesome". For example,

他病得很厉害。
He is seriously sick.
今年夏天热得真厉害。
It is really burning hot this summer.
爸爸又这么厉害，我不想练。
Dad is so severe. I don't want to practice (playing the piano).
这个美国学生的中文真厉害，他说中文说得简直就像个中国人。
This American student's Chinese is awesome. He speaks just like a Chinese.

18

妈妈：好孩子，快去！哎，你轻点儿拉她，啊。

爸爸：走！

妈妈：快去！啊。

爸爸：走！

籁籁：爸，等一会儿。

［开始练琴］

爸爸：练这个。

籁籁：练半个钟头就画画行吗？一个钟头？

爸爸：两个钟头！一分钟也不能少。

（女儿边弹边哭）

……

―――――――― 生词 ――――――――

30. **教子不可强按头**	jiào zǐ bù kě qiáng àn tóu	*Idiom.*	when you teach your children, you shouldn't force them to learn things in which they are not interested
31. **沙发**	shā fā	*N.*	sofa
32. **弹**	tán	*V.*	to play (the piano or a plucked string instrument like guitar)
33. **墙**	qiáng	*N.*	wall

✎ Notes (4)你知道邻居听到你的钢琴声有多羡慕 is an exclamatory remark in which 你知道 means "you should know/realize", and the rest of the sentence means "How envious the neighbors are when they hear you playing the piano". Such an exclamatory remark is usually expressed by "Subject （有）多／多么 Adjective/Verb 啊". For example,

北京多（么）漂亮啊！
How pretty Beijing is!
要是我的同学都能来中国留学那有多好啊！
How wonderful it would be if all my classmates can come to China to study!

34. 贴	tiē	V.	to paste, to glue
35. 练琴	liàn qín	VO.	to practice playing the piano
36. 厉害	lì hai	Adj.	fierce, formidable
37. 从小	cóng xiǎo	PrepP.	since childhood
38. 钢琴	gāng qín	N.	piano
39. 穷	qióng	Adj.	poor
40. 成为	chéng wéi	VP.	to become/to be (in a role or profession)
41. 钢琴家	gāng qín jiā	N.	pianist
42. 当	dāng	V.	to become
43. 画家	huà jiā	N.	painter, artist
44. 小声点儿	xiǎo shēng diǎnr	Adv.	quieter, keep one's voice down
45. 省吃俭用	shěng chī jiǎn yòng	Idiom.	to live frugally (lit. "to economize on food and utility items")
46. 顺着	shùn zhe	VP.	to follow, to obey
47. 邻居	lín jū	N.	neighbor
48. 羡慕	xiàn mù	V.	to envy
49. 声	shēng	N.	sound
50. 知足	zhī zú	V/Adj.	to be content; content
51. 轻点儿	qīng diǎnr	Adv.	gently, softly
52. 拉	lā	V.	to pull, to grab

你会用下面的词吗？
沙发、弹、墙、贴、练琴、厉害、从小、钢琴、穷、成为、钢琴家、当、画家、小声点儿、省吃俭用、邻居、羡慕、声、知足、轻点儿、拉

句型

一、在……(的)环境下 (under... condition, under... circumstances)

> ✍ The structure 在……(的)Noun 下 indicates a certain condition or situation. Here 在……环境下 means "in a ... environment". Other Nouns that can be used in this structure are 情况、条件、帮助、影响、照顾, etc. More examples: 在老师的帮助下，我们的中文有了很大的进步。(With the help of the teachers, we have made great progress with our Chinese.) 在母亲的影响下，她对画画发生了兴趣。(Under the influence of her mother, she has developed an interest in painting).

☞ 很多人说中国的独生子女是"小皇帝"，因为他们都是在一种优越的环境下长大的，常常受到爷爷、奶奶、爸爸、妈妈的溺爱。

1、老大爷在安静、舒服的环境下，休息了两个月，身体很快就好了。
Grandpa rested in a peaceful and comfortable environment for two months, and his health quickly improved.

2、在美国的同学都很羡慕我能在这么好的环境下学习汉语。
My American classmates all envy me because I can study Chinese in such a great environment.

二、受到+V (receive, enjoy, endure, suffer, to be... V-ed)

> ✍ 受到 is a transitive verb that takes verbal-noun objects (typically two-syllables) and conveys a passive meaning. When it collocates with Positive Verbs such as 教育、欢迎、关心、照顾、帮助、鼓励, it means "to receive". When it collocates with Negative Verbs such as 处罚、溺爱、批评、污染、罚款, it can mean "to suffer from". For example, 这些孩子从小就在少年宫受到很好的培养。(These children received good training at the Children's Palace since they were young.) 他们因为不好好学习受到了老师的批评。(They were criticized by the teacher because they didn't study hard).

☞ 很多人说中国的独生子女是"小皇帝"，因为他们都是在一种优越的环境下长大的，常常受到爷爷、奶奶、爸爸、妈妈的溺爱。

1、独生子女的教育问题已经受到社会的重视。

The problems of the single child generation have already received society's attention.

2、在中国，老年人都受到大家的尊重。

In China, the elderly enjoy everyone's respect.

三、按照 NP + V (to V according to/in light of)

> ✍ Unlike its English counterpart "according to" which can take a personal Noun or Pronoun as its object, 按照 must take as its object a non-human noun, although the object may well be associated with a person. In fact, the object often takes the form "personal noun/pronoun + V 的", e.g. 你们得按照导演说的去演。(You must act according to what the director says.) 父母应该让孩子按照自己的兴趣去选择他们的爱好。(Parents should let children select their hobbies according to their own interests).

☞ 他们都希望孩子按照父母的期望发展，甚至让孩子去实现自己没有实现的理想。

1、你应该按照医生说的去吃药、休息。

You should take your medicine and rest according to the doctor's instructions.

2、我们按照老师的要求，到中国学生的宿舍去了解他们的住宿条件。

Following our teacher's request, we went to the Chinese students' dorm to learn about their living conditions.

四、甚至……(even to the extent that...)

> ✍ 甚至, meaning "even to the point of...", is used to introduce a Clause or a Phrase that conveys the extreme extent (or the "last straw") of a certain situation stated in the foregoing clause. The notion of "even..." is often reinforced by the use of 还、都、也、连, etc.

☞ 他们都希望孩子按照父母的期望发展，甚至让孩子去实现自己没有实现的理想。

1、这几年老张有钱了，不但买了房子、电脑，甚至还买了小汽车。

Over the last few years Lao Zhang has become rich. Not only has he bought a house and a computer, but he has even bought a car.

2、这个人真没有礼貌，随便拿别人的东西，甚至把脚放在桌子上。

This person really doesn't have any manners. He casually takes other people's things and even goes so far as to put his feet up on the table.

五、对⋯⋯有影响 (to have influence/impact on...)

> ✍　对⋯⋯（没）有影响 indicates someone or something has/does not have influence/impact on someone or something else.

☞ 这种作法当然对孩子的成长有影响。

1、父母的一举一动对孩子都有很大的影响。

Parents' every action has a great impact on their children.

2、中国人认为味精对身体没有什么影响。

The Chinese people think that MSG is not harmful to one's health.

六、一V就是 (+period of time/amount) (It will be... whenever V)

> ✍　This structure indicates that once an action or event occurs, it goes on for quite some time or a considerable extent. It usually follows a clause that serves as the topic of the entire sentence.

☞ 我不想练琴，一练就是两个钟头，爸爸又这么厉害，我不想练。

1、高志德吃东西不注意，得了急性肠炎，一病就是三天。

Gao Zhide did not pay attention to what he ate and came down with acute enteritis. He was sick for three days.

2、周老师看见中国的书便宜，每次去书店一买就是几十本。

Professor Zhou saw that books in China were cheap, so every time he went to a bookstore he bought dozens of books.

七、可⋯⋯呢／了 (indeed-used for emphasis)

> ✍　This is an Exclamatory Sentence with the part to be emphasized sandwiched between 可 and 呢. What is being emphasized may be an Adjective (as in example 1) or a Verb Phrase (as in example 2 and the sentence in the text "How he wishes you would be a pianist"!)

☞ 他可希望你能成为钢琴家呢。

1、那个医院的设备可现代化呢。

That hospital's facilities are really modern.

2、昨天骑了三个多小时的自行车，可把我累坏了！

Yesterday I rode on a bike for over three hours and got really tired!

八、V得起／V不起 (can/cannot afford to)

> ✍ Verb 得起／Verb 不起 is a verb + complement construction used to indicate whether one can or cannot afford to do something in terms of time or money. The Verbs that often occur in this structure are 买、吃、穿、住、用、玩、看（病）、上（学）、坐（飞机），etc.

☞ 那时候家里穷啊，买不起。

1、学校附近的饭馆都很经济实惠，我们就是天天去吃也吃得起。

The restaurants near the campus all have affordable prices. We can afford to go out and eat everyday.

2、长城饭店的一个房间一晚就要150美元，我是个穷学生，住不起。

Rooms at the Great Wall Hotel cost $150 a night. I'm a poor student so I cannot afford to stay there.

中国的父母为他们的孩子花了很多时间和钱

练习

一、读课文回答问题

1、妈妈过来的时候，籁籁正在做什么？

2、籁籁为什么不想练琴？

3、籁籁的爸爸为什么没能成为钢琴家？

4、籁籁自己的理想是什么？她给妈妈提出了一个什么建议？

5、妈妈同意不同意籁籁的建议？她要籁籁怎么样？

6、籁籁的邻居有没有钢琴？你是怎样知道的？

7、说一说爸爸是怎样要籁籁练琴的？

二、听录音回答问题

1、为什么多半都是爷爷奶奶在照顾王明？

2、爷爷奶奶是怎么对待王明的？

3、周末的时候，王明得做哪几件事？为什么？

4、王明的爸妈给王明买了什么？

5、李荃是谁？

6、为什么王明羡慕李荃？

7、为什么王明有天下最好的东西，可是还是不快乐？

8、王明为什么越来越不爱学习？

三、完成对话

1、A: 怎么？老王也开始学跳舞了？

B:（在……环境下；甚至……）

2、A: 小琴的信说什么？她在中国怎么样？

　　B: （按照……；受到……）

3、A: 北京的女孩子穿得很漂亮嘛！

　　B: （对……有影响；可……呢）

4、A: 小黄，明天是你的生日，请我们全班去硬石咖啡厅(Hard Rock Cafe)吃晚饭吧！

　　B: （一 V 就是……；V 得／不起）

四、阅读短文回答问题

　　我叫马晓星，今年上小学四年级。我班上的同学跟我一样，都是独生子女。我们这一代，最不喜欢听到的就是大人们说他们小时候家里多么多么穷，而我们的生活条件多么优越，想要什么就有什么，应该知足什么的，甚至还有人管我们叫"小皇帝"、"小公主"！每次我听到大人这么说，我就大声地问他们："你们知道我们的生活有多不容易吗？"说真的，我有时候觉得我们的压力太大了。比方说我家吧，我爸我妈都是普通工人，他们年轻那会儿都没有机会上大学，所以对我在学习方面的要求特别严，他们也总是说，我以后一定得上大学，才能找到好工作，挣好多好多的钱。他们也想培养我在音乐、画画方面的爱好，所以省吃俭用为我在少年宫的钢琴班和画画班交了学费，然后每个周末都送我去那儿学，一坐就是一下午。可是其实我对这些一点儿兴趣都没有，星期六星期天的时候，我只想放松一下，看看电视，玩玩球什么的。可是学校的功课太紧张了，我根本没时间看电视；要想玩球吧，邻居家的小朋友也都忙着学这个学那个，没人陪我玩儿。哎，我多希望我们的老师和父母能理解我们，让我们按照自己的爱好去发展啊！

回答问题:

1、跟父母相比，独生子女这一代的生活条件发生了什么变化？
2、你认为，为什么有人管独生子女叫"小皇帝"，"小公主"？
3、马晓星的父母对他在学习方面有什么要求？为什么他们的要求这么严？
4、晓星的父母打算培养晓星的什么爱好？他们是怎么做的？
5、晓星通常怎么过周末？他希望做什么事情？为什么做不到？
6、通过这篇文章，你觉得独生子女的父母应该怎么做才能减轻孩子的压力？

五、翻译

1. Many people say that those who grow up in privileged environments are likely to have more pressure and worries.
2. Most of the single-child generation cannot realize their own dreams because they are expected to develop according to their parents' wishes.
3. I do not think that his profession as a film director has affected his family life.
4. Since my childhood, I dreamed of becoming a pianist. When my mother realized that I had such thoughts, she lived frugally and worked day and night in order to save up enough money to buy me a piano.

独生子女是中国的一种特殊的文化现象

27

六、段落练习

美国大学生也有压力和烦恼

有很多中国人认为美国的大学生活并不紧张，学生也不太用功学习。用你自己的例子来反对这样的看法。

第一段： 提出主题 (topic)
很多人以为……；其实，……；我认为……；一方面……，另一方面……；

第二段： 说明为什么
这是因为……；第一……；比方说……；第二……；为了……，……；第三……

第三段： 你对这个问题的总的看法
因此……；我认为/我的看法是……

有用的词：
名词：现象、环境、压力、烦恼、希望、期望、理想、例子
动词：受到、反映、溺爱、按照、发展、实现、花（时间）、成长、影响、不可
形容词：特殊、优越、完全、顺利

七、作文

《中国的独生子女真是"小皇帝"吗？》

八、讨论

1、你觉得像籁籁这样的生活是不是"小皇帝"式的？为什么？

2、你认为孩子应该按照自己的理想去发展还是应该按照父母的期望去发展？为什么？

3、如果孩子没有这样的爱好，父母能不能像籁籁的爸爸那样去"培养"孩子的爱好？为什么？

4、你的父母对你有什么期望？你自己的理想跟他们的期望一样不一样？如果不一样，你们怎么办？

九、语言实践

采访两个独生子女，了解一下他们的生活、学习，跟他们谈谈
(1) 他们的理想
(2) 他们想做的事
(3) 什么事情让他们有压力
(4) 他们希望有什么样的父母
(5) 如果他们可以跟他们的父母谈谈的话，他们想跟父母说些什么？

中国的独生子女常常受到爷爷、奶奶、爸爸、妈妈的溺爱

独生子女的生活也不完全是"小皇帝"式的

第三课 卖黄瓜的个体户和向"钱"看

人们赚钱的脑子活了

课文

一、简介 ❋

自从八十年代以来，中国人选择职业的自由越来越多。这跟政府的开放政策有很大的关系。过去，人们没有选择，只能在国营单位工作，干好干坏一个样。现在呢，政策活了，出路也多了，想留在国营单位的可以留在那儿，想"下海"当个体户也行。总之，人们赚钱的脑子活了。可是有些人却"活"到一些不应该"活"的地方，甚至只向"钱"看⁽¹⁾，不顾⁽²⁾商业道德。下面的故事就是对这些人的批评。

———❖——— 生词 ———❖———

1. 向钱看	xiàng qián kàn	*Idiom.*	"look toward money," to be obsessed with money
2. 黄瓜	huáng gua	*N.*	cucumber
3. 个体户	gè tǐ hù	*N.*	self-employed people, entrepreneur
4. 年代	nián dài	*N.*	era, decade
5. 以来	yǐ lái	*Conj.*	since...
6. 经济	jīng jì	*N/Adj.*	economy, economics; economical

✎ **Notes** ⁽¹⁾向钱看 ("look toward money", money seeking) is homophonous with 向前看 (looking forward) which was a popular political slogan in the late seventies and early eighties in China. Chinese often use homophones to make a pun on words. Here are a few common examples: 效果 (effect) vs. 笑果 (laughing effect), 气管炎 (bronchitis) vs. 妻管严 ("wife controls strictly", hen-pecked).

⁽²⁾顾 here is a verb which actually means "to attend to", "to take into account", although sometimes it can be translated as "to care". It requires an Object and is usually used with the Adverb 只 before it in the positive and 不 in the negative. For example, 你们不能只顾赚钱，不顾商业道德 (You can't just care about making money and pay no attention to business ethics).

7. 政府	zhèng fǔ	*N.*	government
8. 开放	kāi fàng	*V/Adj.*	to open (vs. to restrict); open, liberal
9. 政策	zhèng cè	*N.*	policy
10. 一个样	yí ge yàng	*Adj.*	the same
11. 活	huó	*Adj.*	flexible, lively, active
12. 出路	chū lù	*N.*	outlet, a way out, opportunity
13. 留	liú	*V.*	to stay
14. 国营	guó yíng	*Adj.*	state-operated
15. 单位	dān wèi	*N.*	work unit
16. 下海	xià hǎi	*VO.*	lit. "to plunge into the sea," to leave government employment and go into the private sector
17. 总之	zǒng zhī	*Adv.*	in short, in a word
18. 赚钱	zhuàn qián	*VO.*	to earn money
19. 却	què	*Adv.*	on the contrary, however
20. 脑子	nǎo zi	*N.*	brain
21. 甚至	shèn zhì	*Adv.*	even to the point of...
22. 不顾	bú gù	*V.*	not care about, not attend to
23. 商业	shāng yè	*N.*	commerce, business
24. 道德	dào dé	*N.*	morals, morality

你会用下面的词吗？
向钱看、黄瓜、个体户、年代、以来、经济、政府、
开放、政策、活、出路、留、国营、单位、下海、总
之、赚钱、脑子、甚至、不顾、商业、道德

二、电视节选 ■

卖黄瓜的个体户

根据电视原文改编

张五原来是一家国营汽车厂的工人。一九八九年他觉得在厂里的出路不好，赚钱不多，就决定下海卖菜。这天，他进了一些黄瓜去菜市场卖……

（北京的菜市场）

张五：买黄瓜了，买黄瓜了。新鲜的黄瓜。大姐，你来点儿黄瓜，六毛五一斤。你来点，六毛五。

大姐：那就来一斤吧。

张五：一斤够谁吃[3]？来二斤吧，您。

大姐：分量你给足啊。

张五：您放心吧。二斤，二斤高高的。

大姐：给你钱。正好啊。

张五：哎，哎，回见，您。

（大姐碰到小穆）

大姐：哎，小穆，你也来买菜了。

小穆：我今天休息。

大姐：哎，你这黄瓜多少钱一斤？

Notes [3] 一斤够谁吃 is a Rhetorical Question which means "One Jin (500 gram) is simply not enough". 足 and 够 both mean "enough", but both can be used only in the predicate of a sentence, and not before a noun to modify it. But the compound 足够 can be used as a noun modifier. For example, 我们有足够的时间练习。 (We have enough time to practice.) In addition, 够 can be used as a transitive verb, meaning "enough for...to..". e.g. 这些菜够我们吃了。 (This is enough food for us.)

34

小穆:	七毛。
大姐:	我这是六毛五,刚在那边买的。哎,你这多少?
小穆:	我这二斤。
大姐:	二斤?我也是二斤。怎么那么少啊?
小穆:	是有点少。咱们去公平秤看看去。

(去公平秤)

工作人员:	少四两。这事儿啊,很可能又是张五这小子干的。

(去找张五)

张五:	哎,怎么着⁽⁴⁾?您二位也来点黄瓜?
工作人员:	你刚才卖给这女同志黄瓜了吗?
张五:	这女同志的黄瓜是我卖的。
工作人员:	来,我们看看你的秤。这是我的证件。
张五:	欢迎检查,欢迎检查。
工作人员:	这秤砣可是磨下去一块啊。根据计量法第二十六条规定,和实施细则第五十一条的规定对你进行处罚,罚款五十,没收计量器具。
工作人员:	你一定要老老实实认错啊。
张五:	嗳,嗳。我认罚,我认罚。
工作人员:	这是收据,啊。

✏️**Notes** ⁽⁴⁾怎么着 is an idiomatic phrase meaning "How is it"? "What about it"? "What is up"? It is mostly used in North China. It is similar to 怎么样 to some extent. For example,

我们去看电影,你怎么着(怎么样)?
We are going to see a movie, what about you?
天黑了,你是回家吃饭还是怎么着(怎么样)?
It is getting dark, are you going home to eat or what?

—◆—— 生词 ——◆—

25. 卖菜	mài cài	*VO.*	to sell vegetables
26. 进	jìn	*V.*	to stock up (merchandise)
27. 新鲜	xīn xiān	*Adj.*	fresh
28. 大姐	dà jiě	*N.*	"elder sister", a polite form of address for a woman about one's own age
29. 来	lái	*V.*	(colloquial) to buy/have
30. 点儿	diǎnr	*Quan.*	(一点儿) some
31. 斤	jīn	*Classifier.*	a unit of weight (=1/2 kilogram)
32. 分量	fèn liàng	*N.*	weight
33. 足	zú	*Adj.*	full, sufficient
34. 高高的	gāo gāo de	*Adj.*	on the high side, a bit more than full measure
35. 哎	ài	*Intj.*	Yes
36. 回见	huí jiàn	*Idiom*	good-bye
37. 小穆	xiǎo mù	*Personal N.*	Little Mu
38. 休息	xiū xi	*V.*	to rest, to take a break
39. 公平秤	gōng píng chèng	*NP.*	"fair scale" (standard scale placed in markets for checking weight)
40. 两	liǎng	*Classifier.*	a unit of weight (= 1/10 斤)
41. 工作人员	gōng zuò rén yuán	*NP.*	staff, employee
42. 可能	kě néng	*Adj/N/Adv.*	possible; possibility; possibly
43. 小子	xiǎo zi	*N.*	fellow, rascal, rogue
44. 怎么着	zěn me zhe	*Q.*	"what's going on"?
45. 秤	chèng	*N.*	scale, steelyard
46. 证件	zhèng jiàn	*N.*	credentials, documents (e.g. I.D., permit, license, etc.)
47. 欢迎	huān yíng	*V.*	to welcome
48. 检查	jiǎn chá	*V.*	to check, to inspect
49. 秤砣	chèng tuó	*N.*	the weight of a steelyard or scale
50. 磨	mó	*V.*	to rub, to grind
51. 根据	gēn jù	*Prep.*	according to
52. 计量法	jì liàng fǎ	*NP.*	measurement regulations

53.	条	tiáo	*Classifier.*	item, article
54.	规定	guī dìng	*V/N.*	to stipulate; regulation, stipulation
55.	实施	shí shī	*V/N.*	to implement; implementation
56.	细则	xì zé	*NP.*	detailed clause
57.	进行	jìn xíng	*V.*	to proceed, to carry out
58.	处罚	chǔ fá	*V/N.*	to exact penalty, to punish; penalty, punishment
59.	罚款	fá kuǎn	*VO/N.*	to exact a fine; fine
60.	没收	mò shōu	*V.*	to confiscate
61.	器具	qì jù	*N.*	implement, utensil
62.	老老实实	lǎo lǎo shí shí	*Adv.*	honestly
63.	认错	rèn cuò	*VO.*	to acknowledge a mistake, to admit a fault
64.	嗳	ài	*Intj.*	Oh! (indicating regret)
65.	认罚	rèn fá	*VO.*	to accept punishment
66.	收据	shōu jù	*N.*	receipt

你会用下面的词吗？
卖菜、进、新鲜、大姐、来、斤、分量、足、高高
的、回见、休息、公平、两、工作人员可能、小子、
怎么着、秤、证件、欢迎、检查、磨、根据、条、规
定、实施、进行、处罚、罚款、没收、器具、老老实
实、认错、收据

句型

一、自从……（以来/以后）(since, from)

> ✍ 自从 refers to a starting point of time in the past and is usually used in combination with 以来 or 以后 to refer to a time frame from a certain point in the past to the point where the remark is made. That "certain point in the past" can be an event like 我到了北京 or a specific time like 三年前，去年八月。以来 occurs more frequently than 以后 in this structure. Moreover, there is a difference in nuance between the two: with 以来, the focus is on the entire time span; with 以后, the focus is on the period after the initiating time or event.

☞ 自从八十年代以来，中国人选择职业的自由越来越多。

1、自从修了三环、四环以来，北京的交通有了一定的改善。
   Beijing's traffic has definitely improved since the Third and Fourth Ring Roads were constructed.

2、自从我买了这本《汉英词典》以后，遇到不认识的字，查起来就方便多了。
   Since I bought this Chinese/English dictionary, it's been very convenient to look up the words that I don't know.

二、A跟B有……关系 (have relation/connection to, be related to)

> ✍ A 跟 B（没）有……的关系 indicates whether two people/events are related or relevant to each other. Modifiers such as 很大、特殊、密切 can be placed before 关系。

☞ 这跟政府的经济政策有很大的关系。

1、我们的进步跟老师的帮助有很大的关系。
   Our improvement has a lot to do with our teacher's assistance.

2、现在计算机跟人们的生活有越来越密切的关系。

Nowadays computers have increasingly become an integral part of people's lives.

三、 V+Adj.$_1$+V+Adj.$_2$+一个样／不一样 (it is [not] the same whether... or...)

> ✍ This structure indicates whether or not the situation is the same under the two circumstances expressed by V + Adj.1 and V + Adj.2 In some cases, an alternative to the V + Adj. component in this structure is Adv. + V, e.g. 位子很多, 早到晚到都一样。(There are lots of seats. It's all the same whether you arrive early or late.)

☞ 过去, 人们没有选择, 只能在国营单位工作, 干好干坏一个样。

1、咱们周末不用上课, 早起晚起一个样。

It doesn't matter if we get up early or late on weekends because we don't have to go to class.

2、学语言就是要多练习, 多练少练不一样。

Studying a language requires a lot of practice. There is a big difference between practicing a lot and just a little.

四、 总之 (in sum, in short)

> ✍ 总之 is used to summarize and usually goes before a conclusive remark. It can appear at the beginning or in the middle of a sentence, followed by a pause in speaking (or a comma in writing).

☞ 总之, 人们赚钱的脑子活了。

1、你的黄瓜又贵又不新鲜, 总之, 我不买。

Your cucumbers are expensive and not fresh. Anyway, I don't want to buy them.

2、到了上下班的时候, 到处都是汽车、电车、出租汽车、马车、摩托车、自行车, 总之, 各种车辆全都挤到马路上来了。

When it's rush hour, there are cars, trolleys, taxis, horse carriages, motorcycles, and bicycles everywhere. In short, every type of vehicle is crowded together on the streets.

五、 却 (but, yet)

> ✍ Adverb 却 is used after the Subject before the Predicate in the second Clause to indicate a contrary situation. It can be reinforced with 但是 or 可是, and is mostly used in written Chinese. For example, 很多人以为独生子女的生活都是 "小皇帝" 式的，但是却不知道他们也有很大的压力和很多的苦恼 (Many people assume that the life of the only child is like that of a "Little Emperor", but they don't know that these children also have a lot of pressures and worries).

☞ 可是有些人却 "活" 到一些不应该 "活" 的地方，甚至只向 "钱" 看，不顾商业道德。

1、 陈教授的父亲已经80岁了，身体却还很健康。

Professor Chen's father is already 80 years old, yet he is still healthy.

2、 虽然这是辆旧车，却非常好骑，一点问题也没有。

Although this is a used bike, it's still very easy to ride and doesn't have a single problem.

六、 来 (used for "order" or "request")

> ✍ 来 is a colloquial word used mostly for ordering a meal or shopping. It means "Please give me ..."

☞ 你来点黄瓜，六毛五一斤。

1、 小姐，请给我们来六两饺子和两瓶可乐。

Miss, please bring us 6 taels of dumplings and two bottles of Coke.

2、 这个菜不错，要不要再来一点儿？

This dish isn't bad. Do you want some more?

七、 根据 + Obj. (according to, on the basis of)

> ✍ 根据 + Obj. is a prepositional phrase meaning "according to...", and the object is often words such as 规定、政策、情况、习惯、经验、决定、化验、核实、反映. Like 按照, no Personal Pronouns or Nouns that refer to people can follow 根据 directly. (Cf. Lesson 2, Sentence Pattern 3.) The prepositional phrase 根据 + Obj. may occur independently before a sentence (as in example 2 below), or before a VP (as in the text example).

☞ 根据计量法第二十六条规定和实施细则第五十一条的规定对你进行处罚。

1、根据字典的解释，这个词可以作名词，也可以作动词。
According to the dictionary, this word can either function as a noun or as a verb.

2、根据小王的了解，北京有差不多八万辆出租车。
According to Xiao Wang's understanding, Beijing has almost eighty thousand taxis.

八、对……进行 + Obj. (to carry out, to conduct, to implement)

> ✍ The object of 进行 is usually a verbal noun that refers to a formal and serious activity, not a casual one or one that lasts for only a short while. It is incorrect to say: *进行玩/*进行吃饭. The verbal noun that follows 进行 is normally disyllabic, such as 批评、教育、帮助、了解、研究、改革、讨论、处罚, etc. and it cannot take another object of its own. To indicate an object of the action being carried out, a prepositional phrase 对 + Obj. is used before 进行, e.g. 对学生进行批评 (to criticize students).

☞ 根据计量法第二十六条规定和实施细则第五十一条的规定对你进行处罚。

1、市场的工作人员除了对张五进行罚款以外，还对他进行了教育。
Besides giving Zhang Wu a fine, the staff at the market also "educated" him.

2、期中考试后，大家对怎样提高我们的汉语水平进行了讨论。
After the midterm, everyone participated in a discussion about how to improve our Chinese proficiency.

卖水果的个体户

41

练习

一、读课文回答问题

1、张五以前在哪儿工作？现在呢？

2、张五说他要卖多少黄瓜给大姐？一共多少钱？

3、小穆买的黄瓜比大姐的贵还是便宜？多还是少？

4、大姐买的黄瓜够不够？一共是多少？

5、大姐和小穆是怎样知道黄瓜少了的？

6、工作人员发现了什么问题？他要对张五怎么样？

7、工作人员最后给了张五什么东西？

二、听录音回答问题

1、老李原来在哪儿工作？

2、老李下海是受了谁的影响？

3、老李一天工作几个钟头？为什么？

4、老李觉得工作很累吗？为什么？

5、老李什么时候可以有自己的车？

6、对老李来说，赚钱要紧还是道德要紧？

三、完成对话

1、A：他为什么每个字才写三次？是什么时候开始这样做的？

  B：（自从……以来；V+ Adj.$_1$+ V+ Adj.$_2$+ 一个样）

2、A: 怎么，你现在只喝水，不喝啤酒了？
　　B: （A和B有关系；总之……）

3、A: 你们学校暑假怎样安排学生的活动？
　　B: （根据……；对……进行V）

四、阅读短文回答问题

> 　　五十年代以后的二、三十年中，要是你问一个中国人他最理想的职业是什么，大多数的人可能会想都不想就回答说，在国营工厂当工人或者在国营单位坐办公室呗。在那个时候，人们没有选择职业的自由。从学校毕业以后只能靠政府分配、安排工作。如果有在工厂或者国营单位办公室工作都会让人羡慕，因为这样的工作很稳定，就算你工作得再差，也不用担心会丢掉工作，很多人会一直在一个单位待到退休，所以老百姓管这样的工作叫"铁饭碗"。那个时候也有开饭馆或者服装店、理发店的个体户，但是他们多数是文化水平不太高，或者是怎么也找不到工作的人，所以社会地位不算高，有的在国营单位的人甚至会看不起这样的个体户。但是八十年代的经济改革改变了这一切，私营经济、个体经济在中国经济中变得越来越重要。国营单位的工资本来就不高，现在跟个体户赚的钱相比差得就更多了，所以有的人离开原来的国营单位"下海"做生意、去当个体户。同时中国人对职业选择的看法也发生了变化。象自己找工作，不满意的时候换工作这样的事越来越被人们接受。现在无论你在国营单位工作还是当个体户，都是你自己的选择。如果今天你再问中国人他们对选择职业的看法，很可能十个人会给你十一个回答，其中有一个还正在考虑换工作呢！

回答问题:
1、三、四十年以前，中国人的理想职业是什么？
2、"铁饭碗"是指什么样的工作？为什么这样的工作让人羡慕？
3、经济改革以后，个体户的社会地位发生了什么变化？为什么？
4、现在中国人对理想职业的看法跟以前相比有什么不同？
5、中国人对选择职业的态度开始发生变化，你认为这种变化会给中国社会带来什么影响？美国的个体户跟中国的个体户有什么不同？

五、翻译

1. In sum, since the 90's, Chinese people have had more and more freedom to "plunge into the sea" and become entrepreneurs.
2. Many college professors criticize the government's open door policy because it (this policy) has made many Chinese become money-seeking and ignore business morality.
3. The peddler was fined 500 RMB by the city because his business is related to the black market.
4. It used to be prestigious to work in a state-owned work unit. Nowadays, more and more Chinese people want to leave their work units. I was told that this is because many people want to choose their own professions.

六、段落练习

> 美国的个体户跟中国的个体户
>
> 第一段： 提出要比较的两个事情
>
> 我要比较一下……； 我认为……； A跟B在……上很不同/一样
>
> 第二段： 从几个不同的方面比较
>
> 根据……； 在中国，自从……以来，……； 以前……，现在……； 一方面……，另一方面……； 然而，在美国，……； 如果……，就……； 尤其是……； 甚至……
>
> 第三段： 最后的结果
>
> 总之，从……方面看……； 我认为/我的看法是……

有用的词:
名词: 个体户、出路，现象、职业、自由、商业道德、压力、政策
动词: 选择、赚钱、受到、按照、发展、实现、影响、反映
形容词: 活、特殊、完全

七、作文

《北京的个体户》
《北京人对个体户的看法》

八、讨论

1、中国的经济发展是什么时候开始的？为什么从那时候起经济就发展得快了？
2、赚钱跟脑子"活"有什么关系？为什么？
3、你觉得像张五这样赚钱好不好？为什么？

九、语言实践

1、采访三个人：个体户、普通的北京人、大学生
　(1) 问问他们去市场买东西的经验，有没有上当受骗的经历？
　(2) 人们"向钱看"的想法对中国的社会有什么影响？
　(3) 如果你发现上当受骗了，你怎么办？
2、去个体户的小摊儿买两样东西，顺便问问他们"下海"以前做什么？下海以后的生活怎么样？请他们谈谈对经济改革的看法。

"下海"当个个体户也不错

政策活了，出路也多了

An Intermediate Chinese Course

第四课 不拘小节的人

我们都是不拘小节的人

课文

一、简介

在中国社会中，人和人的关系非常重要。大多数的人都认为与人相处要互相尊重，也就是说，除了要别人尊重你以外，你也应该尊重别人。我的同事李大亮却不以为然。我和大亮都在国营单位工作，同[1]一个办公室。除了我和大亮以外，办公室还有两个人：小李和老张，我们几个人谁都不喜欢大亮，也没有人跟他合得来。大亮常常跟人说他是一个"不拘小节"的人。"不拘小节"的意思就是不注意生活小事，比如对吃饭、穿衣、梳头这些事情不那么讲究[2]，或者东西不注意放好。大亮常让别人觉得他很不礼貌，而他自己却一点儿都不知道。很多认识大亮的人说像他这样的人并不是不拘小节，而是在生活小事上不注意别人的感觉和反应。作为同事，我们都不好意思当他的面说出他的毛病来。为了让他知道自己做了些什么和别人的反应，我用摄像机把他上班时候的一举一动都录下来了。

Notes [1]同 is a Verb here, meaning "to be in/at the same ...", "share the same ...". 同一个办公室 can be translated as "share/to be in the same office". Other examples are: 同一个学校、同一辆车、同一班飞机、同一个宿舍, etc.

[2]讲究 means "to pay particular attention to or care a lot about something and strive for it", and usually takes Nouns or Verbs that bear an abstract sense as its Object. Words such as 质量 (quality), 态度 (attitude), 方法 (methodology), 速度 (speed), 效率 (efficiency), 卫生 (hygiene) and 衣着 (clothing) are often associated with 讲究. We can also use the preposition 对 to indicate the object of 讲究, as in 对吃饭、穿衣、梳头这些事情不那么讲究.

生词

1. 不拘小节   bù jū xiǎo jié   *Idiom.*   to not be bothered about small matters
2. 与   yǔ   *Conj.*   (formal) and, with (used with noun or NP only)
3. 关系   guān xì   *N.*   relation, relationship, connection
4. 重要   zhòng yào   *Adj.*   important
5. 大多数   dà duō shù   *N.*   great majority, vast majority
6. 认为   rèn wéi   *V.*   to deem, to construe
7. 相处   xiāng chǔ   *V.*   to get along (with one another)
8. 互相   hù xiāng   *Adv.*   mutually
9. 尊重   zūn zhòng   *V.*   to respect
10. 李大亮   lǐ dà liàng   *Personal N.*   Li Daliang
11. 不以为然   bù yǐ wéi rán   *Idiom.*   do not think so, to take exception to
12. 办公室   bàn gōng shì   *N.*   office
13. 合得来   hé de lái   *VP.*   to get along well
14. 意思   yì si   *N.*   meaning
15. 注意   zhù yì   *V.*   to pay attention
16. 穿衣   chuān yī   *VO.*   to wear clothes, apparel
17. 梳头   shū tóu   *VO.*   to comb the hair
18. 讲究   jiǎng jiu   *V.*   to be particular about, to pay attention to
19. 礼貌   lǐ mào   *N/Adj.*   manners; courteous
20. 认识   rèn shi   *V.*   to know (someone)
21. 感觉   gǎn jué   *V/N.*   to feel; feeling, sense perception, to be acquainted with
22. 反应   fǎn yìng   *N.*   reaction, response
23. 作为   zuò wéi   *V/Prep.*   being, in the role of; as
24. 不好意思   bù hǎo yì si   *Adj.*   embarrassed
25. 当……的面   dāng...de miàn   *PrepP.*   to somebody's face, in somebody's presence
26. 毛病   máo bìng   *N.*   shortcoming, defect
27. 摄像机   shè xiàng jī   *N.*   video recorder
28. 举动   jǔ dòng   *N.*   (or 一举一动) (every) behavior

你会用下面的词吗？
不拘小节、与、关系、重要、大多数、认为、相处、互相、尊重、却、不以为然、办公室、合得来、意思、注意、穿衣、梳头、讲究、礼貌、认识、感觉、反应、作为、不好意思、当……的面、毛病、摄像机

"不拘小节" 的意思就是不注意生活小事

二、电视节选 ▨

不拘小节的人

（根据原电视画面编写）

　　这天，大亮利用上班时间去单位的澡堂洗了一个澡。洗完澡回到办公室以后，觉得头发又湿又乱，就想找一把梳子梳梳头。大亮在自己桌子上找不到梳子，就想起同事小李常在办公室里梳头，她一定有梳子。大亮走到小李的办公桌旁边拉开抽屉就翻了起来，翻了半天[3]才找到了梳子。

　　小李从外边进来后看到自己的抽屉被翻得乱七八糟就很生气。她知道这又是同事大亮干的"好事"，就故意问了一句："哎？这是怎么回[4]事？"大亮满不在乎[5]地说："小李，借你的梳子使使[6]"。小李生气地把抽屉关上，一句话都没说就坐下了。

　　过了一会儿，大亮觉得嗓子里有一点儿不舒服，他站起来，打开窗子就往外吐了一口痰。听到他的吐痰声，小李和老张都觉得很恶

Notes [3]半天, literally "half a day", is often used figuratively to mean " quite a long time". It also conveys the speaker's impatience or annoyance. For example, 你上哪儿去了？我等了你半天了 (Where have you been? I have been waiting for you for a long time.)

[4]回 is a Measure Word for matters or actions. For example,

这是另一回事。　　This is another issue.
我去过两回。　　　I have been there twice.

[5]在乎 means "to care about, to take to heart". It is mostly used in Negative Sentences or Rhetorical Questions, and can be modified by 很、非常、不太、满, etc., or be reinforced by 一点儿也. For example, 他一点儿也不在乎 (He doesn't care at all).

[6]使 is a colloquial synonym of 用 (to use), and is used primarily in North China. It often takes Nouns indicating "tools", "utensils" or "apparatus" as its Object. Reduplicating the verb indicates that the action is brief or done lightly.

她不会使筷子，只会使刀叉。
She doesn't know how to use chopsticks, but only knows how to use a fork and knife.
借你的笔使使。
May I borrow your pen (to use for a while)?

心，可是当着大亮的面，谁都不好意思说什么。

　　大亮走回来拿起杯子想喝点水，可是杯子里没水了。他就拿起老张的杯子连问也不问就喝了一口。喝完以后，他又把两只臭脚放在桌子上，一边唱歌，一边看报纸，好像什么事情都没有发生一样。小李真气得忍不住了，说了两个字："讨厌！"老张也赶快加了一句："真是什么人都有啊！"

　　你说大亮到底是个什么人？

———◆——— 生词 ———◆———

29. 澡堂	zǎo táng	N.	public baths, bathhouse
30. 头发	tóu fa	N.	hair
31. 湿	shī	Adj.	wet
32. 乱	luàn	Adj.	messy
33. 梳子	shū zi	N.	comb
34. 拉开	lā kāi	VP.	to pull out, to open
35. 抽屉	chōu tì	N.	drawer
36. 翻	fān	V.	to rummage through, to toss around
37. 乱七八糟	luàn qī bā zāo	Idiom.	at sixes and sevens, in a mess
38. 生气	shēng qì	VP/Adj.	to get angry; angry
39. 故意	gù yì	Adv.	intentionally
40. 句	jù	Classifier.	classifier for sentence
41. 满不在乎	mǎn bú zài hu	Idiom.	not be bothered at all, not care in the least
42. 借	jiè	V.	to borrow, to lend
43. 使使	shǐ shi	V.	to use briefly (cf. Note 6)
44. 嗓子	sǎng zi	N.	throat, voice
45. 往……吐痰	wǎng...tǔ táng	VP.	to spit toward
46. 恶心	ě xīn	Adj.	disgusting, nauseating
47. 臭脚	chòu jiǎo	NP.	stinky foot/feet

48. 一边……一边	yì biān...yì biān	*Adv.*	at the same time, simultaneously
49. 唱歌	chàng gē	*VO.*	to sing (a song)
50. 好像	hǎo xiàng	*Aux/V.*	to seem; to be like
51. 忍不住	rěn bú zhù	*VP.*	to be unable to bear, cannot help but...
52. 讨厌	tǎo yàn	*Adj/V.*	disgusting, annoying; to dislike
53. 赶快	gǎn kuài	*Adv.*	at once, quickly
54. 加	jiā	*V.*	to add
55. 到底	dào dǐ	*Adv.*	after all, in the final analysis (conveys emphasis in questions)

你会用下面的词吗?
澡堂、头发、湿、乱、梳子、拉开、抽屉、翻、乱七八糟、生气、故意、句、满不在乎、借、使使、嗓子、往……吐痰、恶心、臭脚、一边……一边、唱歌、好像、忍不住、讨厌、赶快、加、到底

在中国社会中，人和人的关系非常重要

句型

一、跟/和/与……相处 (get along with...)

> ✍ 相处 is an Intransitive Verb which means "to get along with" or "to interact with". It cannot take an Object but can take a Complement (as in Example 1). Modifiers such as 很难、很好、很容易, etc. can be placed before 相处.

☞ 大多数的人都认为跟人相处要互相尊重，也就是说，除了要别人尊重你以外，你也要尊重别人。

1、这些留学生跟中国老师和留学生宿舍的服务员都相处得很好。
These foreign students get along well with the Chinese teachers and service people in the foreign students' dormitory .

2、我觉得跟不拘小节的人很难相处。
I believe it is hard to get along with people who don't attend to small matters.

二、互相 (mutually, each other)

> ✍ The adverb 互相, meaning "each other", indicates a mutual relationship between two parties. It usually goes before Disyllabic Verbs such as 帮助、关心、照顾、鼓励、学习、检查.

☞ 大多数的人都认为跟人相处要互相尊重，也就是说，除了要别人尊重你以外，你也要尊重别人。

1、周玲和婷婷互相关心，互相帮助，很快就成了好朋友。
Zhou Ling and Tingting quickly became good friends because they cared about and helped each other.

2、因为我们都住在一个宿舍，每天都在一起生活、学习，所以很容易互相帮助。

Because we all live in the same dormitory and because we live and study together every day, it is easy for us to help each other.

三、也就是说 (that is to say, in other words)

> ✍ 也就是说 means "that is to say", "in other words", and is used to elaborate on or paraphrase the preceding sentence or clause.

☞ 大多数的人都认为跟人相处要互相尊重，也就是说，除了要别人尊重你以外，你也应该尊重别人。

1、我们的暑期班有个"语言誓约"，也就是说，每个人都只能说中文，不能说英文。

Our summer school has a "Language Pledge". This means that everyone can only speak Chinese; no one should speak English.

2、小林那天发烧，烧到38度，也就是说，差不多华氏100度。

Xiao Lin had a fever of 38 degrees Celsius that day. That's over 100 degrees Fahrenheit.

四、除了……以外 (besides, except)

> ✍ 除了……以外 can mean "besides, in addition to" or "except, except for", depending on the Verb Phrase that follows. When the Adverb 也 or 还 is used as in the text and Example 1, it is the former. When 都 is associated with the Verb Phrase after 除了……以外, it refers to the latter, as in example 2.

☞ 除了要别人尊重你以外，你也要尊重别人。

1、除了学中文以外，周玲还打算到各地去游览。

Besides studying Chinese, Zhou Ling also plans to visit a number of places.

2、除了王义以外，别的同学都不喜欢吃素。

Except for Wang Yi, all the classmates dislike eating only vegetables.

五、 不以为然 (take exception to, do not agree, do not approve of)

> ✍ 然 here means "是、对". 不以为然 is simply "不认为是对的", indicating objection to something with a sense of disdain. 不以为然 can be modified by 很 or 非常 as in the following examples. 现在不少十三四岁的中学生就开始找男、女朋友了，他很不以为然。 (Now, quite a few middle school students who are thirteen or fourteen years old have begun looking for boyfriends or girlfriends. He disapproves of this strongly.) 美国的小学生经常都不用做功课，很多家长非常不以为然。 (Elementary school students in the United States usually do not need to do homework. Many parents do not approve of such a practice at all.) Recently, a new meaning "to shrug off" has been added to 不以为然. The sentence in the text 我的同事李大亮却不以为然 is such an example.

☞ 大多数的人都认为跟人相处要互相尊重，也就是说，除了要别人尊重你以外，你也应该尊重别人。我的同事李大亮却不以为然。

1、美国人都说感冒了最好喝鸡汤，王义却不以为然。

Americans all say that when you catch a cold you'd better eat chicken soup. Wang Yi doesn't think this is necessary.

2、有的中学生对父母和老师说的话总是不以为然。

Some middle school students always disagree with what their parents and teachers say.

六、 Question Word + 都/也 V (whatever, whoever, wherever, etc.)

> ✍ When linked to the adverb 都 or 也, the Question Word 谁、什么、哪、什么时候、什么地方 or 哪儿 is not used to ask for specific information, but functions as an Indefinite Reference to indicate "all-inclusiveness". It can mean "anybody", "anything", "anyone", "anytime" or "anyplace" in a positive sentence, and "nobody", "nothing", "none", etc. in a negative sentence. The Question Word can function as a Subject, an Object, or an Adverbial as in the following examples:
>
> As Subject: 谁都不喜欢没有礼貌的人。
> Nobody likes people who are impolite.
>
> As Object: 来北京以前，她什么中国电影也没看过。
> Before coming to Beijing, she had not seen any Chinese movies whatsoever.
>
> As Adverbial: 你什么时候都可以给我打电话。
> You may call me at any time.

☞ 除了我和大亮以外，我们办公室还有两个人，小王和老张，可是谁都不喜欢大亮，也没有一个人跟他合得来。

1、老师跟我们住在一起，所以我们什么时候有问题，都可以去问老师。

We live together with our teachers, so whenever we have a question we can always go and ask them.

2、老谢骑着自行车哪儿都跑遍了，最后才买到了这本书。

Lao Xie rode everywhere on his bike before he finally succeeded in buying this book.

七、（跟）……合（谈／处）得来／不来 (can/cannot get along with)

> ✍ This pattern indicates "one can or cannot get along with someone else". The Verbs that can be used with 得来／不来 are limited to interpersonal activities such as 合、谈、and 处.

☞ 大亮跟小王、老张和我都在一个办公室工作，可是谁都不喜欢大亮，也没有一个人跟他合得来。

1、大亮的弟弟小亮也是个不拘小节的人，他跟谁也处不来。

Da Liang's little brother Xiao Liang is also a person who doesn't pay attention to small things and doesn't get along with anyone.

2、虽然我们才认识了两个星期，可是我们很谈得来。

Although we've known each other for only two weeks, we can really have good talks together.

八、像……这样的人 (a person such as....)

> ✍ 像……这样的人, meaning "a person such as ..." or "people like ...", is a noun phrase in which the head noun 人 is preceded by a modifying phrase. We may add a Verb Phrase after 这样 to form a Relative Clause as in: 像李大亮这样不注意别人的感觉和反应的人非常讨厌 (A person such as Li Daliang who pays no attention to others' feelings and reactions is very annoying).

☞ 很多认识大亮的人说像大亮这样的人并不是不注意自己的生活小事，而是在生活上不注意别人的感觉和反应。

1、像小刘这样常常生病的人，一定要有健康保险才行。

A person like Xiao Liu who's always sick should definitely have health insurance.

2、像陈教授这样好客的人，在北京到处都是。

Hospitable people like Professor Chen are found all over Beijing.

九、 不是……而是…… (it is not ... but...; instead of..., it is...)

> ✍ The expression 不是……而是……clarifies an idea by negating "what is not" first, and then specifying "what it is". What follows 不是 and 而是 can be a Nouns Phrase.

☞ 很多认识大亮的人说像大亮这样的人并不是不注意自己的生活小事，而是在生活上不注意别人的感觉和反应。

1、有些中国小孩喜欢吃的不是中国的饺子而是美国的快餐。

What some Chinese children would prefer to eat is not Chinese dumplings but American fast food.

2、我们现在能用中文讨论的不是一般的生活小事而是关于政治、文化的问题了。

Now we are able to discuss politics and culture in Chinese rather than just small matters in daily life.

十、 作为 (as..., being...)

> ✍ 作为 meaning "as...; being...", usually appears at the beginning of a sentence to indicate the role or status of the person(s) who is/are the subject of the main clause. This noun which follows 作为 can function as the Co-Subject of the entire sentence together with the Subject of the main clause that follows the "作为……" phrase immediately.

☞ 作为他的同事，我们都不好意思当他的面说出他的毛病。

1、作为老师，简教授对学生要求很严，但是对他们也非常关心。

As a teacher, Professor Jian is very strict with his students, but he also cares about them a great deal.

2、作为一个留学生，我觉得来中国主要是为了学习而不是玩的。

Being a foreign student, I feel the most important purpose in coming to China is not to play but to study.

十一、当（着）……的面+VP (to VP to one's face, to VP in the presence of)

> ✍ 当（着）(somebody) 的面 means "(to do something) in the presence of somebody", or "(to do something) in front of someone", "face to face". 着 is optional and may be omitted sometimes. This is a prepositional phrase used before a verb phrase to modify it.

☞ 作为他的同事，我们都不好意思当他的面说出他的毛病。

1、婷婷觉得当着这么多人的面唱歌很不好意思。
   Tingting feels embarrassed singing in front of so many people.
2、那个医生不应该当着别的病人的面讨论他得的是什么病。
   That doctor shouldn't discuss the patient's illness in front of the other patients.

这张牌子上写着什么？

练习

一、读课文回答问题

1、大亮什么时候洗的澡？在哪儿洗的澡？

2、大亮为什么用同事小李的梳子？

3、大亮怎么知道小李一定有梳子？

4、大亮为什么往窗子外头吐了一口痰？

5、大亮为什么不用自己的杯子喝水？

6、大亮看报纸的时候还做什么？

7、小李为什么说："讨厌！"？

8、如果你是小李，你会对李大亮说什么？

9、如果你是老张，你会对李大亮怎样？

10、李大亮做的哪些事情你觉得很讨厌？为什么？

11、上班的时候，李小姐、李大亮和老张在做什么？他们像不像在工作？为什么会这样？

二、听录音回答问题

1、小荃为什么不整理自己的屋子？

2、小荃为什么每次要花很多时间找东西？

3、小荃现在住在什么地方？

4、小荃的同屋觉得什么很恶心？

5、小荃的同屋为什么都很生小荃的气？

6、小荃和同屋相处得怎么样？

三、完成对话

1、A: 小张跟男同学相处都没有问题，为什么跟女同学就合不来？
　　B:（跟……相处；却）

2、A: 我只跟她在一个办公室工作，为什么要帮她的忙？
　　B:（作为……；互相V）

3、A: 他做错了，怎么你们都不生气，没有一个人说话？
　　B:（当着……的面；question word+都V）

4、A: 我觉得老师要求太严了。我说的话中国人都听得懂，为什么她还要改我的语法和发音？
　　B:（不是……而是……；也就是说）

5、A: 我认为王小姐说得对，你们觉得怎么样？
　　B:（除了……以外；不以为然）

6、A: 哎，为什么老李没有什么朋友？
　　B:（像……这样的人；跟……V得／不来）

问问中国人什么是"加强思想道德建设"

61

四、阅读短文回答问题

李大亮今年已经快三十了，可还没找到女朋友。其实他个子高高的，长得挺好看，大学毕业，在国营单位的办公室工作，条件算是不错，但是好象没有女孩子喜欢跟他来往。大亮的家人为大亮找女朋友的事情也很着急，尤其是大亮的姐姐。上个星期，大亮的姐姐给他打来电话，说她的学校新来了一位姓王的女老师，要给大亮介绍认识认识。大亮一听很高兴，就说约她这个星期六中午十二点一块儿吃中饭。

星期六很快就到了，上午十一点的时候，大亮的姐姐打电话给大亮，才发现大亮还在睡觉！原来前一天晚上大亮看电视看到三点多才上床。大亮醒了以后还满不在乎地想：让小王等一会儿也没关系，不就是吃饭嘛。平时大亮上班还常常迟到呢。大亮起床以后，穿上衣服、鞋子，看见头发乱七八糟的，想梳头，但是在桌子上、抽屉里翻了半天也没有找到梳子，只好用手整理了一下头发就出门了。

虽然约会的饭馆离大亮的家不算远，但是大亮到的时候已经十二点半了。大亮见到小王，连对不起都没说就开始点菜，他也不问小王爱吃什么，点了几个自己喜欢吃的菜就吃起来了。一边吃饭，大亮一边不停地谈昨天晚上的电视节目，也不管小王感不感兴趣。吃完了饭，要结帐了，大亮才发现忘了带钱包，他往地上吐了一口痰，大声说："糟糕！"小王只好拿自己的钱结了帐。出了饭馆，大亮问小王还要不要跟他一块儿去看电影，小王当着他的面生气地说："不用了，再见！"

你们说，象大亮这样不尊重别人、也没有礼貌的人，能找到女朋友吗？

回答问题：

1、谈谈李大亮的个人条件：学历、工作情况等等？他的家人为了什么事替他着急？

2、李大亮的姐姐为他安排了什么约会？

3、星期六的约会大亮为什么迟到了？

4、你觉得大亮和小王的那顿饭的气氛怎么样？为什么？

5、在你看来，大亮有什么地方做得不合适？应该怎么改？

6、你会给大亮什么建议来帮助他找到女朋友？

五、翻译

1. If you are disgusted by careless people like Li Daliang, you should criticize them to their faces.
2. Although you think that colleagues should respect each other, my friend Xiao Li does not think so.
3. I cannot get along with him because he spits on the floor and puts his feet on the table, but as his friend, I am embarrassed to point these things out in front of him.
4. What surprised me the most was that he does not even know his problem, which is that he does not pay attention to other people's feelings and reactions.

六、段落练习

给李大亮的一封信

收信人的名字: 尊敬的……

第一段: 写信的原因
这封信我主要想说说……

第二段: 用不同的例子说明原因:
自从……以来, ……; 不但……, 而且……; 除了……以外, ……还……; 不是……而是……; 一边……一边……; 甚至……; 结果……

第三段: 我的感觉和看法
为了……, ……; 也就是说……; 如果……, 就……; 尤其是……; 甚至……; 总之, 我认为/我的看法是……; 如果……, 就……

告别语: 祝/敬祝
身体健康/生活愉快/工作顺利

有用的词：
名词：同事、关系、办公室、礼貌、反应、感觉、毛病、一举一动
动词：作为、相处、注意、认识、尊重、不以为然、合得来/合不来
形容词：重要、不好意思、满不在乎、乱七八糟、恶心

七、作文

《什么人是不拘小节的人？》

八、讨论

1、为什么大家都讨厌李大亮？他真的是"不拘小节"吗？你觉得他的问题在哪儿？
2、如果小李和老张是美国人，他们会怎么看李大亮？你觉得中国人和美国人在这些问题上的做法会有什么不同？
3、在生活中，你遇到过像李大亮这样的人没有？你是怎样跟他们相处的？

九、语言实践

1、采访四个人：两个美国学生、两个中国学生，把李大亮的故事讲给他们听，请他们谈谈他们觉得李大亮是一个什么样的人。如果他们是李大亮的同事，他们会对李大亮说什么？比较一下中国学生和美国学生的回答，看看有没有文化上的不同。
2、采访一个中国大学生和一个美国大学生，了解他们有没有过不好相处的同屋？如果有，他们都有过什么样的问题？他们是怎么解决这些问题的？比较一下中国和美国大学生的不同。

An Intermediate Chinese Course

第五课　中国家庭的变化

中国人的家庭观念、婚姻观念和生活方式都开始发生变化

课文

一、简介

　　家庭是中国文化中的一个重要观念，也是中国人的生活中心。过去，因为人们的思想都比较传统，非常看重夫妻、父母和子女之间的关系，所以中国的家庭比较稳定，离婚率也很低。但是八十年代以后，由于改革开放，中国人的家庭观念、婚姻观念和生活方式都开始发生变化，再加上人们的工作压力越来越大，生活节奏越来越快，社会的竞争也越来越激烈。这些不同的因素都在不同程度上影响着中国的家庭生活和家庭关系。从圆圆的故事里，你可以看到，一方面⁽¹⁾，中国的家庭分工还是那种"女人做饭，男人吃饭"的传统方式；另一方面，女性既要外出工作，回家后又要负担家务。这种不合理的分工、紧张的生活节奏和激烈的社会竞争不但影响了中国的夫妻关系和家庭稳定，也给孩子带来很多困惑。

Notes (1) 一方面……（另）一方面…… links up two parallel situations or two aspects of a matter. The two situations/aspects are usually contrasting, and this contrast is reinforced by the use of 又、也, or 还 in the second clause "（另）一方面……". The focus of 一方面……（另）一方面…… is on the coexistence of the two aspects. The two aspects are usually simultaneous, though sometimes one may follow the other. A similar structure is 一边……一边……, but the focus of this latter structure is on the simultaneous occurrence of the two actions. Compare these two sentences:

张五一方面想赚大钱，另一方面又不老实，他的生意怎么能好呢？
On the one hand, Zhang Wu wants to make a lot of money; on the other hand, he is not being honest. How can his business be successful?
她去年在北京一边学中文，一边教英文。
She taught English while learning Chinese when she was in Beijing last year.

生词

1.	观念	guān niàn	*N.*	concept
2.	生活	shēng huó	*N.*	life, living
3.	中心	zhōng xīn	*N.*	center
4.	过去	guò qù	*Adv/N.*	in the past; past
5.	传统	chuán tǒng	*N.*	tradition
6.	看重	kàn zhòng	*V.*	to regard as important, to value
7.	夫妻	fū qī	*N.*	husband and wife
8.	比较	bǐ jiào	*V/Adv.*	to compare; relatively, rather
9.	稳定	wěn dìng	*Adj.*	stable
10.	离婚	lí hūn	*VO/N.*	to divorce; divorce
11.	率	lǜ	*N.*	rate, ratio
12.	改革	gǎi gé	*N/V.*	reform; to reform
13.	婚姻	hūn yīn	*N.*	marriage
14.	方式	fāng shì	*N.*	way, pattern
15.	开始	kāi shǐ	*V/N.*	to start; beginning
16.	再加上	zài jiā shàng	*VP.*	furthermore
17.	节奏	jié zòu	*N.*	pace, rhythm
18.	竞争	jìng zhēng	*V/N/Adj.*	to compete; competition; competitive
19.	激烈	jī liè	*Adj.*	fierce, intense
20.	因素	yīn sù	*N.*	factor
21.	不同程度	bù tóng chéng dù	*Adv.*	to various degrees
22.	圆圆	yuán yuan	*Personal N.*	Yuanyuan
23.	分工	fēn gōng	*VP/N.*	to divide the work; division of labor
24.	女性	nǚ xìng	*N.*	female, women
25.	负担	fù dān	*V/N.*	to bear (a burden); burden
26.	家务	jiā wù	*N.*	housework
27.	不合理	bù hé lǐ	*Adj.*	unreasonable
28.	带来	dài lái	*VP.*	to bring, to lead to
29.	困惑	kùn huò	*N/V.*	perplexity; to feel perturbed

你会用下面的词吗？
观念、生活、中心、过去、传统、看重、夫妻、比较、稳定、离婚、率、改革、婚姻、方式、开始、再加上、节奏、竞争、激烈、因素、不同程度、分工、女性、负担、家务、合理、带来、困惑

女性既要外出工作，回家后又要负担家务

二、电视节选 ▨

我需要一个温暖的家

根据电视原文编写

> （到了吃晚饭的时间，女儿打扫房间）
>
> （敲门声）
>
> 妈妈：圆圆，圆圆，开门。
>
> 圆圆：妈妈，你怎么回来这么晚呢？
>
> 妈妈：我能回来早吗？一个学生家长五点半才离开学校。我在汽车站足足又站了半小时，上了车，挤得骨头都快折了⁽²⁾。哎，你爸爸回来了吗？
>
> 圆圆：没有。
>
> 妈妈：家里有菜吗？
>
> 圆圆：不知道。
>
> 妈妈：干不了⁽³⁾活儿就别添乱，你看你把家和和的。
>
> 圆圆：我刚扫完地。
>
> （门外爸爸喊声）

✏ **Notes** (2)挤得骨头都快折了 is an example of the pattern "V (Adj.) 得+ complement of degree", which is used to indicate that "someone/something is so ... that ...". Here it is a figurative expression describing how crowded a place is ("to the extent that bones are about to break"). The "complement of degree" may be a VP, a sentence, or just a phrase. For example,

他高兴得跳了起来。(VP)

功课多得我没有时间睡觉。(sentence)

There is so much homework that I haven't had time to sleep.

房间乱得不得了。(phrase)

The room is awfully messy.

(3)V + 得了 / V + 不了 (+ Obj.) is a "potential resultative verb" construction meaning "can/cannot do something". The 了 in this structure is pronounced "liao" (not "le"). The Verb in this structure may be an Intransitive Verb such as 走、来、去、玩, etc., or a VO Structure such as 吃饭、睡觉、看书、说话、写字, etc. Note that when VO is used, the Verb and Object are separated by the infix 得 or了, e.g. 吃不了饭, 看得了书.

爸爸：圆圆。

（圆圆开门）

圆圆：爸。

爸爸：嗯。哎呀，这一天，真够呛⁽⁴⁾啊。这一下午连口水都没喝。
哎，我说，晚上吃什么？肚子饿坏了。

妈妈：噢，饿了才回来吃饭，是吧？吃什么？我还问你呢？这又不是
饭馆，想吃什么就有什么！

爸爸：哎，我说，你的话是怎么说的，啊？我这不顺便问问吗，你发
什么火啊？我这一天容易吗？喊！

妈妈：你不容易，我容易？好，大厂长，以后你也挣个万儿八千的拿
回来，我给你当保姆，保证你进门就吃。

爸爸：你……这厂子里的事儿啊，就够我挠头的了，回家还看你的脸
子⁽⁵⁾。你，你也太不近人情了吧！

妈妈：我不近人情？你近人情？你也去盯盯一天8节课的讲台去，你
也做做一天三顿饭，你也操心一下这一家三口人的四季衣裳。

爸爸：你还有完没完，啊？越说你越来劲儿了，我看你是有病⁽⁶⁾！

妈妈：你才有病呢！你的病就跟你们厂子似的，没治！

Notes ⁽⁴⁾够呛 is a colloquial expression used primarily in North China. It indicates that a situation is so unpleasant that it could make one choke, i.e., to the extent of being "unbearable" or "terribly serious". It can function as a Predicate or a Complement. For example,

挤得够呛。	It is terribly crowded.
今天真够呛。	Today was really unbearable.

⁽⁵⁾脸子, a synonym of the more widely used 脸色, is a word used in North China to refer to the unpleasant look of someone's facial expression. "看……的脸色/脸子" literally means "to look at someone's facial expression", implying that one must adjust/accommodate one's speech or behavior according to that someone's mood or temper.

⁽⁶⁾ "(Somebody) 有病" is a Beijing colloquial expression which means "Someone is crazy". This expression must be used with caution lest you inadvertently offend that "somebody".

圆圆：妈，您别说了！爸，你们别吵了。你们一吵，我的心里头就乱得[7]慌。

爸爸：去！去！去！这儿没你的事儿，快走！啊？你说，我一回家，啊？你就找碴儿。

妈妈：我找碴儿？是我找碴儿还是你找碴儿？

爸爸：你找碴儿呗！

妈妈：我看是你找碴儿！

爸爸：我怎么找碴儿了？

妈妈；那当然啦！

爸爸：厂里那么多事儿，你说我不管谁管呢？

妈妈：厂里？厂里需要你管，是吧？

爸爸：那当然的啦！

妈妈：好啊！你卷铺盖[8]卷儿上厂里住去啊！走啊！

爸爸：有你这么说话的吗？

妈妈：我怎么了？

爸爸：你还老师呢！

妈妈：老师怎么了？

爸爸：为人师表？啊？你让圆圆说说。

妈妈：说说就说说！

爸爸：圆圆！你评评！

Notes [7]Adj./V + 得慌 is another example of Complement of Degree. Used mostly in colloquial Chinese, it indicates an extreme situation causing one to become '慌' (bewildered, flustered). Some Adjectives and Verbs commonly associated with "……得慌" are 乱、忙、累、闷、饿、热、疼、堵, etc.

[8]Originally 铺盖 meant "bedding" and 卷铺盖 meant "to roll up one's bedding". Now 卷铺盖 is used mostly figuratively to mean that someone is fired from a job and has to pack up to leave.

妈妈：圆圆，你来！

爸爸：妈妈：圆圆！圆圆！

［爸爸妈妈互相看，圆圆不在房间，到外边去了］

［孩子们玩的声音］

儿童：看你往哪儿跑？

［圆圆看孩子们高兴地玩］

［一个家庭，爸爸正在给母女二人照相］

爸爸：我喊一二三就开始照，一二三！

［圆圆羡慕地看着别的孩子跟爸爸妈妈一起玩］

—————— 生词 ——————

30. 需要	xū yào	V/N.	to need; need
31. 温暖	wēn nuǎn	Adj.	warm
32. 打扫	dǎ sǎo	V.	to sweep, to clean
33. 敲门	qiāo mén	VO.	to knock on the door
34. 家长	jiā zhǎng	N.	parents, the head of a family
35. 离开	lí kāi	V.	to leave
36. 足足	zú zú	Adv.	fully, as much as
37. 挤	jǐ	V/Adj.	to squeeze; crowded
38. 骨头	gǔ tou	N.	bone
39. 折	shé	V.	to break, to snap
40. 活儿	huór	N.	(colloquial) work
41. 添乱	tiān luàn	VO.	to add to a mess
42. 和和	huò huo	VP.	(colloquial) to mix, to make a mess
43. 扫地	sǎo dì	VO.	to sweep the floor
44. 喊声	hǎn shēng	NP.	the sound of shouting
45. 嗯	ng	Intj.	mm..., hm... (indicating one heard what the other person said)

46. 哎呀	ài ya	*Intj.*	Aah! Ooh! (indicating surprise, or just suddenly remembering something
47. 够呛	gòu qiàng	*Adj.*	(colloquial) lit. "enough to make one choke", unbearable, terrible
48. 口	kǒu	*Classifier.*	(=一口) a mouthful of...
49. 饿坏	è huài	*VP.*	starving, extremely hungry
50. 噢	ào	*Intj.*	Oh! (indicating sudden realization)
51. 顺便	shùn biàn	*Adv.*	conveniently, in passing, along the way
52. 发火	fā huǒ	*VO.*	to get angry, to lose one's temper
53. 厂长	chǎng zhǎng	*N.*	factory chief
54. 嘁	qī	*Intj.*	Geez! (expressing exasperation)
55. 挣	zhèng	*V.*	to earn
56. 万儿八千	wànr bā qiān	*Idiom.*	(colloquial) eight thousand or ten thousand dollars, a lot of money
57. 保姆	bǎo mǔ	*N.*	nanny, maid
58. 保证	bǎo zhèng	*V.*	to guarantee, to assure
59. 挠头	náo tóu	*VO/Adj.*	to scratch one's head; vexing, brain-racking
60. 看……的脸子	kàn...liǎn zi	*N.*	lit. "to look at so-and-so's (ugly) face", to bear so-and-so's temper/mood (cf. Note 5)
61. 不近人情	bú jìn rén qíng	*Idiom.*	lit. "not in line with human feelings", unreasonable
62. 盯盯	dīng ding	*V.*	to fix one's eyes on, to persevere in a difficult/tedious task
63. 节	jié	*Classifier.*	(for a class period)
64. 讲台	jiǎng tái	*N.*	classroom or lecture platform
65. 顿	dùn	*Classifier.*	(for a meal, a round of scolding, etc.)
66. 操心	cāo xīn	*V.*	to worry about, to take pains with
67. 四季	sì jì	*N.*	four seasons, all seasons
68. 衣裳	yī shang	*N/V.*	clothes; clothing
69. 来劲儿	lái jìnr	*VO/Adj.*	(colloquial) to surge in

73

			energy/zeal/gusto; to be fired up
70. ……似的	shì de	*Prep.*	as if..., just like...as (cf. Sentence Pattern 9)
71. 没治	méi zhì	*VP.*	beyond remedy, no cure
72. 吵	chǎo	*V/Adj.*	to quarrel (often followed by object 架), to make a lot of noise; noisy
73. 乱得慌	luàn de huāng	*VP.*	awfully jumbled, extremely upset
74. 找碴儿	zhǎo chár	*VO.*	(colloquial) to find fault, to pick a quarrel
75. 呗	bei	*Intj.*	sentence-final particle to expressing obviousness
76. 卷铺盖卷儿	juǎn pū gai juǎnr	*Idiom.*	(colloquial) lit. "to roll up one's bedroll", to pack up (and leave) (cf. Note 9)
77. 为人师表	wéi rén shī biǎo	*Idiom.*	to serve as a teacher, to act as an example for others (师表: an exemplary teacher, a role model)
78. 评评	píng ping	*V.*	to judge, to evaluate
79. 外边	wài biān	*N.*	outside
80. 玩	wán	*V.*	to play
81. 照相	zhào xiàng	*VO.*	to take pictures

你会用下面的词吗？
需要、温暖、打扫、敲门、家长、离开、足足、挤、骨头、活儿、添乱、扫地、喊声、嗯、哎呀、够呛、饿坏、顺便、发火、厂长、挣、保姆、保证、不近人情、盯盯、节、讲、台、顿、操心、衣裳、似的、没治、吵、乱得慌、找碴儿、为人师表、评评、外边、玩、照相

句型

一、看重 (to pay great attention to, to value)

> 看重 means "to regard as important", "to value (somebody or something)", and can be modified by 很、非常、不太, etc. The object of 看重 can be a Personal Noun or Pronoun, as well as a concrete or abstract noun, such as 成绩、关系、能力、方式、感情、技术, and 质量.

☞ 过去，因为人们的思想都比较传统，非常看重夫妻、父母和子女之间的关系，所以中国的家庭比较稳定，离婚率也很低。

1、这个学校的学生都很看重自己的学习成绩。
The students in this school pay a lot of attention to their grades.

2、虽然她还是个新演员，但是导演已经非常看重她了。
Although she is a new actress, the director already thinks highly of her.

二、由于 (due to, as a result of)

> 由于…… is a formal way to indicate a reason, and is used mostly in written Chinese. It usually occurs in the first clause of a two-clause sentence to introduce the reason, with the result/outcome stated in the second clause. Like its more commonplace synonym 因为, it is often coupled with 所以 in the second clause. The two clauses stating the cause and result may be reversed, and 因为 may be used in the second clause to indicate the reason behind the situation stated in the first clause. However, 由于 is transformed to 是由于 when used in the second clause to state the reason.

☞ 由于改革开放，中国人的家庭观念、婚姻观念和生活方式都开始发生变化。

1、由于很多司机不遵守交通规则，使交通阻塞更加严重。
Traffic congestion has become more severe as a result of many drivers not complying with traffic rules.

2、由于受到西方文化的影响，中国人现在过生日也吃蛋糕了。

Due to the influence of Western culture, the Chinese people now also eat birthday cake when celebrating birthdays.

三、（再）加上 (in addition, moreover)

> ✍ （再）加上 is a phrase used to introduce one or more factors in addition to what has already been stated in the preceding sentence. It means "in addition", "more over" or simply "plus". 她本来就很聪明，加上老师的帮助，所以进步很快。(She was quite smart to begin with. On top of that, the teacher helped her, so she has made rapid progress.) 李大亮很不礼貌，不尊重别人，加上他对别人的批评不以为然，所以大家都讨厌他。(Li Daliang is very impolite, and does not respect others. In addition, he shrugs off others' criticism, and therefore, everybody loathes him.)

☞ 但是八十年代以后，由于改革开放，中国人的家庭观念、婚姻观念和生活方式都开始发生变化，再加上人们的工作压力越来越大，生活节奏越来越快，社会的竞争也越来越激烈。

1、她本来就很聪明，再加上老师的帮助和她自己的努力，她的电脑技术提高得很快。

She was quite smart to begin with, but through her own effort and with the teacher's help, her computer skills have improved tremendously.

2、她刚到美国的时候，英文不好，学习的压力很大，再加上她的经济情况也不好，所以才六个月她就决定回国了。

When she first came to the U.S., her English was poor and the pressure from school work was great. In addition, her economic situation was not good. So she decided to return home after just six months.

四、既……又…… (both...and..., neither... nor...)

> ✍ 既……又…… is used to link up two Verb Phrases or Adjectives to juxtapose two aspects of a person or thing. It is similar to 不但……而且……. However, 既……又…… can be used only when the two aspects share the same subject, whereas 不但……而且…… can be used whether or not the two VP's have the same subject. E.g. 在中国，不但女人做家务，而且很多男人也做家务。(In China, not only women do housework, so do a lot of men.) 既……又…… cannot be used instead of 不但……而且…… in the above sentence. 也 or 且 may be used in lieu of 又 in the 既……又…… structure, but they are less common.

☞ 一方面，中国的家庭分工还是那种"女人做饭，男人吃饭"的传统方式；另一方面，女性既要外出工作，回家后又要负担家务。

1、 在北京我常常去公园跟老人聊天，这样既可以练习说中文，又可以了解中国文化。

I often went to the park to chat with elderly people when I was in Beijing. In this way, I could both practice Chinese and learn about Chinese culture.

2、 李大亮既不注意自己的举动，又不注意别人的反应，怎么会有人喜欢他呢？

Li Daliang never pays attention to what he does, nor to other's reactions. How can people like him?

五、 足足 V 了 (+period of time/amount) (fully, as much as..., not a bit less than...)

> ✍ 足足 is an Adverb, used before a Verb Phrase with a quantifier to underscore the large amount (of time, money, etc.) in the statement. It is similar to 整整 in meaning.

☞ 我在汽车站又足足站了半小时。

1、 昨天她给朋友打电话足足打了两个多钟头。

Yesterday she gave her friend a phone call that lasted for over two hours.

2、 他下海当个体户以后，足足赚了十几万块钱。

After he became a private entrepreneur, he earned well over 100,000 *yuan*.

六、 连……都 / 也 (even)

> ✍ 连……, meaning "even ...", is used to state an extreme case. It must be used in conjunction with 都 or 也. Grammatically, 连 is an adverb (or coverb), and therefore must precede the main verb of the sentence, even though what follows 连 may be the object of the sentence, as in the text and Example 1. What follows 连 may also be the subject of the sentence, as in 连三岁的孩子都会唱这个歌 (Even three year old kids can sing this song.); or an Adverbial as in example 2.

☞ 这一下午连口水都没喝。

1、 周玲来北京已经五个星期了，连一句英文都没说过。

Zhou Ling has been in Beijing for 5 weeks already and has not spoken even one word of English.

77

2、圆圆的爸爸很忙，连星期天也要回厂里工作。

    Yuanyuan's father is very busy; he has to go to work at the factory even on Sundays.

七、又不／没+V (used in negation for emphasis)

> ✍ 又 is used in a Rhetorical Question or a Negative Sentence to emphasize negation.

☞ 这又不是饭馆，想吃什么就有什么！

1、他又不会弹钢琴，买钢琴做什么？

    Why do you want to buy a piano? He can't even play it.

2、你是怎么知道的？我又没有告诉过你！

    How did you know? I never told you.

八、够……V 的 (sufficient to V, plenty enough for someone to V)

> ✍ "够V" means "enough to V"; and if a personal noun or pronoun is inserted between 够 and the verb, then the meaning becomes "enough for...to V". The expression often ends with 的 or 了 or both, to convey the sense that the amount or degree is more than enough, in fact, almost too much.

☞ 这厂子的事儿啊，就够我挠头的了，回家还要看你的脸子。

1、我们每天交这么多的作业，也够老师改的了。

    Since we hand in so much work every day, it is plenty/enough for the teacher to correct.

2、星期五有语言实践报告，够咱们准备的了。

    On Fridays we have language practicum; it is plenty/enough for us to prepare.

九、跟……似的 (to be like...)

> ✍ This structure is used to liken the subject or topic of the sentence to the "thing" (a Noun, Pronoun, or Verb Phrase) inserted between 跟 or 像 and 似的. 跟 and 像 are interchangeable in this pattern. When 似的 is preceded by a Verb Phrase, 跟/像 may be omitted from this pattern, e.g. 挤得骨头都快折了似的. (It's so crowded that it's like my bones were about to break.)

☞ 你的病跟你们厂子似的，没治！

1、这是什么药，怎么像糖似的？

What kind of medicine is this? Why does it taste so much like candy?

2、她说话说得特别好听，跟唱歌似的。

When she speaks it sounds especially pleasant, as though she's singing.

十、还……呢 (used to convey ridicule or disdain)

> ✍ This pattern is used to sarcastically ridicule or to express disdain for - someone or something. It conveys the sense that the subject is unworthy of its name or title, or unfit to do something. Grammatically, what comes between 还 and 呢 should be a VP. But when that VP is an equative verb (e.g. 是、当、作 + N, then the equative verb may be dropped in colloquial speech, as in the text and example 2.

☞ 你还老师呢！

1、他连交通规则都不懂，还开出租汽车呢！

He doesn't even understand traffic rules, how could he drive a taxi!

2、你还画家呢！一个月挣不到一千块钱。

You, an artist? Yeah, right! You can't earn even a thousand RMB a month!

练习

一、读课文回答问题

1、妈妈为什么很晚才回家？

2、妈妈回家的时候，圆圆正在做什么？妈妈看见了高兴不高兴？

3、为什么爸爸回家后就跟妈妈吵起架来了？

4、爸爸为什么觉得妈妈不近人情？

5、你觉得妈妈是不是不近人情？为什么？

6、圆圆看到爸爸、妈妈吵架，心里觉得怎么样？她做了什么？

7、爸爸妈妈听完圆圆的话以后，还吵架吗？

8、爸爸妈妈到底吵什么？妈妈觉得爸爸不应该做什么？爸爸呢？

9、爸爸妈妈找圆圆的时候，她到哪儿去了？她看到了什么？她心里会想什么？

10、从圆圆的家庭来看，你觉得中国人的家庭关系怎么样，有什么样的家庭分工？

二、听录音回答问题

1、为什么"女人做饭，男人吃饭"的传统观念不再合理了？

2、什么样的家庭是最理想的家庭？

3、什么样的男人愿意留在家里照顾孩子？

4、为什么有的父母让孩子在外边吃饭？

5、为什么父母工作很忙的孩子容易有问题？

6、为什么两人都忙着工作的夫妻容易离婚？

三、完成对话

1、A：我们走了多长时间了？怎么还不到天安门？

  B：（足足V了time；由于）

2、A：什么？这些小孩七岁了还不会自己洗澡？

  B：（来自；连……都……）

3、A：我只有80块钱，吃饺子可以吗？

  B：（又不／没V；够……V的）

4、A：他们说那个饭馆是最干净、最方便、最实惠的。

  B：（还……呢；跟……似的）

四、阅读短文回答问题

中国的妇女解放

在中国过去几千年的传统社会中，由于受到"男主外，女主内"的传统思想的影响，丈夫负责出去工作、赚钱、养家，而妻子只能以家庭为生活中心，她们很少有机会上学受教育，也不能出去工作，整天待在家里既要做家务又要照顾老人和孩子。很多妇女没有任何经济收入，年轻的时候靠丈夫，老了以后靠孩子，自己什么事情都不能决定。

到了五十年代，一方面，中国政府要求妇女走出家庭，参加工作；另一方面由于政府实行低工资政策，丈夫一个人赚的钱根本就不够养家，所以很多妇女在这个时候开始出门工作。从那时起，无论是在农村还是在城市，无论是在工厂还是在学校，到处都可以看到女性工作者。因为妇女有了经济收入，在家里开始有了地位。但是这也使家庭分工更不公平，因为像做饭、照顾孩子、整理房间等家务大部分还是由妻子来完成的。每天妇女除了工作，回家以后还要操心全家人的三顿饭，四季衣裳，还有孩子的教育，可以说，她们的负担更重了。

回答问题:

1、中国传统观念中的"男主外、女主内"思想是什么意思?在那些年代,丈夫和妻子的分工是什么样的?

2、你认为这种分工的不同反映了中国传统社会里男女地位的什么特点?

3、妇女在旧式家庭中受到什么样的限制?

4、为什么自从五十年代以来,出去工作的妇女越来越多?这给她们的生活带来了什么变化?

5、你认为现代的职业妇女面临什么困难?请你分别从政府、单位、丈夫的角度谈一谈怎么才能解决这些问题?

五、 翻译

1. What he said reflected an important Chinese concept: that family is the center of one's life and the basis of society.

2. By the way（对了）, may I ask who in your family cooks the three meals for the day and takes care of the family's seasonal clothing?

3. Do you think economic reform and the opening up of the country have had an impact on the Chinese family structure?

4. Due to the following reasons (原因 yuán yīn), many social changes are gradually affecting the structure of Chinese families: first, the working hours are getting longer; second, life's pace is getting faster; third, the competition is becoming more fierce.

六、段落练习

我对男女平等的 (equality) 看法

第一段：提出个人的看法
　　　　我个人的看法是……；在不同程度上，……；也就是说……

第二段：说明为什么我的看法是有道理的
　　　　由于……；一方面……，另一方面……；再加上……；
　　　　所以……；不但……也……；还有……；除了……以
　　　　外，……还……

第三段：总结 (summary)
　　　　简单地说，……；无论……都……；既……又……

有用的词：
名词：思想、观念、生活、方式、因素、分工、家务，节奏、竞争
动词：看重、发生、负担、作为、需要、相处、注意、尊重、不以
　　　为然、
形容词：重要、很传统、稳定、激烈、温暖

七、作文

《经济发展对家庭的影响》

八、讨论

1、圆圆的爸爸妈妈吵架的原因是什么？这跟经济改革、国家开放有没有关系？为什么？

2、在美国，先生和太太吵架的事情多不多？多数的原因是什么？

3、要是圆圆的妈妈不用去工作，只待在家里，她还会跟圆圆的爸爸吵架吗？为什么？

4、父母吵架对孩子有什么影响？如果你是圆圆，会怎么样做？

5、中国的家庭生活、关系和结构 (jié gòu, structure) 在改革开放以后发生了什么样的变化？你认为这种变化对家庭和社会都很好吗？

九、语言实践

1、采访两个小学生或者中学生，了解一下他们父母的工作情况，看看他们有多少时间和他们的爸爸、妈妈待在一起？他们希望有一个什么样的家？

2、采访几位60岁以上的中国人和你的中国家庭
   (1) 五、六十年代中国家庭的情况是怎么样的？一般有几口人？家里的事情谁做得多？家人之间的关系怎么样？
   (2) 现在的家庭里的事情谁做得多？为什么？
   (3) 请你的中国爸爸谈谈对妻子满意的地方和不满意的地方。（如果不方便和他们谈这个问题，那你能不能谈谈你自己的父母）
   (4) 请你的中国妈妈谈谈对丈夫满意的地方和不满意的地方。（如果不方便和他们谈这个问题，那你能不能谈谈你自己的父母）
   (5) 比较一下五、六十年代的中国家庭跟现在的中国家庭有什么不同？

传统的家庭分工是女人看孩子做饭

第六课 下岗女工

张静就是千千万万个下岗女工当中的一个

课文

一、简介

> 这几年，中国出现了一个新词——"下岗"。下岗本来的意思是走下或者离开工作岗位，现在是失业的代名词。下岗人员是指那些原来有工作单位，后来因为单位体制改革、人员过多等原因而失去工作的人。
>
> 通常，下岗人员可以从国家或者原工作单位领到一笔下岗费或者在一段时间内每月可以领一定的生活费。很多人下了岗以后都要面临一个重新就业的问题，比如参加职业培训以便另找工作，下海当个体户，或者去外地打工。下岗人员重新就业是很不容易的，下岗女工就更困难了，因为她们多数[1]已经三四十岁了，没有什么学历[2]，也没有什么特别的技术，所以很难找到合适的工作，张静就是千千万万个下岗女工当中的一个。

Notes [1] 多数 is a Numeral which means "the majority" or "most". It is used in two ways: 1) as a Noun Modifier, e.g. 多数(的)学生 (most of the students), 多数(的)女工 (most of the women workers); 2) as a NP, e.g. 我们学校的学生，多数是 18-22岁。 (Most ACC students are 18-22 in age.) 我们是多数。 (We are in the majority.) 多半 is a synonym of 多数, and may be used in all but one of the contexts mentioned above. The one exception is as predicate nominative, e.g. it is incorrect to say * 我们是多半。 In addition, 多半 (but not 多数) can also be used to mean "most probably"; e.g.:

周末她多半都不在宿舍。
She is mostly not in the dormitory on the weekend.
已经十一点了，小林今天晚上多半不会来了。
It is already 11 o'clock. Xiao Lin most likely won't come tonight.

— ◆ — 生词 — ◆ —

1. 下岗	xià gǎng	*VO.*	to be laid off, to leave one's post
2. 女工	nǚ gōng	*NP.*	female worker
3. 出现	chū xiàn	*V.*	to appear, to emerge
4. 新词	xīn cí	*NP.*	new term
5. 本来	běn lái	*Adj/Adv.*	original; originally
6. 岗位	gǎng wèi	*N.*	post, position
7. 代名词	dài míng cí	*N.*	pronoun, substitute word
8. 失业	shī yè	*VP.*	to lose one's job, to be unemployed
9. 人员	rén yuán	*N.*	personnel, staff
10. 指	zhǐ	*V.*	to designate, to signify
11. 体制	tǐ zhì	*N.*	system
12. 过多	guò duō	*Adj.*	excessive, in surplus
13. 等	děng	*N.*	etc., and so on
14. 原因	yuán yīn	*N.*	reason
15. 失去	shī qù	*V.*	to lose
16. 通常	tōng cháng	*Adv.*	usually, generally
17. 国家	guó jiā	*N.*	country
18. 领到	lǐng dào	*VP.*	to receive
19. 笔	bǐ	*Classifier.*	a sum (of money)
20. 费	fèi	*N.*	fee, expense

Notes (2) In 没有什么学历, 什么 is not used as an interrogative pronoun, but in its indefinite sense. In a positive sentence or a Yes/No Question, it indicates "something". In a negative sentence, it indicates "anything". This "indefinite" usage applies to other question words (谁, 哪儿, etc.) as well. For example,

我没跟谁说话。
I didn't speak to anyone.
今天我没去哪儿，就在宿舍里学习。
I didn't go anywhere today, just stayed in the dorm and studied.
我饿了，想吃点什么。
I'm hungry, and want to eat something.
他们好像在讨论什么。
They seem to be discussing something.
我不买什么，只是看看。
I'm not buying anything, just browsing.
她们没有什么技术，所以找工作很难。
They don't have any skills, so it is very hard to find a job.

21.	段	duàn	Classifier.	a period (of time), section, segment
22.	一定的	yí dìng de	Adj.	a certain (amount, time, etc.), fixed
23.	面临	miàn lín	V.	to face (an impending crisis/dilemma)
24.	重新	chóng xīn	Adv.	again, anew, afresh
25.	就业	jiù yè	VP.	to obtain employment, to take up an occupation
26.	参加	cān jiā	V.	to participate, to join in
27.	培训	péi xùn	V/N.	to train; training
28.	以便	yǐ biàn	PrepP.	so that, in order to
29.	外地	wài dì	NP.	other locations (within the country), non-local
30.	打工	dǎ gōng	VP.	to work (at menial or odd jobs)
31.	其中	qí zhōng	Prep.	among (which, them, etc.), in (which, it, etc.)
32.	岁	suì	N.	years of age
33.	技术	jì shù	N.	skill, technology
34.	中年	zhōng nián	N.	middle age
35.	学历	xué lì	N.	educational background
36.	合适	hé shì	Adj.	appropriate, suitable, qualified
37.	千千万万	qiān qiān wàn wàn	Adj.	"thousands and ten thousands", multitudes
38.	当中	dāng zhōng	Prep.	among, in the midst

你会用下面的词吗？
下岗、女工、出现、新词、本来、岗位、代名词、失业、人员、指、体制、过多、等、原因、失去、通常、国家、领到、笔、费、段、一定的、面临、重新、就业、参加、培训、以便、外地、打工、其中、岁、技术、中年、学历、合适、千千万万、当中

二、报纸节选

下岗女工

（根据《华声日报》原文改编）

今年35岁的张静，下岗已经五年了，一直没找到合适的工作。五月的一天，她又来到东城区职业介绍服务中心碰运气。张静原来在北京市地毯二厂工作，厂里有500多个工人，下岗了400多。记者找到下岗的张静，问了她下面几个问题：

———————◆———————

记者：下岗后这四、五年日子怎么样？

张静：这四五年日子可真不好过。下岗后我每月拿二十块钱，哪儿够花的。我上有老人，下有孩子。既要养活老人，又要应付孩子的学费，每月都是紧巴巴的。儿子今年十岁，光英语课一年的学费就得两千块。没办法，只好拿出我的全部下岗费两千块交这笔钱。这还不算，现在马上又要房改，得一下子拿出三四万块买房子，我上哪儿找这笔钱呢？

记者：在下岗的这四五年里，你做过什么工作吗？

张静：做过。当过电话员、导购等等[3]。在外边打工，要看人家的脸

Notes [3]等等 is a Particle used at the end of a list of items to indicate that the list is not exhaustive . It is similar to "etc.", "and so on and so forth" in meaning. 等 alone means the same thing, but the tone is milder. For example,

这个大学比较有名的专业主要有电脑、数学、中文、生物等。
The famous departments in this college include computer science, mathematics, Chinese, biology, and so on.
记者采访了小张、小王、小李、小陈等几位同学。
The reporter interviewed several students including Xiao Zhang, Xiao Wang, and Xiao Li.

The rep

色⁽⁴⁾，就像当孙子⁽⁵⁾似的，心里真不是滋味。在远大公司，上午我还在接电话，下午老板就对我说"你明天不要来了"。我心里觉得很奇怪：当时要我们来的时候老板说急着要人，怎么刚干了两个月就不缺人了？后来我们才知道在头两个月里，我们拿试用期工资六百块，到第三个月，该涨到九百块了，老板就又去雇用新人了。

记者：今天在这儿找到合适的工作了吗？

张静：没有。今天我又白来一趟。你看，上百个招工单位，合适的工种全要三十五岁以下的，哪儿有我们的工作呀？我只符合保险公司的要人条件，但是我干不了这种到处跑的工作。当清洁工，一个月才三四百块，对我们的生活根本不管用。想自己干，又没有资金，也没有人给我投资。上早市卖早点，我还拉不下脸⁽⁶⁾来。我现在挺苦恼的，再晃晃，就四十了。到了那个年龄，找工作就更难了。像我这样的人，起码代表一部分人，代表我这个年龄段的下岗女工。

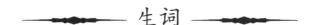

生词

38. 华声日（月）报　huá shēng rì (yuè) bào　*NP.*　Hua Sheng Daily (Monthly) (cf. Lesson 10)

Notes ⁽⁴⁾看……的脸色 is similar to 看……的脸子 (Lesson 5) in meaning, except that it is more commonly used and not just limited to Northern China. (Cf. Lesson 5, Note 5)

⁽⁵⁾孙子, originally "grandson," is used figuratively here to mean "someone with no status, low man on the totem pole". In an extended family in traditional China, three generations usually lived under the same roof. As the youngest ones in the family, grandsons had the lowest status and had to obey everyone else. Thus, 象孙子似的 indicates that one has to kowtow to others, just like a grandson in a big family.

⁽⁶⁾拉下脸, lit. "to give up one's face", is a colloquial expression which means "to compromise one's dignity". So 拉不下脸 means "unable to forego one's dignity (to do something lowly)".

39. 改变	gǎi biàn	*V./N.*	to adapt; adaptation
40. 东城区	dōng chéng qū	*Place N.*	East City District
41. 服务中心	fú wù zhōng xīn	*NP.*	service center
42. 碰运气	pèng yùn qì	*VO.*	to try one's luck
43. 地毯	dì tǎn	*N.*	carpet
44. 日子	rì zi	*N.*	life, livelihood (**过日子**: to get by from day to day
45. 养活	yǎng huó	*VP.*	to support, to provide a living (for someone)
46. 应付	yìng fu	*V.*	to deal with, to cope with
47. 学费	xué fèi	*N.*	tuition
48. 紧巴巴	jǐn bā bā	*Adj.*	very tight
49. 光	guāng	*Adv.*	only, just
50. 办法	bàn fǎ	*N.*	way, means
51. 全部	quán bù	*Adj.*	all
52. 算	suàn	*V.*	to count
53. 房改	fáng gǎi	*NP.*	housing reform
54. 一下子	yí xià zi	*Adv.*	all of a sudden
55. 电话员	diàn huà yuán	*N.*	telephone operator
56. 导购	dǎo gòu	*N.*	"purchase advisor", merchandise pusher
57. 脸色	liǎn sè	*N.*	facial expression (usually unpleasant), facial colors (indicating state of health)
58. 孙子	sūn zi	*N.*	grandson
59. 像……似的	xiàng...shì de	*Prep.*	as if
60. 不是滋味	bú shì zī wèi	*Idiom.*	to be left with a bad taste in one's mouth, to be dismayed, to feel bad
61. 远大公司	yuǎn dà gōng sī	*NP.*	Yuan Da Company
62. 接电话	jiē diàn huà	*VO.*	to answer the phone
63. 老板	lǎo bǎn	*N.*	boss
64. 急	jí	*Adj.*	urgent
65. 缺	quē	*V.*	to be short of, to lack

66. 头	tóu	Adj.	first (in the sense of "initial, earliest")
67. 试用期	shì yòng qī	N.	"trial use" period, probation period
68. 工资	gōng zī	N.	wages
69. 涨到	zhǎng dào	VP.	to go up to, to rise to
70. 雇用	gù yòng	V.	to hire
71. 白	bái	Adv.	in vain, for nothing
72. 趟	tàng	Classifier.	classifier (for a trip)
73. 招工	zhāo gōng	VO.	to recruit workers
74. 工种	gōng zhǒng	NP.	kind of job
75. 符合	fú hé	V.	to correspond with, to match, to meet (requirements)
76. 保险公司	bǎo xiǎn gōng sī	NP.	insurance company
77. 要人条件	yào rén tiáo jiàn	NP.	hiring requirements
78. 到处	dào chù	Adv.	everywhere
79. 清洁工	qīng jié gōng	N.	sanitation worker
80. 根本	gēn běn	Adv.	simply, (not) ... at all
81. 不管用	bù guǎn yòng	Idiom.	of no use, useless
82. 资金	zī jīn	N.	resources, capital
83. 投资	tóu zī	VO.	to invest
84. 早市	zǎo shì	NP.	morning market
85. 早点	zǎo diǎn	N.	breakfast
86. 拉不下脸	lā bù xià liǎn	Idiom.	cannot lower one's "face", unable to forego one's dignity
87. 苦恼	kǔ nǎo	Adj.	vexed, worried
88. 晃晃	huàng huang	VP.	to wander aimlessly
89. 年龄	nián líng	N.	age
90. 起码	qǐ mǎ	Adv.	at least
91. 代表	dài biǎo	V/N.	to represent; representative
92. 一部分	yí bù fèn	NP.	one segment
93. 年龄段	nián líng duàn	NP.	age group

你会用下面的词吗？
一直、服务中心、碰运气、地毯、厂、日子、花、养活、应付、学费、办法、全部、笔、算、房改、当、电话员、脸色、孙子、滋味、接电话、老板、急、缺、试用期、涨到、雇、用、白、一趟、招工、工种、符合、保险公司、要人条件、到处、清洁工、根本、不管用、资金、投资、早市、早点、苦恼、年龄、起码、代表、一部分、年龄段

很多人下了岗以后都要面临一个重新就业的问题

句型

一、本来 (original, originally)

> ✍ 本来 can be both an Adjective and an Adverb. As an Adjective, it can be used as a Noun modifier, but not as a Predicate. For example, we can say 本来的意思 (the original meaning) or 本来的颜色 (the original color) but not *你的想法很本来。(Your idea is very original.) As an Adverb, it is "movable", i.e., it can go either before the Subject or before the Verb.

☞ 下岗本来的意思是走下或者离开工作岗位，现在是失业的代名词。

1、她本来只是个普通的女工，现在是这家饭馆的老板了。

Originally, she was only a common worker; now she is the boss of this restaurant.

2、有的父母把所有的希望都放在孩子身上，甚至想让孩子去实现自己本来想实现但是又没能实现的理想。

Some parents put all their hopes on their children, even making their children realize the dreams that they themselves wanted to but could not realize.

二、是指…… （的意思）(to refer to, to designate)

> ✍ 指, lit. "to point to...", is a Transitive Verb meaning "to refer to, to indicate, to designate". It often follows 是, to give an explanation of the subject or topic of the sentence. Due to the explanatory function of 指, its object may be quite elaborate, and it may consist of a Noun Phrase, a Verb Phrase, or a Clause.

☞ 下岗人员是指那些原来有工作单位，后来因为单位体制改革，人员过多等原因而失去工作的人。

1、 "不拘小节" 是指一个人对吃饭、穿衣、梳头等生活小事不注意的意思。

"Not bothering about small matters" refers to a person who does not pay attention to little things in life, such as what kind of food they eat, what they wear, combing their hair, and so on.

2、"他的眼睛在吃冰淇淋"是指他正在看他喜欢的女孩子。

    "His eyes are eating ice cream" means that he is looking at the girl he likes.

三、因（为）……而…… (due to, owing to, because)

> This pattern is a more formal version of the "因为……所以……" structure, but it differs from the latter in two ways: 1) "因为……而……" has a "literary" flavor and is used mostly in written Chinese. The 因为 in this pattern may be abbreviated to just 因, which further increases the literary flavor. 2) The subject in the two parts of the structure "因为……而……" must be one and the same, and therefore it is only stated in the first clause; whereas the subject in the two clauses of the "因为……所以……" structure may or may not be the same.

☞ 下岗人员是指那些原来有工作单位，后来因为单位体制改革，人员过多等原因而失去工作的人。

1、目前中国的农村还有不少的孩子因为家里穷而不能上学。

    In China's countryside today, there are still many children who, due to family poverty, are unable to attend school.

2、圆圆的爸爸妈妈因工作的压力和紧张的生活节奏而常常吵架。

    Due to work related pressures and life's frantic pace, Yuanyuan's parents often argue.

四、面临 (to be facing, to encounter)

> In modern Chinese, 面临, lit. "to face", is used primarily in its figurative sense of "to be confronted with, to be up against (an impending crisis, dilemma, challenge, etc.)" It usually takes as its object such Abstract Nouns as 困难、问题、情况、危机, etc.

☞ 很多人下岗以后都要面临一个重新就业的问题，……

1、我们面临的竞争将会越来越激烈。

    The competition we are facing will become fiercer and fiercer.

2、这几年不少国营工厂都因为体制改革而面临着很多困难。

    In recent years, many state-owned factories have been faced with many difficulties due to reforms of the system.

五、 重新 (again, re + V)

> The Adverb 重新 is made up of 重 (repeat) and 新 (new). It is translated as "again", "anew", or "Re+Verb" depending on its context. For example, 重新打扫 (clean all over again), 重新检查 (re-examine), and 重新结婚 (remarry).

☞ 很多人下岗以后都要面临一个重新就业的问题，……

1、 这些工人过去都没有摸过电脑，所以必须重新培训，才能开始工作。
These workers have never touched a computer before, so they need to be retrained before starting work.

2、 根据情况的变化，老师又重新安排了暑期班的教学计划。
According to the changes in the situation, our teacher rearranged the teaching plan for the summer session.

六、 上有……下有…… (with...and...at both ends (above and below))

> 上有……下有…… is an idiomatic expression, indicating the relationships one has with those above and those below oneself in terms of age or social status. This structure may also apply to non-personal situations, e.g. 上有天堂，下有苏杭 (There's heaven above, and Suzhou and Hangzhou below.) 上有政策，下有对策 (There are policies at the top, and strategies down below.)

☞ 我上有老人下有孩子。

1、 老师，上有校长，下有我们，你就放心吧。
Teacher, with the principal above you , and us, your students below you, you can just relax.

2、 上有工厂厂长，下有几千工人，这样的事情她也不太好办啊。
It is not easy for her to handle matters like this with the director of the factory on one side and thousands of workers on the other.

七、 光⋯⋯就⋯⋯ (merely, just)

> ✍ 光 is a synonym of 就, both mean "merely", "just". But 光 is more colloquial, while 就 is more commonplace. Moreover, 光 is used with noun phrases just as often as with verb phrases, whereas 就 is used mostly with verb phrases. In the pattern "光⋯⋯就⋯⋯", the two are used in tandem to accentuate the small extent/size/quantity stated after 光 and the large extent/size/quantity stated after 就.

☞ 儿子今年十岁，光英语课一年的学费就得两千块。

1、 这一课的练习真难，光翻译就花了我一个半小时。
   The exercises of this lesson are really hard. The translation section alone took me an hour and a half.

2、 失业的问题越来越严重，光这个厂就下岗了400多人。
   The unemployment problem is getting more and more serious. 400 people got laid off from this factory alone.

八、 只好 (to have no alternative but...)

> ✍ The adverb 只好 is normally used just before the Verb, indicating that the action stated by the verb is the only available option. The situation leading to the limited option is usually stated in a preceding clause or phrase. More often than not, the subject of both the restricting factor and the limited option is one and the same, so it is stated only in the first part (e.g. examples 1 and 2 below). However, a subject may also occur in the 只好 clause, sometimes even after the adverb 只好; e.g. 功课太多了，我只好不去了。(There's too much homework, I have no choice but to not go); 别人都太忙了，只好我自己去。(Others are all too busy, there's no choice but to go myself.)

☞ 没办法，只好拿出我的全部下岗费两千块交了这笔钱。

1、 卖黄瓜的张五因为违反 (violate) 了计量法的规定，只好老老实实认错受罚。
   Zhang Wu, who sells cucumbers, has no alternative but to admit his guilt and pay the fine because he has violated the "Measure Regulation".

2、 她下岗以后，找不到合适的工作，只好去外地打工。
   After she was laid off, she could not find a suitable job, so she had no choice but to go elsewhere to take on odd jobs.

九、 白+V (in vain, for nothing)

> ✍ The primary meaning of 白 is "white", but as an Adverb, it indicates that one has failed to achieve the intended result or goal, and is commonly translated as "in vain" or "for nothing". This adverb may be intensified by reduplication, e.g. 我在这儿白白等了半个小时. (I wasted half a hour waiting here for nothing.) 白 is usually used before a verb, but sometimes it can be used with an Adj., e.g. 你别白难过了，他下岗后当上个体户，赚的钱比从前多多了. (You don't need to feel bad for nothing. After he was laid off, he became a private entrepreneur and is making a lot more money than before.)

☞ 今天我又白来一趟。

1、像大亮这样的人一点也不注意别人的感觉和反应，你说他也是白说，所以我才用摄像机把他的一举一动录下来，让他自己看看。

Daliang is the type of person who never pays attention to other people's feelings and reactions, so it is pointless to talk to him. And that's why I recorded his actions on tape to let him look at it himself.

2、如果我们不好好利用北京的环境学中文，就白来中国了。

If we don't take advantage of Beijing's environment to study Chinese, we come to China for nothing.

十、 （不）符合……（条件／要求）(not) to conform to/in accord with (conditions/requirements)

> ✍ The Verb 符合, meaning "to conform to, to be in accord with", takes as its object such abstract nouns as 条件、要求、实际、事实, etc.

☞ 我只符合保险公司的要人条件，但是我干不了这种到处跑的工作。

1、经过职业培训，这些新工人都已经符合我们公司的雇用条件了。

After professional training, these new workers now meet the job qualifications of our company.

2、张五的称砣磨去了一块，不符合计量法的要求，所以受到了处罚。

Zhang Wu violated the measurement regulation because a piece of the weight on his scale was ground off, so he had to pay a penalty.

十一、对……（不）管用 (to be of (no) use, to be (in) effective)

> ✍ 管用 is a colloquial word which means "useful, effective". It is often preceded by a Prepositional phrase "对……" to indicate the intended target situation.

☞ 当清洁工，一个月才三四百块，对我们的生活根本不管用。

1、这种药对拉肚子很管用。
This type of medicine is very effective for diarrhea.

2、你觉得每天看中文电视对提高听力管用不管用？
Do you think watching Chinese television every day will help improve listening skills?

十二、起码 (minimum, at least)

> ✍ 起码 can be an Adjective or an Adverb. As an Adjective, it means "the minimum..." and usually occurs with 的, as in 起码的要求 (the minimum requirement). When it is an Adverb, it means "at least". 最 may be added to 起码 (as either an adverb or an adjective) to intensify it, as in example 1.

☞ 像我这样的人，起码代表一部分人，代表我这个年龄段的下岗女工。

1、我们公司雇用新工人最起码的条件是会用电脑。
The minimum qualification for being hired at our company is the ability to use computers.

2、现在一个人每月的生活费起码也要两三百块钱，这些下岗费根本就不管用。
The monthly expenses of each individual are at least two to three hundred yuan nowadays, so the unemployment compensation is not much help at all.

练习

一、读课文回答问题

1、张静原来在哪儿工作？下岗多长时间了？
2、张静家里有些什么人？
3、张静把全部下岗费拿去做什么了？
4、张静下岗以后做过哪些工作？她为什么心里觉得不是滋味？
5、为什么远大公司的老板叫张静第二天不要去了？
6、在职业介绍服务中心招工的单位有多少？他们多半要找多大年纪的人？
7、张静为什么不想到保险公司工作也不想当清洁工？

二、听录音回答问题

1、为什么很多女性结婚以后愿意待在家里？
2、为什么有的女性在孩子离开家后不知道怎么安排自己的生活？
3、三、四十岁的女性重新就业会面临什么样的问题？
4、什么原因让有的女性在孩子长大后又重新回学校念书？
5、要想找个理想的工作得有什么样的条件？

三、完成对话

1、A：她下岗以后为什么不去当个体户，而要当清洁工？
　　B：（本来；只好）

2、A："小皇帝"是什么意思？
　　B：（是指；因……而……）

3、A：我花了几十块钱买这些药，可是吃了以后肚子还是不舒服。

B：（对……不管用；白＋V）

4、A：你们单位的体制改革进行得怎么样了？

B：（面临；光……就……）

5、A：这些工人已经工作半年多了，为什么还要参加职业培训呢？

B：（不符合……条件；重新）

6、A：你看这位女厂长多大岁数？

B：（上有……下有……；起码）

四、阅读短文回答问题

下岗人员的再就业问题已经成为中国政府面临的必须解决的问题，因为如果这个问题不能得到正确解决，就会影响到老百姓的日常生活甚至社会的稳定。通常单位在工作人员下岗的时候，会发给下岗工人一笔下岗费，并且在以后的一段时间内发给下岗人员一定的生活费。有的单位也会给下岗人员介绍一个工作，比方说在大饭店里打扫卫生或者去商场做导购等等。要是下岗人员不愿意去这样的地方工作，政府就不会再为他们安排其它的工作了。

下岗人员再就业难有好几个原因，一是工作少，下岗人员多，尤其是年龄大、没有技术的下岗人员多，当然就竞争不过有学历、有技术的年轻人；二是有的下岗人员怕苦、怕累，怕工资少，也拉不下脸来做一些服务性的工作。在北京流行着这样一个说法，说有的下岗工人在找工作的时候是"路远了不去，活儿累了不去，钱少了不去。"所以在各个职业介绍所常常可以看到，一方面下岗人员抱怨说下岗以后日子不好过，很苦恼，急着找到工作，另一方面介绍所给他们介绍工作的时候，他们又这个也不想做，那个也不想做。其实在北京、上海这样的大城市，工作机会还是很多的，从在菜市场卖菜到在饭馆当服务员，从当清洁工到送牛奶、送报纸，都可以赚钱。但是现在在这样的岗位上，工作着的大多数是不怕苦、不怕累的外地人，很少能看到本地的下岗人员。所以，要想完全解决下岗人员再就业的问题，除了要提高这些人员的学历和技术水平，增加工作机会以后，还必须改变有的人的观念。

回答问题：

1、通常单位怎么处理职工的下岗问题？

2、从年龄、学历、技术的方面来看，为什么下岗人员在在就业的时候会遇到种种困难？

3、为什么很多下岗人员宁可在家待着，也不愿意去从事一些服务性的工作？

4、你认为怎么才能改变这些人的观念？

五、 翻译

1. Old Zhang doesn't look right today. What is going on with him? He should have gone to work at 8:00, but he is still home.

2. I heard that almost all of those in his factory who are over forty and have no college education were laid off.

3. If Old Zhang lost his job, his family would find it difficult to live. He has both his parents and children to support. After all these years of working for the factory, he has to find a new job. It is really hard for him.

4. Many people are now facing the problem of unemployment. In Old Zhang's factory alone, 70% of the workers have lost their jobs. I guess this is the natural result of the reform in China.

"下岗" 现在是失业的代名词

六、段落练习

美国的蓝领人和白领人

第一段： 什么是蓝领人和白领人
　　　　……是指……；……本来的意思是……；……………是的
　　　　代名词

第二段： 说明蓝领人和白领人在工作上都有什么特点和不同
　　　　在不同程度上，……；因为……的原因，……；就有了
　　　　……；以便……；光……就……；再加上……；比如…
　　　　…；其中……；所以……；不但……也……；
第三段： 这两种人在社会上的需要和作用
　　　　总之……；在一段时间内，……；甚至……

有用的词：

名词： 工作单位、公司、体制、观念、原因、职业、方式、学
　　　　历、技术、费、分工、打工、工种、节奏、竞争

动词： 雇用、符合、代表、打工、到、面临、培训、参加、失
　　　　去、选择、重新

形容词： 过多、不容易、很困难、合适、全部、苦恼、好过/不
　　　　好过

副词： 本来、起码，根本

七、作文

《下岗工人×××的一天》
《中国国营单位的工人下岗问题》

八、讨论

1、为什么中国这几年会出现"下岗"（失业）的情况？你认为这是好事还是坏事？为什么？

2、为什么用"下岗"这个词代替"失业"？你还知道哪些像这样表示不愉快 (unpleasant) 的事情的代名词呢？

3、如果你是张静，你会不会把你全部的下岗费拿出来给儿子交英语课的学费？为什么？

4、张静找不到工作，跟她自己的条件有什么关系？为什么？

九、语言实践

1、到饭馆、街上的小摊儿或自由市场采访2-3名下岗工人，了解一下他们现在的生活情况怎么样？他们参加过职业培训没有？参加过哪种培训？以后有什么打算？

2、到职业介绍所采访2-3名下岗女工，了解一下她们现在的生活情况和对再就业的想法。她们是不是打算参加职业培训？找工作容易吗？会不会受到歧视 (discrimination)？

下岗女工很难找到合适的工作

An Intermediate Chinese Course

第七课　她再也不想结婚了

那时候怎么就那么甘心？

课文

一、简介

> 徐慧是北京一家有名的广告公司的秘书，今年三十七岁。九年前她跟丈夫离婚了，一个人带着孩子跟婆婆一起生活了快十年。徐慧最近有了一个男友，虽然他们的关系很好，还合伙买了房子，但是俩人都不打算结婚，也许因为他们都有离婚的经历吧。下面是徐慧讲述的她自己离婚的故事。

—————— 生词 ——————

1. 结婚	jié hūn	*VP.*	to get married
2. 徐慧	xú huì	*Personal N.*	Xu Hui
3. 广告	guǎng gào	*N.*	advertisement
4. 秘书	mì shū	*N.*	secretary
5. 丈夫	zhàng fu	*N.*	husband
6. 带	dài	*V.*	(refer to children) to look after, to raise
7. 婆婆	pó po	*N.*	mother-in-law
8. 男友	nán péng yǒu	*NP.*	boyfriend
9. 合伙	hé huǒ	*VP.*	to pool resources, to partner up
10. 也许	yě xǔ	*Adv.*	perhaps
11. 经历	jīng lì	*N.*	experience

你会用下面的词吗？
结婚、广告、秘书、丈夫、带、婆婆、男友、合伙、也许、经历

106

二、故事节选 ✂ （根据安顿《绝对隐私》片段改编）

　　我前夫是一个大学的英语老师，个子挺高的，谁都说他长得帅。他教我们那年，我上大学四年级。第一天见到他，我就爱上他了。后来他也说，那个班的学生就数我最出众。毕业第二年，我就嫁[(1)]给他了。我的家在南京，为了跟他结婚，我拼命找门路[(2)]留京，最后找到一个出版社团委的工作，连专业都丢了。

　　那时候怎么就那么甘心？说出来你都觉得可笑。我经常在下班前找个理由早走，到他回家必须经过的一个路口去等他。假如我先到家了，就把厨房的窗户开着，每隔一会儿就趴在那儿看看，看见他走进楼里才关上窗户。

　　那段时间我大概就是那种被幸福冲昏了头的女人吧。可惜好景不长。我二十八岁那年，我们决定要孩子，我是一月怀孕的。我丈夫，不对，是我前夫，在七月的时候提出离婚。他说他要去加拿大。一个女孩子帮他办出去。这个女孩子是他的学生，就和当年的我一样。不同的是，女孩子的家在加拿大，所以他要走的唯一前提就是和那个女孩结婚。他说他也没办法，实在太想出国了，找了这么多年才找到这么一个门路。再不出去，他就只有在国内当一辈子老师。

✎**Notes** [(1)]嫁 (to marry) only refers to a woman marrying a man, whereas 结婚 is gender-neutral. 结婚 is a VO and cannot in turn take another object. 嫁 can take an obj., in which case it means "to marry off...", "嫁给……" means " (for a woman) to marry so-and-so". The counterpart of a man marrying a woman (i.e. taking a wife) is 娶.

　　他们明年就要嫁女儿了。
　　They are going to marry off their daughter next year.
　　她想嫁给一个有钱的个体户。
　　She wants to marry a wealthy entrepreneur.

　　[(2)]门路 means literally "doorway, road/path". It is used mostly figuratively to refer to "social connections" (for personal gain such as getting things done or securing a job) or ways to solve a problem. The verb to use with the first meaning is 找 or 走, and the verb to use with the second meaning is 摸 (to grope for) or 开.

到今天我都记得听到这话时我的第一个反应就是双手捂住了肚子。可是不知道为什么，我就是哭不出来。我心里明白，他是真的不要我了。当天晚上我们俩就各睡各的了。我只说了一句话："让我想想"。奇怪的是那天晚上我睡得特别好，一夜无梦。第二天早上他没去上班。我也不知道自己是怎么想通的，看着他那严肃的样子，我知道不答应也没有用，还不如好合好散⁽³⁾。我就说行，你放心地走吧，孩子生出来我先带着。

我们是在一个星期以后办的离婚。我挺着大肚子跟他去街道办事处，就是当年我们结婚的那个地方。因为我的坚持离婚办得很顺利。我们最后一次见面是在他走之前，那时候他好象已经又结婚了。我没想到难过的人会是他。临走的时候，他说他一定会寄钱给我和孩子。我说你看情况吧，我无所谓⁽⁴⁾。他最后问我，为什么不留他。我说他想过好日子不是什么错，但是连没见面的孩子都舍得下的人，我能留得住吗？那天他是哭着走的。

生词

12. 前夫	qián fū	NP.	former husband
13. 个子	gè zi	N.	(refer to a person) height, build
14. 长得……	zhǎng de	VP.	to be physically...(describing a person's physical attributes)
15. 帅	shuài	Adj.	handsome

Notes ⁽³⁾好合好散: This special structure links up a pair of antonyms with a reduplicated adverb, indicating a result or subsequent event (2nd part) that follows a first event (1st part). For example, 好散 (separating peacefully) follows or results from 好合 (joining nicely). Other examples are 早睡早起 (sleep early and get up early), 晚来晚走 (come late and leave late), 多劳多得 (work more and gain more), etc.

⁽⁴⁾无所谓 is similar in meaning to 不在乎. 觉得没有什么关系, indicating that the speaker does not care.

16. 数	shǔ	*V.*	to count, to reckon...as...(cf. Sentence Pattern 2)
17. 出众	chū zhòng	*Adj.*	"stand out in a crowd", outstanding
18. 毕业	bì yè	*V.*	to graduate
19. 嫁	jià	*V.*	(of a woman) to marry
20. 南京	nán jīng	*Place N.*	Nanjing
21. 拼命	pīn mìng	*Adv.*	with all one's might, exerting one's utmost
22. 找门路	zhǎo mén lù	*VO/Idiom.*	(门路: channel, connections) to look for ways, to solicit help from potential backers
23. 留京	liú jīng	*VO.*	to stay in Beijing
24. 最后	zuì hòu	*Adv.*	finally
25. 出版社	chū bǎn shè	*N.*	publisher
26. 团委	tuán wěi	*N.*	committee of the Communist Youth League (short for 共青团委员会)
27. 专业	zhuān yè	*N.*	(academic) specialty, major
28. 丢	diū	*V.*	to lose, to (academic) specialty, to abandon
29. 甘心	gān xīn	*Adj.*	willingly
30. 可笑	kě xiào	*Adj.*	ridiculous, laughable
31. 经常	jīng cháng	*Adv.*	frequently, often
32. 下班	xià bān	*VO.*	to go off work
33. 理由	lǐ yóu	*N.*	reason
34. 经过	jīng guò	*V.*	to pass by
35. 路口	lù kǒu	*N.*	intersection
36. 假如	jiǎ rú	*Conj.*	if
37. 厨房	chú fáng	*N.*	kitchen
38. 窗户	chuāng hù	*N.*	window
39. 隔	gé	*V.*	to separate (by a partition), to be apart by (an interval or distance)
40. 趴	pā	*V.*	to lean over on (a ledge), to bend over, to lie prone
41. 楼	lóu	*N/Classifier.*	building; story, floor

42. 幸福	xìnq fú	Adj/N.	happy, content, to enjoy good fortune; happiness
43. 冲昏了头	chōng hūn le tóu	Idiom.	dizzy (with excitement or joy)
44. 可惜	kě xī	Adv/Adj.	it's a pity that..., too bad...
45. 好景不长	hǎo jǐng bù cháng	Idiom.	good times don't last long
46. 怀孕	huái yùn	VO.	to become pregnant
47. 提出	tí chū	V.	to put forward (a proposal), to bring up (an issue)
48. 加拿大	jiā ná dà	N.	Canada
49. 办	bàn	V.	to handle, to arrange
50. 当年	dāng nián	N.	in that year (当...: on/in/at that particular...)
51. 唯一	wéi yī	Adj.	only, sole
52. 前提	qián tí	N.	premise, prerequisite
53. 实在	shí zài	Adv.	really, truly
54. 出国	chū guó	VO.	to go abroad
55. 国内	guó nèi	NP/Adj.	in one's own country; domestic
56. 一辈子	yí bèi zi	N.	all one's life
57. 双手	shuāng shǒu	NP.	both hands
58. 捂住	wǔ zhù	VP.	to cover (with one's hands)
59. 肚子	dù zi	N.	belly, stomach
60. 哭	kū	V.	to cry
61. 明白	míng bai	V/Adj.	to understand; clear
62. 无梦	wú mèng	VP.	to have no dream (无: 没有)
63. 想通	xiǎng tōng	VP.	to straighten out one's thinking, to be reconciled/resigned to a reality
64. 严肃	yán sù	Adj.	serious, earnest
65. 样子	yàng zi	N.	manner, demeanor, appearance, shape
66. 答应	dā yìng	V/N.	to consent; consent
67. 好合好散	hǎo hé hǎo sàn	Idiom.	(refer to a couple) to part friends after having gotten along well together
68. 挺	tǐng	V.	to hold up/out (a part of one's body)

			straight, to endure stoically
69. 街道	jiē dào	N.	street (social service agency in urban China) neighborhood, community
70. 办事处	bàn shì chù	N.	office, agency
71. 坚持	jiān chí	V/N.	to insist, to persist; insistence, persistence
72. 没想到	méi xiǎng dào	Idiom.	unexpected, by surprise
73. 难过	nán guò	Adj.	to feel bad, to have a hard time
74. 临走	lín zǒu	VP.	just before leaving (临……: about to..., on the verge of...)
75. 寄钱	jì qián	VO.	to send money (寄: to mail)
76. 看情况	kàn qíng kuàng	Idiom.	"to look at the situation", depending on the situation
77. 无所谓	wú suǒ wèi	Idiom.	to be indifferent, it doesn't matter
78. 舍得下	shě de xià	VP.	to be willing to part with, not to begrudge (舍不得: can't bear to part with)

你会用下面的词吗？
前夫、个子、帅、出众、毕业、嫁、南京、拼命、找门路、最后、出版社、专业、丢、甘心、可笑、经常、下班、理由、经过、路口、假如、厨房、隔、一会儿、趴、楼、幸福、可惜、好景不长、怀孕、提出、加拿大、办、当年、唯一、前提、实在、出国、国内、一辈子、双手、捂住、哭、明白、无梦、想通、严肃、样子、答应、街道、办事处、坚持、没想到、难过、临走、寄钱、看情况、无所谓、留

句型

一、 跟……结婚／离婚 (to be married to/to divorce somebody)

> ✍ Unlike their English counterparts, both 结婚 and 离婚 are Intransitive Verbs that cannot take an Object. The Preposition 跟 should be used to introduce an Object.

☞ 九年前她跟丈夫离婚了，一个人带着孩子跟婆婆一起生活了快十年。

1、 有的人为了出国，就跟外国人结婚，可是出国以后，又马上跟他们离婚。

Some people marry foreigners in order to go overseas; once they get there they divorce the person.

2、 过去，有些地方同姓的人是不能结婚的，也就是说，姓张的不能跟姓张的结婚，姓李的也不能跟姓李的结婚。

In the past, there were some places that wouldn't allow people with the same surname to marry each other. In other words, someone with the surname Zhang couldn't marry another person with the surname Zhang. And the same applied to the people with the surname Li.

二、 数N+Adj. (to reckoned/count N as...)

> ✍ "数" is used in a special sense of the word "count" in this structure, which states that "something/someone is reckoned to be (the most...when compared with others in a group or class)".

☞ 后来他也说，那个班就数我最出众。

1、 老师说中文语法就数 "了" 最难了。

The teacher said "le" is reckoned to be the most difficult point in Chinese grammar.

2、 很多人认为中国的电影导演中，最有名的要数张艺谋了。

Many people consider Zhang Yimou to be the most famous among Chinese film directors.

三、拼命 (to go all out, to do one's utmost)

> ✍ "拼命", literally "to put one's life on the line", indicates that someone goes all out to do something as if it's a matter of life and death. It usually takes a Verb Phrase as its Object, but it can also occur without an object, as in examples 3 and 4 below.

☞ 我的家在南京，为了跟他结婚，我拼命找门路留京……

1、籁籁的爸爸为了让她成为钢琴家，每天都拼命强迫她练琴。

In order to make her become a pianist, Lailai's father goes all out everyday to force her to practice piano.

2、她下岗后拼命找工作，可是都没找到合适的。

Although she did her utmost to find a job since she was laid off, she never found a suitable one.

3、他干什么事总是很拼命！

He goes all out in whatever he does!

4、我想通了，拼命是没用的。

I've thought it through, it's useless to go all out.

四、怎么就这么 / 那么…… (how come it is/was so/that...)

> ✍ This idiomatic expression, meaning literally "how come ...is so..." is used to convey deprecation or contempt for something perverse, irregular, or irrational. Note that the tone or nuance of the sentence changes if 怎么 (how come) is replaced by 为什么 (why), in which case the speaker is simply asking for a reason or explanation.

☞ 那时候怎么就那么甘心，说出来你都觉得可笑。

1、现在才五月，怎么就这么热了。

It is only May now, how come it is so hot already?

2、大亮这个人怎么那么讨厌，一点儿也不尊重别人，也不讲究文明礼貌。

How come Daliang is so annoying: he has absolutely no respect for others, and he has no regard for civility and etiquette either.

113

五、假如（／如果／要是）……（的话）(if...then...)

> ✍ 假如、如果、and 要是 all mean "if", but 假如 occurs more frequently in written form and 要是 in spoken form. In colloquial speech, any of the three may be coupled with "的话" at the end of the hypothetical clause.

☞ 假如我先到家了，就把厨房的窗户开着，……

1、 现在还有不少中国人只想要男孩，不想要女孩，可是假如大家都只生男孩不生女孩的话，二十年以后，他们的孩子还能结婚吗？

There are still a great number of Chinese who prefer boys over girls. But if everybody has only boys but no girls, then how will their children be able to get married in 20 years?

2、 假如中国只有五亿人，就不用象现在这样控制人口的增长，这个问题也就不存在了。

If China's population were only 500,000,000, then China wouldn't have to control population growth like this now, and this problem wouldn't exist.

六、 被 (used in a passive sentence to introduce the agent of an action)

> ✍ One way to express the passive voice in Chinese is by using the sentence pattern "Subj. 被 (agent) VP", in which the subject is the recipient of the action, and the agent of the action may optionally be introduced as the object of the preposition 被. The subject of the sentence as well as the agent of the action may be something other than a person, as illustrated by the passive voice sentence below and the example from the text. The main difference between a passive voice sentence and its corresponding active voice sentence is that the latter focuses on "what did so-and-so do" and the former focuses on "what was done to so-and-so (and by whom)"; e.g.:
>
> Active Voice:
>   工作人员没收了张五的秤。
>   The staff member confiscated Zhang Wu's scale.
>
> Passive Voice:
>   张五的秤被（工作人员）没收了。
>   Zhang Wu's scale was confiscated (by the staff member).
>
> A common pitfall for students of Chinese is to equate the passive voice in English with the 被 structure in Chinese. In fact, the passive voice in English can be translated into three types of sentences in Chinese, and the 被 structure is only one of the three. One distinctive characteristic of

the 被 structure is that it usually carries a negative connotation, indicating that the action is something that's inflicted upon the recipient. In modern usage - perhaps due to influence from English - the 被 structure is now used occasionally without a negative connotation.

With negative connotation:
她的钱被男朋友花完了。
Her money has been used up by her boyfriend.

李大亮被人打了。
Li Daling was beaten.

Without negative connotation:
他被选上了班长。
He was elected class president.

In English, the passive voice is often used with no negative connotation at all, and it is simply a way to state "what has happened to...", or "what was done to..." The Chinese equivalent to this type of sentence is the "topic-comment" sentence, in which the topic is not the agent but the recipient of action (i.e. person or thing acted upon).

票都卖完了。 The tickets are all sold out.
你的自行车找到了。 Your bicycle has been found.
作业做好了。 The homework is done.

In the English equivalent of the above sentences, the recipient of action is the subject of the sentence. But in Chinese, the NP at the beginning of this type of sentence is regarded as a "topic" to distinguish it from a subject, which is normally the agent of action. Moreover, in this type of topic-comment sentence, an agent of action may be inserted as the subject of the "comment" portion of the sentence; e.g. 周末的作业，我星期六就做完了。 (The homework for the weekend, I've finished it already by Saturday.) This type of sentence differs from the standard "subj + V + obj." sentence in that one focuses on the agent of action and the other on the recipient of action.
A third way in which the passive voice is used in English is to specify the agent of an action done on the subject of the sentence; e.g. "This book was written by my teacher". There is also no negative connotation in this type of sentence. In Chinese, this type of sentence is expressed by using the "Subj. 是 agent 的" or the "Subj. 是由-agent 的" structure; e.g. 1) 这本书是我的老师写的。 2) 学生上的课是由自己选的。 (Courses taken by students are chosen by themselves.)

☞ 那段时间我大概就是那种被幸福冲昏了头的女人吧。

1、小真的钱包在纽约被人抢走了。
Xiao Zhen's wallet was snatched by someone in New York.

2、他不遵守语言誓约，被罚了一次。
He was punished once for violating the language pledge.

七、（唯一的）前提是…… (the (only) prerequisite/premise is...)

> In this structure, 前提是 means "the prerequisite or premise is". 唯一 (the only, sole) is an Adjective used only as a Noun modifier (not as a predicate). 的 is usually tacked onto modifying elements of 前提. The modifying elements can be an Adjective, a Verb phrase, and a Clause. For example, 要去中国旅行，唯一的前提是得到中国的签证。(adjective) (If one wants to travel to China, the only prerequisite is to obtain a Chinese visa.) 解决问题的前提是先分析问题。(verb phrase) (The prerequisite for solving the problem is to first analyze the problem.) 中国发展经济的前提是要遵守国家的人口政策。(sentence) (The prerequisite for China to develop its economy is for the whole nation to abide by the national population policy.)

☞ 不同的是，女孩子的家在加拿大，所以他要走的唯一前提就是跟那个女孩子结婚。

1、你要别人尊敬你，唯一的前提是你得先尊重别人。

If you want others to respect you, the only prerequisite is that you must respect others first.

2、解决这个问题的前提是大家坐下来好好地把事情说清楚，吵架是没有用的。

The prerequisite to solving this problem is for everyone to sit down and talk things out clearly. Quarreling is not going to help.

八、实在 (indeed, really)

> 实在 is an Adverb which means "indeed" or "really", and is used to modify a Verb Phrase or Adjective in the predicate of the sentence.

☞ 他说他也没办法，实在太想出国了，找了这么多年才找到这个门路。

1、象张静这样的下岗女工想找一份合适的工作实在太难了。

It is really hard for an unemployed female worker like Zhang Jing to find a suitable job.

2、我实在不明白她为什么会跟那个不爱孩子，只想自己出国的人结婚。

Indeed, I really don't understand why she would want to marry someone who doesn't love (his own) child and just wants to go abroad himself.

九、各V各的 (each V his/her own...)

> ✍ 各 puts the focus on each individual one within a group. The structure 各 V. 各的 indicates that each one does something on his/her own.

☞ 当天晚上我们就各睡各的了。

1、美国人上饭馆吃饭一般都是各付各的，很少象中国人那样你请我，我请你的。

Americans usually go Dutch when they eat out, unlike the Chinese who always vie with each other to pay the bill.

2、他们虽然是夫妻，可是在很多问题上都各有各的想法，而且常常是各做各的，所以常常吵架。

Although they are a married couple, they have their own opinions on many issues and they each do their own thing. Therefore they quarrel all the time.

十、临V的时候／以前 (when...is about to..., just before...)

> ✍ "临 V 的时候/前" is a prepositional phrase headed by the Preposition 临. It precedes either the entire sentence or just before the verb phrase, in both cases to indicate that the timing of the main event in the sentence is "when...is about to..." or "just before..."

☞ 临走的时候，他说他一定会寄钱给我和孩子，……

1、临开车的时候，陈明的妈妈还去给他买了很多梨。

Just before the train was about to depart, Chen Ming's mother went to buy him a lot of pears.

2、徐慧的前夫是在他的孩子临出生前跟另一个女孩结婚的。

Xu Hui's ex-husband married another girl just before his baby was about to be born.

十一、看情况 (depends on the situation, to act accordingly)

> ✍ Here 看 means "to depend on". It usually follows 要, 得 or 就, and must take a Noun, a Verb, or a Clause as its Object.

☞ ……我说你看情况吧，我无所谓。

117

1、现在还在下大雨，飞机能不能起飞得看情况。

It is still pouring right now, whether the plane will depart depends on the weather condition.

2、毕业以后上研究所还是去工作，我要看情况再决定。

Whether I decide to go to graduate school or start working after graduation depends on the situation.

十二、舍得下 / 不下 ((not) to be willing to part with/ to give up)

> ✍ The Verb 舍 means "to give up", "to abandon". 舍得下 and 舍不下 are the positive and negative form of the Potential Complement.

☞ 我说他想过好日子不是什么错，但是连没见面的孩子都舍得下的人，我能留得住吗？

1、如果你舍得下自己的专业，舍得下这稳定的工作，那就下海去当个体户吧。

If you are willing to give up your profession and this stable job, you should go ahead and become a private entrepreneur.

2、虽然她也想过离婚，但是她舍不下孩子，舍不下这个家。

Although she thought of getting a divorce, she is not willing to give up her child and her family.

你放心地走吧，孩子生出来我先带着

118

练习

一、读课文回答问题

1、徐慧是怎么认识她前夫的？她前夫长得怎么样？

2、徐慧的家在哪儿？她为什么决定留在北京？

3、徐慧为什么以前经常在下班前找个理由早走？

4、徐慧的前夫什么时候提出离婚？他要跟谁结婚？

5、徐慧的前夫为什么不想在国内当一辈子老师？

二、听录音回答问题

听力(一)

1、"媳妇"是什么意思？

2、在传统社会里，媳妇跟谁的关系最重要？为什么？

3、以前的男人结婚后跟太太住在哪儿？

4、为什么现在婆婆和媳妇的关系不那么紧张了？

5、现代婆婆和媳妇的关系好起来了吗？他们的关系怎么样？

6、要是媳妇上班，好的婆婆会帮什么忙？

听力(二)

1、现代人的家庭观念、婚姻观念和以前有什么不同？

2、有人比较晚结婚或是不想结婚，原因是什么？

3、为什么有人结婚以后不想要孩子？

4、有了孩子就要担心哪些事情？

三、完成对话 👫

1、A：听说她刚离了婚又要结婚了？
　　B：（实在；跟……结婚）

2、A：你认为哪种类型的中文课对你帮助最大？你希望你的大学也有这样的课吗？
　　B：（数；假如……的话）

3、A：来中国以前，我在纽约机场跟父母见面的时候，差一点儿就哭了。
　　B：（临……的时候；舍得下／舍不下）

4、A：她们是从科索沃（Kosavo）跑出来的吗？为什么她们的爸爸、哥哥不跟她们一起跑呢？
　　B：（被；各V各的）

5、A：李大亮又翻老张的抽屉了。我们要不要告诉老张？
　　B：（怎么就那么……；看情况）

四、阅读短文回答问题 🧑‍💼

中国人常说，家庭是社会的最小单位。婚姻产生家庭，所以在一个国家中，人们的婚姻观念和家庭观念通常能反映出这个国家的传统。在中国几千年的传统社会中，青年男女的婚姻大事，只能由双方的父母来决定。有的青年男女，在结婚以前，甚至连面都没有见过，更不用说互相了解了。自己喜欢的对象，要是父母不同意，也不可以跟那个人结婚。这种没有爱情的婚姻，在传统的中国社会是非常普遍的，而且也常常可以维持下来。原因主要是由于中国的家庭结构决定了父母是家庭的中心，儿女并没有决定权，他们必须尊重父母的选择。另外，中国女性从小就受到"嫁鸡随鸡，嫁狗随狗"的家庭熏陶，意思是说，不管丈夫是一个什么样的人，只要是跟他结婚了，就得听他的话，尽妻子的责任。所以在那个时代，家庭一般来说都比较稳定。即使是不幸福的夫妻，也很少会想到离婚。从二十世纪开始，中国的社会、经济、观念等各个方面都开始发生变化，中国人的婚姻和家庭观念也随着时代的变化在不断变化着。现在，人们不但可以按照自己的意愿结婚，自由离婚，而且还可以一辈子不结婚做单身。这种变化可以说完全改变了中国几千年的传统。

回答问题：

1、家庭观念为什么能反映出国家和国家之间传统的不同？

2、在中国的传统社会中，青年男女怎么来决定他们的婚姻大事？

3、为什么在传统社会，没有爱情的婚姻可以维持下来？

4、"嫁鸡随鸡，嫁狗随狗"这句俗语有什么意思？

5、在你看来，婚姻自由对社会发展有没有好处？为什么？

五、翻译

1. Chen Ming and Li Hong have been married for about ten years, but their relationship is getting worse.

2. Li Hong not only worked late but also worked almost every weekend. She was rarely home, and this made Chen Ming really unhappy.

3. In order to make her husband happy, Li Hong decided to give up her job and stay at home even though that wasn't really acceptable to her.

4. Starting last month, Li Hong stayed home to be with Chen Ming. But their happiness did not last very long. Chen Ming fell in love with another woman.

5. However, he did not want to bring up divorce with Li Hong simply because he could not leave his child behind. If you were Chen Ming, what would you do?

六、段落练习

我的理想婚姻

第一段： 我的理想婚姻是什么样的？
我的理想婚姻是……；也就是说……；不但……，而且……

第二段： 用例子说明理想婚姻的前提和条件
……唯一的前提是……；……是……的根本条件；……虽然……，但是……；假如……；上有……下有……；再加上……；所以……；不但……也……；还有……；

第三段： 我的希望
可以说……；无论……都……；既……又……

有用的词：
名词： 条件、幸福、婚姻、夫妻、孩子、家庭、生活、方式、因素、分工、家务、前提、理由
动词： 看重、明白、办、跟……结婚、提出、作为、需要、相处、尊重、无所谓
形容词： 帅、温暖、出众、可笑、唯一
成语： 好合好散

七、作文

《我的中国父母对离婚的看法》
《结婚、离婚和社会变化》

八、讨论

1、徐慧跟她的男友合伙买了房子但是不结婚，你觉得这种情况奇怪不奇怪？为什么？
2、从徐慧怀孕到丈夫提出离婚只有半年的时间，他跟那个女孩好是不是这半年的事情？这说明了什么？
3、你觉得徐慧的前夫是一个什么样的人？他为什么走的时候哭了？
4、如果你是徐慧，你会怎样对待"你的"前夫？你会怎么办？

九、语言实践

1、采访一位父亲或母亲，请他（她）谈谈对离婚的看法、现代社会离婚的原因和离婚跟人们带来的社会压力。
2、采访一位中学生，请他谈谈对父母离婚的看法，别的同学对单亲家庭的孩子的看法。
3、请有关人员（民政部门或新闻单位）跟大家谈谈离婚问题。
  (1)现在中国人对婚姻的看法，现在中国的离婚率
  (2)现在人们离婚的主要原因

第一天见到他，我就爱上他了

想过好日子不是什么错

An Intermediate Chinese Course

第八课 现代科学技术

电脑的使用已经越来越普遍了

课文

一、简介

> 以前在中国，电脑是什么，多数人连听都没听说过。可是最近几年，电脑在中国发展得非常快。电脑不但是工作的基本工具，而且也慢慢进入了普通老百姓的家庭，成了很多家庭的必需品。现在除了家家⁽¹⁾买电脑外，人人也都在谈"上网"。据⁽²⁾说，北京现在有电脑的家庭差不多占百分之五十，办理上网的人也越来越多。每月只要花一百多块钱，就可以通过⁽³⁾自己的电脑和电话在因特网上尽情⁽⁴⁾浏览和收发

Notes ⁽¹⁾家家 and 人人: 家家 and 人人: A colloquial way to express the idea "every..." is to reduplicate the measure word. This is synonymous with "每+ (一) measure word", e.g. 家家= 每(一)家, 天天= 每(一)天, 年年 = 每(一)年, 个个= 每(一)个. In the above examples, 家、天、年, and 个 are all measure words. The noun 人 is an exception in that it too can follow this pattern for measure words, hence 人人= 每人=每(一)个人. The reduplicated measure word and the form "每+ (一) measure word" can function only as the subject of a sentence, not as the object. To express "every..." as an object, the form "每+ (一) measure word + NP" is used, e.g. 我要谢谢你们每一个人 (I should thank every one of you.).

⁽²⁾据 is synonymous with 根据, meaning "according to, in light of". It is used primarily in written Chinese. 据may be followed by a noun (e.g. 据新闻报道 "according to news reports"); a verb (e.g. 据说 "it is said"); or a clause (e.g. 据他说 "according to what he said", 据学生反映 "according to what students reported").

⁽³⁾通过 is a verb meaning "to pass through", as in 上飞机前必须通过护照检查 "One must go through passport check before boarding the plane". But is often used as a preposition, meaning "through..., by means of ...", to introduce a means or channel through which a certain result is achieved. The object of the preposition 通过 can be a Noun Phrase, Verb Phrase or a clause.

他们通过各种办法学习电脑技术。
They learned computer skills through various methods.
通过做习题，从山的理科成绩提高了。
Through working on exercises, Cong Shan's grades in science have improved.
通过朋友介绍，她在一家公司找到了工作。
She found a job in a company through a friend's introduction.

电子邮件。在中小学，电脑的使用虽然还在初级阶段，但是已经越来越普遍了。从下面的《电脑与中学生》的报道我们就可以知道中国也在拼命追赶世界高科技的发展。你认为这种情况对中国的社会发展与进步有好处吗？

———◆——— 生词 ———◆———

1. 科学	kē xué	N.	science
2. 电脑	diàn nǎo	N.	computer
3. 基本	jī běn	Adj.	basic
4. 工具	gōng jù	N.	tool
5. 进入	jìn rù	V.	to enter
6. 老百姓	lǎo bǎi xìng	N.	common people, ordinary people
7. 必需品	bì xū pǐn	N.	necessity, necessary item
8. 上网	shàng wǎng	VO.	to get on the web
9. 据说	jù shuō	VP.	it is said, it is reported
10. 占	zhàn	V.	to occupy
11. 百分之……	bǎi fēn zhī	NP.	... percent
12. 办理	bàn lǐ	V.	to handle, to make arrangements
13. 通过	tōng guò	V/Prep.	to go through, to pass; by means of, through
14. 因特网	yīn tè wǎng	N.	internet
15. 尽情	jìn qíng	Adv.	as one wishes, to one's heart's content
16. 浏览	liú lǎn	V.	to browse, to peruse
17. 收发	shōu fā	V.	to receive and send
18. 电子邮件	diàn zǐ yóu jiàn	N.	e-mail

✎ Notes ⁽⁴⁾尽情 functions as an Adverb, and means "as one wishes, to one's heart's content". It is normally associated with Verbs that have a positive connotation, such as 浏览 (browse), 表现 (display; demonstrate), 参加 (participate), 交流 (exchange), etc.

127

19. 使用	shǐ yòng	V/N.	to use, to utilize; usage
20. 初级	chū jí	Adj.	beginning level, elementary
21. 阶段	jiē duàn	N.	stage, phase, period
22. 普遍	pǔ biàn	Adj.	common, widespread
23. 报道	bào dào	V/N.	to report; report
24. 追赶	zhuī gǎn	V.	to chase and catch up with
25. 世界	shì jiè	N.	world
26. 高	gāo	Adj.	high, advanced
27. 科技	kē jì	Abbrev.	(＝科学技术) science and technology

你会用下面的词吗？
科学、电脑、基本、工具、进入、老百姓、必需品、上网、据说、占、办理、通过、因特网、尽情、浏览、收发、电子邮件、使用、初级、阶段、普遍、报道、追赶、世界、高科技

电脑已经进入了普通老百姓的家庭

128

二、电视节选

电脑与中学生

根据电视原文改编

一个偶然的机会，我认识了两位二十中学初二年级的学生，了解到他们利用计算机对课堂教学的内容进行复习和预习，他们的学习成绩和兴趣都有了明显的提高。这便[5]促成了我们对二十中学的采访。

据介绍，从山和于思远是二十中学初二年级的学生。他们因为对计算机共同的爱好而[6]成为知己的朋友。

———◆———

（采访从山）

"我是全方位的，比如说，生物啊，语文啊，数学啊，我都可以通过它的题库来进行学习。另外，每次学习完以后，你的成绩，你的结果，都会在系统里给你储存，这样就便于[7]——你随时随地掌握你自

Notes [5]便 is one of the many words that have come down from classical Chinese and are still used in modern Chinese, particularly in formal, written Chinese. As an Adverb, it is synonymous with 就.

这便促成了我们对二十中学的采访。
This then led to our visit to the #20 Middle School.
她很聪明，两天便学会用电脑了。
She is very smart and learned to use the computer in just two days.

[6]而 is another classical word which remains in use today. It serves as a pivotal word that links up a prepositional phrase or clause stating a purpose/cause/manner/result with the action or event stated in the predicate of the sentence. The phrase or clause leading up to "而……" is often introduced by a preposition or conjunction like 为, 因, 通过, etc.

工厂为解决下岗工人重新就业的问题而组织了各种培训班。
In order to solve the problem of re-employment for the laid off workers, the factory organized various training classes for them.
他们因为对计算机的共同爱好而成为知己的朋友。
They became bosom buddies due to their shared love of computers.
我们希望通过经济改革而进一步提高中国的科技水平。
We hope to further elevate the level of science and technology in China through economic reform.

己的学习情况，所以我就用这样的办法。因为我的理科比较差，经常做一些数学题，这样我就能提高我的理科成绩"。

今年寒假，从山别出心裁地利用计算机把老师布置的作业一一[8]打印出来交了上去，当时也还不知道老师对这件事是什么样的态度。

"老师是怎么样评价这件事的？"

"老师说：'这样很好，利用了高科技来辅助自己的学习'。老师的反应是比较好的"。

———◆———

（采访老师）

"我在这方面[9]是很支持他们的。因为我觉得我是九十年代初毕业的大学生，已经是在拼命地追赶这个时代了。他们这一代中学生呢，作为跨世纪的人才应该是顺应这个时代的，所以说这方面我非常支持他们，并且在课下鼓励他们。我觉得这是社会的一个大趋势"。

Notes [7]于, like 便 and 而 above, is another word from classical Chinese. In classical Chinese, it functions as a "generic preposition", meaning "at, in, with, than, etc". In modern Chinese, it is frequently suffixed to a verb or adjective to mean "V/Adj.+at/in/for..." Since the combination X-于 is a disyllabic word, what follows is typically also a disyllabic word to preserve the rhythm. For example, 便于掌握新技术 = 对新技术的掌握很方便 (*convenient for* mastering new technology); 善于鼓励学生 = 很会鼓励学生 (*good at* encouraging students); 忙于准备考试 = 忙着准备考试 (*busy with* preparing for exams).

[8]一一, meaning "one by one" or "individually", functions as an adverb. The verb which follows it is typically disyllabic – perhaps to preserve the two-syllable rhythm. For example, 一一打印 (to print out individually), 一一介绍 (to introduce one after another). Other Verbs commonly used with 一一 are 办理、掌握、布置、检查、指出, etc.

[9]在这方面/在……方面: This is a Prepositional Phrase meaning "in the aspect of..., with regard to..." Like all prepositional phrases in Chinese, it serves a coverbial function and therefore occurs before the verb phrase.

我在这方面是很支持他们的。
I am very supportive (of them) in this respect.
老师说我们在听力方面有了很大的进步，但是在发音和语法方面还要多注意。
The teacher said that we have made great progress in listening comprehension, but still need to pay more attention to the aspects of pronunciation and grammar.

—◆— 生词 —◆—

28. 偶然	ǒu rán	*Adj.*	coincidental, accidental, fortuitous
29. 计算机	jì suàn jī	*N.*	(=电脑) computer
30. 课堂教学	kè táng jiào xué	*NP.*	classroom teaching
31. 内容	nèi róng	*N.*	content
32. 复习	fù xí	*V/N.*	to review; review
33. 预习	yù xí	*V/N.*	to preview; preview
34. 明显	míng xiǎn	*Adj.*	obvious, evident
35. 便	biàn	*Adv.*	therefore
36. 促成	cù chéng	*V.*	to help bring about, to make possible
37. 据	jù	*Prep.*	according to
38. 介绍	jiè shào	*V/N.*	to introduce; introduction
39. 从山	cóng shān	*Personal N.*	Cong Shan
40. 于思远	yú sī yuǎn	*Personal N.*	Yu Siyuan
41. 共同	gòng tóng	*Adj/Adv.*	common, shared, mutual; together, jointly
42. 知己	zhī jǐ	*N.*	(lit. "to know self") bosom friend
43. 全方位	quán fāng wèi	*N/Adj.*	all directions; comprehensive
44. 生物	shēng wù	*N.*	biology
45. 语文	yǔ wén	*N.*	language and literature
46. 数学	shù xué	*N.*	mathematics
47. 题库	tí kù	*N.*	a pool of questions
48. 系统	xì tǒng	*N.*	system
49. 储存	chǔ cún	*V.*	to store, to stock
50. 便于	biàn yú	*Adv.*	easy to, convenient for
51. 随时随地	suí shí suí dì	*Adv.*	at any time and any place
52. 掌握	zhǎng wò	*V.*	to grasp, to master
53. 理科	lǐ kē	*N.*	science (vs. humanities and arts as an academic area)
54. 寒假	hán jià	*N.*	winter break
55. 别出心裁	bié chū xīn cái	*Idiom.*	to adopt an original approach, to take a different tack

56. 布置	bù zhì	V.	to assign, to arrange
57. 一一	yī yī	Adv.	one by one
58. 打印	dǎ yìn	V.	to type and print out
59. 交	jiāo	V.	to turn in (assignment)
60. 态度	tài du	N.	attitude
61. 评价	píng jià	V/N.	to evaluate, to appraise; evaluation
62. 辅助	fǔ zhù	V.	to assist
63. 支持	zhī chí	V/N.	to support; support
64. 跨世纪	kuà shì jì	VO.	to straddle two centuries, to cross over to a new century
65. 人才	rén cái	N.	qualified and/or trained personnel, talented person
66. 顺应	shùn yìng	V.	to adapt to, to conform to
67. 鼓励	gǔ lì	V/N.	to encourage; encouragement
68. 趋势	qū shì	N.	trend, tendency

你会用下面的词吗?
偶然、计算机、课堂、教学、内容、复习、预习、明显、便、促成、据、介绍、共同、知己、全方位、生物、语文、数学、系统、储存、便于、随时随地、掌握、理科、寒假、布置、一一、打印、交、态度、评价、辅助、支持、跨世纪、人才、顺应、鼓励、趋势

句型

一、成了 (to have become)

> ✎ The Verb 成 never occurs alone, but usually with the particle 了, or in combination with a preceding verb (e.g. 变成，改成，促成，造成). The verb + 成 combination may also occur with the particle 了 to indicate perfect tense. 成了 means "to have become..., to have turned into...", whereas "verb+成" means "to V into..., to lead to..."

☞ 到了九十年代，电脑不但成了工作的基本工具，而且还慢慢进入了普通老百姓的家庭。

1、这些个体户到处摆摊卖东西，看，这马路都变成市场了！

These private entrepreneurs set up stands everywhere to sell things. Look, this road has been transformed into a market!

2、籁籁不想当钢琴家，可是每天都得练两个钟头的琴。她成了她父母要实现他们自己理想的工具了。

Lailai doesn't want to become a pianist, but every day she has to practice playing the piano for two hours. She has become a tool for her parents to achieve their own dreams.

二、占……（百分之……） (to constitute, to account for...(per cent))

> ✎ The Verb 占 means "to occupy (a certain position, rank, or situation)", and by extension, it means "to constitute, to account for (a certain proportion)". For example, 占优势 (to occupy a dominant position); 占第三位 (to rank number 3); 占百分之五十 (to account for 50%).

☞ 据说，北京市现在有电脑的家庭差不多占百分之六，办理上网的人也越来越多。

1、这个工厂下岗的女工占了全厂人数的百分之三十。

Female workers laid off from this factory constitute 30% of this factory's work force.

2、这个城市有电脑的家庭目前只占百分之六左右，所以电脑的市场很大。

Presently, families that have computers only constitute 6% of the households in this town, so there is a big (potential) market for computers here.

三、（一个）偶然（的机会）(coincidentally, by chance)

> ✍ 偶然can function as an adjective or adverb. As an adjective, it means "coincidental/accidental, fortuitous", and can function as a noun modifier (e.g. 一个偶然的机会 "a fortuitous opportunity"; 偶然的现象 "accidental phenomenon") or as the predicate in a sentence (e.g. 这件事非常偶然 "This event is very fortuitous".) As an adverb, it means "by chance, coincidentally, fortuitously", as in example 2.

☞ 一个偶然的机会，我认识了两位二十中学初二年级的学生，了解到他们利用计算机对课堂教学的内容进行复习和预习。

1、一个偶然的机会，他发现了那个咖啡厅有好几台电脑。

By chance, he discovered that the coffee-house has several computers.

2、周玲在飞机上偶然遇到了大学的同学王义。

By chance Zhou Ling ran into his college classmate Wang Yi on the plane.

四、利用NP+VP (utilize... to..., make use of... to...)

> ✍ 利用, a transitive verb meaning "to utilize" or "to make practical use of", is often used as a coverb in a the structure "利用 + NP+ VP". The object of 利用 is typically something like 时间、机会、暑假、计算机、设备, etc. 利用 may also be used as the main verb in a 把 structure, e.g. "把时间利用起来".

☞ 一个偶然的机会，我认识了两位二十中学初二年级的学生，了解到他们利用计算机对课堂的内容进行复习和预习。

1、中国的学生现在也开始利用暑假打工挣钱了。

Now China's students have also started to use their summers to work and earn money.

2、我利用这个机会给父母和朋友买了很多礼物。

I used this opportunity to buy a lot of gifts for my parents and friends.

五、促成 (help to bring about, to make possible)

> ✍ 促成 is a Transitive Verb, and its object may be either a Noun Phrase or a Clause. 促成 carries a nuance of "accomplishment", so the meaning of the sentence is generally positive.

☞ 这便促成了我们对二十中学的采访。

1、这篇《家用电脑与上网》的报道促成了因特网在中国的大发展。
   The report entitled "Personal Computers and Using Internet" helped bring about a great development in the use of Internet in China.

2、她来中国留学是她的男朋友帮忙促成的。
   It was her boyfriend's assistance that made it possible for her to come to China to study.

六、便于+VP/clause (easy to, convenient for)

> ✍ The 便 in 便于 is a contraction of 方便, meaning "convenient" Hence, 便于 means "convenient for…, easy to…" Some typical verbs which follows 便于 are: 使用、了解、掌握、储存、解决、采访、检查、准备、照顾, etc. Note the disyllabic rhythm in the "便于+ V" combination.

☞ 这样就便于你随时随地掌握你自己的学习情况，所以我就用这样的办法。

1、这种洗衣机质量好，噪声 (zào shēng, noise) 低，便于使用，而且价格便宜，所以很受欢迎。
   This type of washing machine's quality is very good. It's quiet, easy to use, and the price is cheap. Therefore it is popular.

2、老师跟我们住在一起，这就便于老师随时了解学生的问题。
   The teachers live together with us. This makes it easy for the teachers to understand the students' problems at all times.

七、随时随地 (at all times and all places)

> ✍ In the phrase 随时随地, 时 is a contraction of 时间, and 地 is for 地方. The phrase is used as an adverbial before a Verb Phrase, to indicate "at all times and all places, no matter when and where".

☞这样就便于你随时随地掌握你自己的学习情况，所以我就用这样的办法。

1、你一个人去纽约，随时随地都要注意安全。

You're going to New York by yourself. You must pay attention to your safety at all times and places.

2、这种电话非常方便，随时随地都可以打。

This type of telephone is very convenient: one can make calls any time and any place.

除了家家买电脑外，人人也都在谈"上网"

练习

一、读课文回答问题

1、"我"是怎样认识这两个中学生的？什么事情促成了我们对二十中学的采访？
2、从山和于思远是怎样成为好朋友的？
3、为什么从山说自己是"全方位的"？
4、他觉得电脑对学习有什么好处？
5、从山怎样提高他的理科成绩？
6、老师对利用计算机辅助学习有什么反应？
7、为什么老师会支持学生这样做？

二、听录音回答问题

1、很多人每天一到办公室就做的第一件事是什么？
2、为什么说电子邮件让人跟人的关系越来越近？
3、人们可以利用因特网做哪些事情？
4、电子邮件和因特网给现代人带来了什么压力？
5、学生花太多时间浏览因特网会有什么不好的影响？

三、完成对话

1、A: 张四每天都在街上摆摊叫卖，一干就是十几个钟头。
   B: （因为……而……；拼命）

2、A: 什么？她现在是电视节目主持人了？
   B: （一个偶然的机会；成了）

3、A: 唉，这些学生怎么不用笔写作业？

B: （利用 NP + VP；便于）

4、A: 听说在北京"打的"很方便，是吗？

B: （随时随地）

四、阅读短文回答问题

仅仅在十多年以前，电脑还被中国普通老百姓视为专用的办公设备，与老百姓的生活还相当遥远。但是最近几年，电脑在中国的速度快得让人吃惊。电脑不但在公司、学校早已普及，银行、飞机场、火车站等公共服务性机构也已经实现电脑联网，就连在普通家庭中，电脑也不再是奢侈品，尤其是在经济收入较高，孩子又在中学、大学上学的家庭，家用电脑几乎是一种必需品。多数父母都舍得花一大笔钱购置电脑，目的不是为了便于自己使用，而是因为他们相信掌握电脑技术对孩子的智力发展有很大的好处，另外，他们也希望孩子能够通过因特网了解各种各样的信息。中国的学校教育鼓励、支持学习电脑知识、掌握电脑技术，大多数的学校都为学生开设电脑课，受到学生们的欢迎。

但是电脑的普及也带来了一些问题。有的学生并不利用电脑来辅助自己的学习，提高学习成绩和培养使用电脑的兴趣，而是利用电脑来玩游戏。很多孩子一回家就打开电脑玩游戏，一玩就是好几个钟头，根本就没有时间和精神来做功课，更不用说进行预习和复习了。父母发现了这种情况以后，常常会不允许孩子在家玩电脑游戏，可是孩子们就去街上的网吧玩。根据法律，网吧是不可以让未成年人（十八岁以下）进入的，但是很多网吧的老板为了赚钱，谁都让进。结果这些孩子下课以后就不回家，直接去网吧，甚至在白天逃课（不去上课）上网吧。

回答问题：

1、请你从不同方面说明现在电脑在中国的普及情况？

2、父母舍得花钱购买家用电脑的主要目的是什么？

3、学校对电脑使用和电脑教学一般是什么样的态度？

4、电脑也带来了什么样的问题？

5、你认为电脑的发展会给中国社会带来什么样的影响？

五、翻译

1. By coincidence, the TV station learned that the economics professor uses the computer to help students study and review their course-content. So they came to the school to interview him.
2. Thirty years ago, most people in China had never seen a TV set, but now it has not only entered into the common people's households, but it has also brought great changes to family life.
3. From the developments and changes in this company, one can see that China is trying with all its might to catch up with the advanced technology of the world.
4. As an entrepreneur, it is important that I have the latest information at all times (getting the latest information at all times is very important to me). In this way, I can understand the general trend of the economy.

六、段落练习

电脑为什么会给中学生带来问题？

根据上面"四"中的短文写一段话说明为什么电脑会给中学生带来问题。

第一段： 提出问题
在我看来……； ……的原因是……； 占……百分之……； 结果……

第二段： 说明原因
原因之一是……； 虽然……，但是……； 原因之二是……； 不是……而是……； 这样，……； 再加上……； 随时随地……，所以……； 促成……；

第三段： 我的看法
总之……； 如果……将会……； 不但……而且……； 只有……才……

有用的词:

名词: 电脑、网吧、电子邮件、工具、必需品、老百姓、条件、
　　　时间、精神、趋势、好处、科技

动词: 上网、进入、收发、据说、办理、通过、浏览、使用、便
　　　于、掌握、支持、鼓励

副词: 尽情、随时随地、别出心裁

七、作文

《电脑在大学中的使用》

八、讨论

1、美国中学生利用电脑进行学习和复习的情况普遍吗？他们还用电脑做什么？

2、你有没有利用电脑学中文的经验？如果有的话，你做过什么？如果没有，你希望电脑能怎样帮助你学中文？

3、从山的老师说："作为跨世纪的人才应该顺应这个时代"，你同意吗？怎样做才能顺应这个时代？

九、语言实践

去首都经贸大学的电脑中心或者有电脑设备的地方去采访一下那儿的工作人员和学生。

采访工作人员:

(1) 了解一下学校电脑中心的设备，看看他们的电脑是什么阶段的电脑（初级、中级、还是高级）？学校每年给多少钱？每天有多少老师和学生用电脑？他们用电脑做什么等。

(2) 他们用什么方法了解电脑的最新信息，怎么鼓励和支持学生使用电脑来提高学习
　　成绩和进行研究？

(3) 他们对使用电脑的看法：他们觉得电脑会不会对中国的经济发展有好处？有什么
　　处？

采访学生:

(1) 他们用什么电脑？用电脑做什么工作？

(2) 他们用自己的电脑还是学校的电脑？他们觉得用电脑对他们的学习有好处还是坏
　　处？

北京现在有电脑的家庭差不多占百分之五十，网吧 (Internet Cafe) 也越来越多

通过自己的电脑和电话可以在因特网上尽情浏览和收发电子邮件

在中小学，电脑的使用虽然还在初级阶段，但是已经越来越普遍了

An Intermediate Chinese Course

第九课　文化比较

妈妈为什么要这样？

课文

一、简介

父母应该不应该看孩子的信？父母应该不应该对孩子的任何事情都过问？不同的文化对这些问题有不同的回答，语言也最能反映这种文化的不同。就拿英文来说，"privacy" 这个词的意思是指在某[1]种情况下[2]，一个人不受别人的干扰，也不受别人的存在或者活动的影响，而且不希望别人知道、打听甚至议论自己的事情。而在中文里，由于这样的观念不存在，所以就没有一个跟英文 "privacy" 对应的词。有人[3]把 "privacy" 翻译成 "隐私"。其实这个词并没有准确地表达英文的原

Notes [1]某, like the word "X" in English, is used to refer to a certain person, place, time, or thing which shall remain unnamed for lack of more specific information or for deliberate withholding of information. Grammatically, it functions in two ways: 1) As an indefinite specifier, meaning "a certain (person, place, etc.)", e.g. 某位老师 (a certain teacher, who shall remain unnamed), 北京某地 (somewhere in Beijing), 在某种程度上 (to a certain extent), 在某种情况下 (under certain circumstances). 2) As a "proxy" in part of a name, e.g. 张某 (Zhang so-and-so, probably with a single syllable given name), 张某某 (Zhang so-and-so, with two syllables in the given name). However, 某 is not used as proxy for the surname when followed by the given name, e.g. *某大亮 is simply not said.

[2]This phrase is an example of the structure "在……（的）Noun下" discussed in Lesson 2, Sentence Pattern 1. It indicates a certain condition or situation under which the main event of the sentence takes place. The noun in this structure is typically an abstract noun such as 情况、条件、环境, or a verbal noun such as 帮助、关心、照顾、鼓励、影响.

[3]有人: This word means "someone" in the sense of an undesignated or unknown certain person, and is used only as the subject of a sentence (not as an object). The negative form of 有人 is 没(有)人 (no one/nobody). For example, 昨天没人给你打电话 (No one phoned you yesterday.) 有的人, which is also used only in subject position, means something slightly different from 有人. 有的人 means "some people, some among a group of people", implying that some other people are different from them; e.g. 有人不遵守语言誓约 (Someone is not abiding by the language pledge) vs. 有的人不遵守语言誓约 (Some of the people are not abiding by the language pledge (implying that others are)).

意。因为 "隐" 的意思是藏起来，"私" 的意思是属于[4]个人的、秘密的、不公开的。很显然，"隐私" 这个词并不是 "privacy" 的最合适的翻译。

在美国，"privacy" 被认为是人天生的权利，也是人与人之间的一种关系。一个人不能没有 "privacy"，这就是说，一个人需要有一定的属于自己的时间和空间，别人也应该尊重他/她的这种权利。这种属于个人的时间和空间在美国的家庭和社会中十分重要，而在中国，"privacy" 的观念在家庭中几乎是不存在的，因为父母和孩子的关系一方面是上对下的关系，一方面又非常亲近。因此，按照传统的观念，父母跟孩子之间是不应该有距离的，父母有权过问孩子的每一件事情。

可是现在，时代不同了，很多新的观念产生了，西方的观念也开始进入中国，逐渐动摇了中国的传统观念。这篇课文中李小玲的态度就反映了不同年龄的中国人对 "privacy" 的态度。

生词

1. 过问	guò wèn	V.	to concern oneself with, to take an interest in
2. 回答	huí dá	V/N.	to answer; answer
3. 某种	mǒu zhǒng	NP.	certain kind (某: a certain...)
4. 干扰	gān rǎo	V/N.	to disturb, to interfere; interference
5. 存在	cún zài	V/N.	to exist; existence
6. 活动	huó dòng	V/N/Adj.	to move about, to exercise; activity; active

---

Notes [4]属于 is a Transitive Verb and its Object is typically a Noun indicating a person, an institution/organization, or an establishment.

7. 打听	dǎ tīng	*V.*	to inquire about
8. 议论	yì lùn	*V/N.*	to discuss (at length); to gossip about
9. 对应	duì yìng	*Adj.*	equivalent, corresponding
10. 翻译	fān yì	*V/N.*	to translate; translation
11. 隐私	yǐn sī	*N.*	one's secrets, confidential private matters
12. 准确	zhǔn què	*Adj/Adv.*	accurate; accurately
13. 表达	biǎo dá	*V.*	to express, to convey
14. 原意	yuán yì	*NP.*	original meaning/intention
15. 藏起来	cáng qǐ lái	*VP.*	to hide
16. 属于	shǔ yú	*VP.*	to belong to
17. 秘密	mì mì	*N.*	secret
18. 公开	gōng kāi	*Adj/V.*	public, open (vs. confidential); to make public
19. 显然	xiǎn rán	*Adv.*	apparently, obviously
20. 天生的	tiān shēng de	*Adj.*	inherent, innate, god-given
21. 权利	quán lì	*N.*	right
22. 之间	zhī jiān	*Prep.*	among..., between...
23. 空间	kōng jiān	*N.*	space
24. 上对下	shàng duì xià	*Idiom.*	superior to subordinate
25. 亲近	qīn jìn	*Adj.*	close, intimate
26. 距离	jù lí	*N.*	distance
27. 有权	yǒu quán	*VO.*	to have the right
28. 时代	shí dài	*N.*	times, era
29. 产生	chǎn shēng	*V.*	to emerge, to produce
30. 动摇	dòng yáo	*V.*	to waver, to shift, to loosen up
31. 篇	piān	*Classifier.*	measure word for articles

你会用下面的词吗？
过问、回答、某种、干扰、存在、活动、打听、议论、
对应、翻译、隐私、准确、表达、原意、藏起来、属
于、秘密、公开、显然、天生的、权利、之间、空间、
上对下、亲近、距离、有权、时代、产生、动摇、篇

二、电视节选

妈妈为什么要这样？

根据电视画面编写

李小玲今年十四岁，去年刚刚考上了四中，四中是北京最好的中学之一。她很喜欢交朋友，学习也很好。上中学以后，小玲比以前忙多了，要想聊天谈心就只有靠⁽⁵⁾写信或者打电话了。这天，小玲放学回家，看到信箱里有一封同学的来信，心里非常高兴。她拿着信一进门，妈妈就看见了，问："谁来的信？"小玲回答说："同学"。妈妈紧跟着又问了一句："同学？男同学，女同学？"小玲不耐烦地回答说："哎呀，女同学"。这时，电话铃响了，小玲放下手里的信就去接电话。

妈妈把小玲的信拿起来，先看了半天信封，后来就拆开信念了起来。等小玲回来的时候，妈妈正在一页一页地仔细看小玲的信。小玲气得脸通红，一句话都说不出来。可是妈妈对小玲的不高兴不但没有反应，反而还又问了一句："谁来的电话"？

———◆◆◆——— 生词 ———◆◆◆———

32. 交朋友	jiāo péng you	*VO.*	to make friends
33. 聊天	liáo tiān	*VO.*	to chat
34. 谈心	tán xīn	*VO.*	to have heart-to-heart talk
35. 靠	kào	*V.*	to rely on, to lean on
36. 放学	fàng xué	*VO.*	to be let out of school

Notes ⁽⁵⁾靠 originally meant "to lean on", but is now used mostly in its figurative sense of "to depend on; to rely on (somebody or something to get things done or achieve a certain result)". It is a transitive verb, and its object is typically a Noun or noun phrase referring to a person, tool, means, etc.

37. 信箱	xìn xiāng	N.	mailbox
38. 紧跟	jǐn gēn	VP.	to follow closely
39. 不耐烦	bú nài fán	Adj.	impatient, irritated, annoyed
40. 哎呀	ài yā	Intj.	indicating impatience or annoyance
41. 电话铃	diàn huà líng	NP.	telephone ring
42. 响	xiǎng	V/Adj.	to ring, to sound off; loud
43. 信封	xìn fēng	N.	envelope
44. 拆信	chāi xìn	VO.	to open a letter
45. 页	yè	Classifier.	page
46. 仔细	zǐ xì	Adj/Adv.	careful; carefully
47. 脸通红	liǎn tōng hóng	Idiom.	face flush (with anger or embarrassment)
48. 反而	fǎn ér	Adv.	on the contrary, contrary to norm

你会用下面的词吗？
交朋友、聊天、谈心、靠、放学、信箱、紧跟、不耐烦、哎呀、电话铃、响、信封、拆信、页、仔细、脸通红、反而

时代不同了，很多新的观念产生了

句型

一、把……翻译成…… (to translate...into/as...)

> ✍ The sentence pattern of choice for expressing the idea of turning one thing into another is "把……Verb 成……" The verb in this pattern represents the action that brings about the change, e.g. 翻译成 (translate into), 做成 (make into), 改成 (change into), 写成一本书 (write into a book).

☞ 有人把"privacy"翻译成"隐私"。其实，这个词并没有准确地表达英文的原意。

1、我觉得把 computer 翻译成"电脑"比"电子计算机"更合适。
   I feel that translating the word "computer" as "electronic brain" is more suitable than as "electronic calculator".

2、她现在已经能够把写给家里的英文信翻译成中文了。
   Now, she can translate the English letters she writes home into Chinese.

二、被（……）（认为） (cf. Lesson 7, Sentence Pattern 6)

> ✍ The 被 structure was thoroughly discussed in Lesson 7, Sentence Pattern 6. As pointed out earlier, this structure has been extended beyond sentences with negative connotations in modern Chinese. Here are some additional examples of 被 being used with neutral or positive connotations: 被认为 (to be considered), 被选为 (to be elected as), 被感动 (to be touched/moved), 被发现 (to be discovered), 被接受 (to be accepted), 被承认 (to be recognized).

☞ 在美国，"privacy"被认为是人天生的权利，也是人跟人之间的一种关系。

1、现代科学技术是属于全世界的，这个观念已经被世界上大多数的科学家接受了。

Modern science and technology belong to the entire world. This concept has already been accepted by the majority of scientists in the world.

2、你知道这种病是什么时候被发现的吗？

Do you know when this type of disease was discovered?

三、 (Sentence/clause) 而 (+Sentence/clause) (..., and yet, while on the other hand, ...)

> ✍ 而, a word from classical Chinese, is used in modern Chinese as a conjunction to indicate a variety of relationships. Here, it indicates a contrary relationship between two clauses.

☞ 这种属于个人的时间和空间在美国的家庭和社会中十分重要，而在中国，"privacy" 的观念在家庭中几乎是不存在的。

1、我们都觉得李大亮对人很不礼貌，而他自己却认为这是生活小事，不是什么大问题。

We all think that Li Daliang is very rude to others, but he thinks that this is just a small matter in life and therefore no big deal.

2、过去大多数中国人连电脑都没见过，而现在"上网"已经是一件很普通的事情了。

In the past most Chinese people had never seen a computer, but now going online is a rather common thing.

四、 A和（／跟）B……之间 (between A and B)

> ✍ "……之间" and "中间" can both be translated as "between", but there are differences between them in meaning and usage. 之间 is always preceded by either "A 和/跟 B" or a plural noun (e.g. 父子、朋友、夫妻、师生), and implies a vis-a-vis relationship between A and B or among members of the plural noun group. 中间 has broader usage than 之间. It may refer to the "space" (physical or abstract) in the between two or more parties, or convey the idea of "within, in the middle of, amidst" a single entity. 中间 is in itself a noun, and if it is preceded by a NP, that NP functions as its modifier, so the particle 的may be added between them, e.g. 两个饭馆(的)中间有一个书店 (There's a bookstore between the two restaurants.) Moreover, 中间 (but not 之间) may be used without a preceding NP, e.g. 中间的那个 (the one in the middle), (中间有个市场) (there's a market in the middle), 最好放在中间 (It's best to put it in the center.)

☞ 因此，按照传统的观念，父母跟孩子之间是不应该有距离的。

1、由于中国文化和西方文化之间有很多不同的地方，所以像 "privacy" 这样的文化观念就很难翻译得好。

Due to many differences between Chinese and Western cultures, concepts like "privacy" are very hard to translate.

2、最近，这两个国家之间的关系有了很大的改善。

Recently, the relations between these two nations have greatly improved.

五、有（／无）权+V (have the right/no right to V)

> 有权 is a VO compound meaning "to have the right/power". It frequently functions as a transitive verb, in which case its object is typically a verbal noun. The antonym of 有权 is 无权 or 没有权利

☞ 父母有权过问孩子的每一件事情。

1、在美国，虽然说每个人都有权受教育，可是有的孩子还是不能上学。

Even though it is said that everyone in America has the right to an education, there are still some children who are unable to attend school.

2、中国人认为，这是他们自己的事情，外国人无权过问。

Chinese people consider this to be their own affair, and foreigners don't have the right to get involved.

六、对……的态度 (attitude toward...)

> This is a NP in which the prepositional phrase "对-object" modifies the noun 态度. The object of the preposition 对 is the person or issue toward which the subject's attitude is directed.

☞ 这篇课文中李小玲的态度就反映了不同年龄的中国人对"privacy"的态度。

1、张力发现，如果你会用汉语点菜，服务员对你的态度就会不一样。

Zhang Li discovered that if you can use Mandarin to order food, waiters will take a different attitude toward you.

2、这两个中学生开始的时候也不知道老师对他们用计算机做作业是什么样的态度。

When these two students started using computers to do their homework, they didn't know what their teacher's attitude would be.

七、……之一 (one of the...)

> 之, a particle from classical Chinese, has found its way into many words in modern Chinese. Its basic meaning is similar to 的, so 之一 is equivalent to "……的一个". Other examples of 之 in the modern vocabulary are: ……之间、百分之……、……之后、总之 (in sum).

☞ 李小玲今年十四岁, 去年刚考上北京最好的中学之一: 四中。

1、大批工人下岗是近年来中国经济改革面临的问题之一。

One of the problems that China is facing in its economic reform in recent years is that a large number of workers are being laid off.

2、谢添是中国有名的导演之一。

Xie Tian is one of China's famous film directors.

八、（不但）……反而…… (not only..., on the contrary...)

> 反而 is a conjunction used in the second clause of a sentence to indicate a situation that is contrary to expectations or the norm. It is often used in tandem with 不但 (not only) in the first clause; e.g., 对于别人的隐私, 他不但不保密, 反而到处跟人议论 (He can't keep secrets about other's privacy, on the contrary, he gossips about it everywhere); 上课时他不但自己不注意听课, 反而干扰别的同学 (During class, not only does he not pay attention to the lecture but he also disrupts the other students.) The nuance of "contrariness" conveyed by this pair of conjunctions is more intense than the more commonly used "不但……而且……" structure.

☞ 可是妈妈对小铃的不高兴不但没有什么反应, 反而还又问了一句: "谁来的电话？"

1、黄文海考上大学以后, 不但不好好学习, 反而经常不上课, 跟朋友一起去跳舞、喝酒。

After having passed the entrance exam and entered college, Huang Wen-hai did not take his studies seriously. Instead, he often skipped classes and went dancing and drinking with his friends.

2、小孩都有这样的特点，有时候大人不让做的事情，他们反而更想做。

Children all have this characteristic: The more their parents prohibit them from doing something, the more they want to try it.

在中国一个人很难有属于自己的时间和空间

练习

★ HW: 一、读课文回答问题

1、小玲回来的时候，手里拿着什么？

2、小玲妈妈问小玲什么？你觉得妈妈为什么要问这样的问题？

3、小玲是怎样回答她妈妈的？她心里会是怎么想的？

4、小玲接电话的时候，她妈妈在做什么？

5、小玲对妈妈这样的做法有什么反应？

6、小玲心里想说什么？她为什么没有说出来？

7、你觉得小玲妈妈为什么要这样做？

二、听录音回答问题

1、在中国老师和学生的关系跟什么一样？

2、"一日为师，终身为父"是什么意思？

3、为什么毕业生要请老师吃饭？

4、在中国学生怎么叫老师？在美国呢？

5、老师在中国的社会地位怎么样？在美国呢？

6、在美国老师可以公开学生的成绩吗？在中国呢？

7、要是学生功课学不好，美国老师和中国老师有什么不同的看法？

三、完成对话

1、A: 为什么中国人管独生子女叫"小皇帝"？

　　B: （是指；被……）

2、A: 英文"丢脸"怎么说？翻译以后的意思跟中文一样不一样？

    B: （把……翻译成……；……之间）

3、A: 美国人都可以过问政府的事情吗？

    B: （有权 V）

4、A: 他们为什么要采访那些中学生？

    B: （对……的态度）

四、阅读短文回答问题

> 翻开《现代汉语词典》，"隐私"的定义是"不愿告人的或不愿公开的个人的事"，但是，在计划经济体制下产生的工作单位，"隐私"的观念根本就不存在，也是不应该存在的。
>
> 在中国实行计划经济的年代，普通人参加工作以后，就被严格地控制在单位的手中，单位负责职工的生、老、病、死。职工有义务向单位报告自己的一举一动，甚至观点态度，而单位有权证明、过问并且干涉职工的所有的社会活动，甚至婚姻也不例外。因此，一个人到了法定结婚年龄，准备结婚的时候，必须要让单位知道，让单位开出证明，才可以办理好结婚手续，离婚的时候过程也是完全一样。向单位报告结婚的时候还好，毕竟是一件喜事，多数人愿意通知自己的朋友与同事。但是当婚姻出现问题，准备离婚的时候，双方必须要先找各自领导谈话，请他们批准，写证明信或者同意书，然后才能分手。这样就等于把一个原本属于个人隐私的事情公开化(publicize)了。随着社会的开放和西方文化的影响，单位在人们生活中的作用越来越小，人们的隐私意识却越来越强，都希望个人隐私权能得到单位和社会的尊重。

回答问题:

1、根据《现代汉语词典》的解释，"隐私"是指什么？

2、你认为《现代汉语词典》对"隐私"的解释合适不合适？为什么？

3、为什么说在严格实行计划经济的单位，"隐私"观念根本就不存在？

4、在你看来，职工的婚姻情况属于不属于个人隐私？单位有没有权利掌握职工的婚姻情况？为什么？

5、你认为在中国这样一个社会，怎么样才能既尊重个人的隐私权？你有什么好办法？

五、翻译

1. Freedom of speech (言论自由) is considered to be a person's god-given right by nature. Obviously, such a concept does not exist in China.

2. Taking "xiàng qián kàn" for example, it originally referred to looking forward, but now it means "to look for money". Such a phrase did not exist in the old days.

3. According to the traditional Chinese concept, there should not be any distance between parents and their children. Parents have every right to ask their children about anything.

4. The film directed by Xie Tian reflects the attitude of people from different age groups toward the concept of "family".

父母和孩子的关系一方面是上对下的关系，一方面又非常亲近

六、段落练习

父母到底尊重不尊重孩子的 "隐私" －问卷调查 (survey questionnaire)

找二十个中国或者美国的中学生回答下面的问题:

1、你的父母拆不拆你的信?
2、你给朋友打电话的时候, 你的父母注意不注意听你们的谈话?
3、你不在的时候, 你的父母翻不翻你的东西?
4、你的父母问不问你的朋友的情况?
5、你对你的父母的做法有什么反应?
6、如果你的父母没有经过你的同意就看你的信, 你对他们有什么看法?你会对他们说什么?

第一段: 说明问卷调查的时间、地点、准备工作、参加者等等

第二段: 报告问卷调查的情况
百分之……认为……;他们的回答是……;其中百分之……认为……;原因是……;

第三段: 分析问卷调查
根据……, 把……V成……;原因之一是……;原因之二是……

第四段: 报告结果
通过……的分析;在……之间, 对……的态度, 有……不同;因此, ……

七、作文

《给小玲的妈妈的一封信》
《中国人对 privacy 的看法》

八、讨论

1、如果你是小玲，你会对妈妈说些什么？

2、美国的父母对孩子的这些事情过问不过问？为什么美国父母跟中国父母的做法不一样？

3、你认为父母对孩子的事情应该不应该过问？为什么？

4、你觉得有哪些事情是父母应该过问的？为什么？如果不过问，将会怎么样？

九、语言实践

1、采访三个大学生，问问他们对 "privacy" 的看法。他们的父母对这个问题有什么看法？你认为中国有没有 "privacy"。

2、设计 (design) 十个问题问五个二十岁、五个四十岁和五个五十岁的中国人，看看他们到底知道不知道 "privacy" 这个观念？他们对这个观念的理解跟美国人的一样吗？从这些回答中看看中国人对 "privacy" 这个观念的看法。

第十课　中国的摇滚乐歌手
－崔健

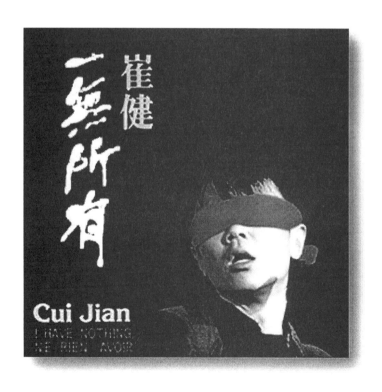

崔健，这个名字在中国可以说是无人不知。他是有名的摇滚乐歌手，也被人称为中国的"摇滚之父"。

课文

一、简介

崔健，这个名字在中国可以说是无人不知。他是有名的摇滚乐歌手，也被人称为中国的"摇滚之父"。从八十年代起，崔健就开始用摇滚乐和他的歌来表现自己的强烈情感和批判精神。他用一首自己写的"一无所有"(1)唱红了全国。十几年过去了，他对现在的社会、音乐以及他自己又有什么新的评价和批判呢？下面的采访可以让你多少了解一些这方面的情况。

生词

1. 摇滚乐	yáo gǔn yuè	NP.	rock and roll
2. 歌手	gē shǒu	N.	singer
3. 崔健	cuī jiàn	Personal N.	Cui Jian
4. 无人不知	wú rén bù zhī	Idiom.	没有人不知道, well known
5. 称为	chēng wéi	VP.	to be called as
6. ……之父	zhī fù	NP.	……的父亲, father of...
7. 表现	biǎo xiàn	V/N.	to display, to express; manifestation
8. 强烈	qiáng liè	Adj.	strong, intense, fierce
9. 情感	qíng gǎn	N.	feeling
10. 批判	pī pàn	V/N.	to criticize; criticism

✎ Notes (1)一无所有: 无, a word from classical Chinese, is equivalent to 没有 in modern Chinese. Like many single-syllable classical Chinese words, it has become a component in many disyllabic words and four-character idioms or phrases in modern Chinese, particular words and phrases used primarily in the written form.; e.g. 无权、无名、无意、无效、无关、一无所有、无论如何、无人不知、一夜无梦.

11. 精神	jīng shén	*N.*	spirit
12. 首	shǒu	*Classifier.*	classifier for song or poem
13. 一无所有	yī wú suǒ yǒu	*Idiom.*	to have nothing, the title of one of Cui Jian's songs
14. 唱红	chàng hóng	*VP.*	to make a song popular by singing
15. 全国	quán guó	*NP.*	the whole country
16. 音乐	yīn yuè	*N.*	music
17. 以及	yǐ jí	*Prep.*	and, as well as...
18. 自身	zì shēn	*N.*	oneself
19. 多少	duō shǎo	*Adv.*	more or less

你会用下面的词吗？
摇滚乐、歌手、无人不知、称为、表现、强烈、情感、批判、精神、首、一无所有、唱红、全国、以及、音乐、自身、评价、多少

崔健和他的乐队

161

二、报纸节选

中国摇滚乐歌手 - 崔健

根据《华声月报》原文改编

记者：　你如何评价摇滚乐？

崔健：　它本身是流行音乐的一种，是与商业结合的产物，是有影响的文化现象。从文化上讲，它是比较直接、简单、强烈的情感表现。我的摇滚比较个人化[(2)]，我比较喜欢把我的愤怒以及一些个人的情感通过音乐表现出来。说白了，就是比较具批判性[(3)]。

记者：　中国的摇滚呢？

崔健：　这很难讲，因为现在中国的摇滚没有真正完全发展起来，没有系统化，比如演出机制……甚至一些酒吧里的小型非正式演出都没有建立起来。原创歌曲社会地位比较低。虽然摇滚在中国已经有十多年了，但仍处于萌发阶段。

记者：　你印象中感觉最好的年代是什么时候？

崔健：　我觉得这十年我过得比较愉快。如果这十年让我选的话，应

Notes [(2)]化 is a suffix attached to a Noun or an Adjective to form a Verb. Its original meaning is "to transform", so it functions like the suffix "-ize" in English, although it is used more broadly than the English suffix "–ize". Just about all English words ending in "-ize" can be translated into a -化 word in Chinese, but not vice versa. For example:

Noun + 化:　　个人化 (individualize), 系统化 (systematize), 现代化 (modernize), 电脑化 (computerize), 美国化 (Americanize), etc.

Adjective +化:　绿化 (making a place green by planting trees), 美化 (beautify), 简单化 (simplify), 软化 (soften), 老化 (aging)

[(3)]性 is a suffix attached to a word to form a new Noun. Its original meaning is "gender, characteristic". As a suffix, it refers to a specific quality, characteristic, nature, or property. For example, 理性 (rational faculty), 感性 (sensitivity), 创造性 (creativity), 规律性 (regularity; law), 批判性 (nature of criticism), 艺术性 (artistic nature).

该是一九九二年。一九九二年自己的歌出得比较多，又有全国巡回演出。但我觉得就因为那时候过得太愉快，好象很多事很容易，造成现在的一些压力，一些理性的东西。但这是潮起潮落的规律，我不可能总是在浪尖⁽⁴⁾上。我现在也很高兴，可以很理性地看我的过去，而对未来的理解比过去更客观。

记者： 你最愤怒的时候是什么时候？

崔健： 看一个人睁眼说谎的时候，你还没办法，因为谎言的力量比你征服他的力量大多了。比如有些人为了阻止我演出而编造了一些谎言，他会给我一些他自己都不相信的理由，那时候我只能去骂。因为与其听他说谎，倒不如大骂一顿⁽⁵⁾最让我舒服。但后来我发现这也许能给你带来一些美好的回忆，但不会有好的结果。比如我一个朋友的父亲对艺术、对音乐有很大的偏见，他不让自己的孩子搞音乐。我和他针锋相对地争论，最后彻底激怒了他。于是他就给文化部写信，破坏我们本来就很少的演出机会。

记者： 很多人说你的创作和政治有很大的关联，你怎么看？

崔健： 首先，一个人关心自己的生存环境是天经地义的事。一个男人关心自己的生存环境就像女人关心颜色一样，而且这甚至

Notes (4) 浪尖 means literally "the tip of the wave". Here 在浪尖上 is used figuratively to mean "to be on top (of something turbulent), to be at the pinnacle of popularity".

(5)顿, a Measure Word, applies to two categories of things: 1) a meal or feast, e.g. 吃一顿饭 (having a meal), 喝了一大顿 (had a great round of drinking); 2) a round or bout of attack, e.g. 打 (beating), 批评 (criticizing), 骂 (scolding), and 说 (reprimanding), etc. There are two other measure words – 场 and 番 – that indicate a session or a stint of some activity, e.g. 病了一场 (had a bout of illness), 讨论了一番 (had a round of discussion). It is through lots of practice with examples that students learn to distinguish among these three measure words.

是赢得女人尊重的一种方式。

记者：你去过那么多国家，最喜欢哪儿？

崔健：最喜欢纽约，它是疯狂的城市。

记者：对中国的未来怎么看？

崔健：大家都是中国人，你是，我也是，谁也别跑。光靠我们的前辈，我们的后辈还不行，还不够！应该共同努力，共同创造一个生存环境。

——◆—— 生词 ——◆——

20. 如何	rú hé	Adv.	(literary) how
21. 本身	běn shēn	N.	oneself, itself
22. 流行音乐	liú xíng yīn yuè	NP.	pop music
23. 结合	jié hé	V/N.	to integrate; integration
24. 产物	chǎn wù	N.	product
25. 直接	zhí jiē	Adv/Adj.	directly; direct
26. 简单	jiǎn dān	Adj.	simple
27. 个人化	gè rén huà	V/Adj.	to individualize/personalize; individualized
28. 愤怒	fèn nù	N.	anger, wrath
29. 说白了	shuō bái le	Idiom.	to speak frankly, to be perfectly candid
30. 具	jù	V.	(literary) to possess, to have
31. 批判性	pī pàn xìng	N.	critical character
32. 真正	zhēn zhèng	Ad/Advj.	real, really
33. 系统化	xì tǒng huà	V/Adj.	to systematize; systematic
34. 机制	jī zhì	N.	mechanism
35. 演出	yǎn chū	V.	to perform
36. 酒吧	jiǔ bā	N.	bar
37. 小型	xiǎo xíng	Adj.	small scale
38. 非正式	fēi zhèng shì	Adj.	informal, unofficial, casual

39. 歌曲	gē qǔ	N.	song
40. 建立	jiàn lì	V.	to establish
41. 原创	yuán chuàng	NP.	original creation
42. 地位	dì wèi	N.	status
43. 仍	réng	Adv.	(literary) still
44. 处于	chǔ yú	VP.	(literary) to be situated (in a certain stage or circumstance)
45. 萌发阶段	méng fā jiē duàn	NP.	budding stage
46. 愉快	yú kuài	Adj.	happy, pleasant
47. 出	chū	V.	to produce
48. 巡回	xún huí	V.	to go on tour (for performance), to make a circuit
49. 造成	zào chéng	VP.	to cause, to result in
50. 理性	lǐ xìng	N/Adj.	rational nature; rational (vs. emotional)
51. 潮起潮落	cháo qǐ cháo luò	Idiom.	the flowing and ebbing of the tide, natural rhythm
52. 规律	guī lǜ	N.	regular pattern, regularity
53. 浪尖	làng jiān	NP.	pinnacle of the wave, height of the trend
54. 未来	wèi lái	N/Adj.	future
55. 理解	lǐ jiě	V.	to comprehend
56. 客观	kè guān	N/Adj.	objectivity; objective
57. 睁眼	zhēng yǎn	VO.	to open one's eyes, with eyes wide open
58. 说谎	shuō huǎng	VO.	to tell a lie
59. 谎言	huǎng yán	N.	lie
60. 力量	lì liàng	N.	power, strength
61. 征服	zhēng fú	V.	to overcome, to conquer
62. 阻止	zǔ zhǐ	V.	to block, to obstruct
63. 编造	biān zào	V.	to fabricate
64. 骂	mà	V.	to scold, to curse
65. 与其A倒不如B	yǔ qí...dào bù rú	Conj.	(literary) A is not as good as B
66. 舒服	shū fu	Adj.	comfortable
67. 美好	měi hǎo	Adj.	beautiful
68. 回忆	huí yì	V/N.	to recall; memories

69. 结果	jié guǒ	N.	result, outcome
70. 艺术	yì shù	N.	arts
71. 偏见	piān jiàn	N.	bias, prejudice
72. 搞	gǎo	V.	(colloquial) to do, to be engaged in
73. 针锋相对	zhēn fēng xiāng duì	Idiom.	to give tit for tat, to be diametrically opposed
74. 争论	zhēng lùn	V/N.	to debate, to argue; debate, argument
75. 彻底	chè dǐ	Adv.	completely, thoroughly
76. 激怒	jī nù	V.	to enrage, to infuriate
77. 于是	yú shì	Conj.	therefore, thereupon
78. 文化部	wén huà bù	N.	Ministry of Culture
79. 破坏	pò huài	V.	to destroy, to sabotage
80. 创作	chuàng zuò	V/N.	to create; creative work
81. 政治	zhèng zhì	N.	politics
82. 关联	guān lián	V/N.	to be inter-related; connection, relevance
83. 首先	shǒu xiān	Adv.	first, first of all
84. 关心	guān xīn	V/N.	to be concerned with, to care about; concern
85. 生存环境	shēng cún huán jìng	NP.	environment for existence or survival
86. 天经地义	tiān jīng dì yì	Idiom.	principles of heaven and earth, law of nature
87. 颜色	yán sè	N.	color
88. 赢得	yíng dé	VP.	to win, to obtain (through struggles)
89. 疯狂	fēng kuáng	Adj.	crazy, wild
90. 谁也别跑	shéi yě bié bǎo	idiom	don't anybody run away
91. 前辈	qián bèi	N.	the older generation
92. 后辈	hòu bèi	N.	the younger generation
93. 努力	nǔ lì	V.	to make great efforts, to try hard
94. 创造	chuàng zào	V.	to create

你会用下面的词吗？
如何、本身、流行音乐、结合、产物、影响、文化现象、直接、愤怒、说白了、批判性、发展、系统化、演出、酒吧、小型、非正式、建立、地位、仍、处于、萌发阶段、感觉、愉快、造成、理性、规律、未来、理解、客观、睁眼、说谎、谎言、征服、力量、阻止、编造、理由、骂、与其……倒不如、顿、舒服、美好、回忆、结果、艺术、偏见、搞、争论、最后、激怒、于是、文化部、破坏、本来、创作、政治、关联、首先、关心、生存环境、颜色、赢得、疯狂、前辈、后辈、共同、努力、创造

摇滚音乐是流行音乐的一种

句型

一、 （被）称为 (to be called ……), 称……（为）……/把……称为……(to call...(as)...)

> ✍ 称 and 叫/叫作 both mean "to call (by the name of)...", but 称 is used primarily in written form. In Chinese, there are several different ways to express the idea of calling so-and-so by the name of such-and-such:
>
> "He is called Little Tiger":
> 他叫(作)小老虎。
> 他被叫作小老虎
> 他被称为小老虎
>
> "We call him Little Tiger":
> 我们叫他作小老虎。
> 我们把他叫作小老虎。
>
> 我们称他小老虎。
> 我们把他称为小老虎。
>
> Notice that in the two-clause sentence 他是有名的摇滚乐手，也被人称为中国的"摇滚之父"，the 被……称为 pattern is used in the second clause. The choice of passive voice is not random, but actually serves to retain cohesiveness in the discourse. When two consecutive clauses have the same subject, the subject may be omitted in the second clause, and the first clause would then naturally flow into the second clause, creating a greater sense of cohesion. Here the Subject of the first clause is 他 (崔健), and the 被……称为 pattern allows the subject to remain the same (and therefore unstated) in the second clause.

☞ 他是有名的摇滚乐手，也被人称为中国的"摇滚之父"。

1、因为她不拘小节，所以被大家称为"傻大姐"。
She is called "Silly Big Sister" by everyone because she is a careless person.

2、北京人称有钱人为"大款"。／北京人把有钱人称为"大款"。
People in Beijing call the rich guys "Big Bucks".

二、（对⋯⋯有⋯⋯的）评价 (to have a...(qualitative) evaluation of...)

> ✍ The word 评价 can function as a transitive Verb or a Noun . When it functions as a transitive Verb, it means "to evaluate, to assess." For example, 他们要重新评价这部电影 (They want to re-evaluate this movie.). When it functions as a Noun, it is often modified by a Prepositional Phrase "对⋯⋯" indicating the person or thing being evaluated, e.g. 对这位老师的评价(evaluation of this teacher). Another pattern in which 评价 plays a role is "对⋯⋯有⋯⋯(的)评价" (to have a...(qualitative) evaluation of...), e.g. 你对他的摇滚音乐有什么评价？ (What is your assessment of his rock music?)

☞十几年过去了，他对现在的社会、音乐以及他自己又有什么新的评价和批判呢？

1、学生们对这个暑期班有很高的评价。

The students speak highly of this summer program.

2、大家对这个人在中国历史上的作用都有不同的评价。

Everyone has a different assessment of this person's role in Chinese history.

三、与（／跟）⋯⋯结合 (to combine/integrate...with...)

> ✍ 结合 means "to merge, to integrate", and is often preceded by a Prepositional phrase "与/ 跟⋯⋯" indicating the entity with which the aforementioned thing is being merged or integrated. 跟 is used mostly in speaking, while 与 is generally used in writing.

☞它本身是流行音乐的一种，是与商业结合的产物，是有影响的文化现象。

1、如果学习汉语不跟了解中国文化结合起来，是很难学得好的。

It is hard to master Chinese if you don't integrate the culture with the language.

2、他们想把中国的传统医学与现代的电脑技术结合起来，治疗爱滋病。

They want to combine traditional Chinese medicine with modern computer technology to cure AIDS.

四、从……来讲（／说）(speaking from the perspective of..., in terms of...)

> ✍ The phrase 从……（上）来讲/说 means "to speak from a certain perspective or aspect", and that "certain perspective or aspect" is typically indicated by an abstract noun such as 文化、艺术、经济、技术、政治、内容、质量, etc.

☞ 从文化上讲，它是比较直接、简单、强烈的情感表现。

1、近年来大批的工人下岗，从经济上讲，是体制改革和市场经济发展的结果。

A lot of workers have gotten laid off in recent years. From the perspective of economics, this is a result of reform of the system and development of the market economy.

2、现在用电脑来做这样的事情，从技术上说，是完全可能的。

In terms of technology, it is now absolutely possible to use a computer to do something like this.

五、（把……通过……）表现 (to express/show...through/by means of...)

> ✍ The Verb 表现 is usually followed by either an Object, as in 他表现了强烈的批判精神 (He has demonstrated a strong critical spirit), or a Complement, as in 把个人的感情表现出来 (to express one's personal feelings).

☞ 我比较喜欢把我的愤怒以及一些个人的情感通过音乐表现出来。

1、从八十年代起，崔健就开始用摇滚乐和他的歌来表现自己强烈的情感和批判精神。

From the 1980s on, Cui Jian began to use rock music and his songs to express his strong emotions and critical spirit.

2、文化和语言是分不开的，而且很多时候，文化是通过语言来表现的。

Culture and language are inseparable. Often times, culture is reflected through language.

六、处于……阶段 (to be at the stage of...)

> ✍ 处于 means "to be situated in/at", and is used to indicate the temporal, spatial, or circumstantial location of the subject. 处于 is a rather formal word, and is therefore used mainly in writing. Its equivalent in the spoken vernacular is 处在, e.g. 处在这种环境（中） (under this circumstances), but this word is not used frequently.

☞ 虽然摇滚在中国已经有十多年了，但仍处于萌发阶段。

1、处于恋爱阶段的人常常会觉得自己是世界上最幸福的人。
People who are in love often feel that they are the happiest people in the world.

2、改革开放以后，中国有了非常大的进步，可是还是处于发展的阶段。
Although China has made great progress since reforms and opening up began, it is still in a developmental stage.

七、造成（压力／后果／影响） (to cause pressure/ consequence/ influence...)

> ✍ 造成 is a Causative Verb. As such, it is always followed by an object, which can be a Noun, a Verb, or a Clause; and the object is typically something abstract. For example, 造成严重的污染 (to cause serious pollution), 造成说谎 (to cause lying), 造成很多工人下岗 (to cause many workers to be laid off).

☞ 但是我觉得就因为那时候过得太愉快，好象很多事很容易，造成现在的压力，一些理性的东西。

1、有些人认为这样大的音乐会会给青少年造成很坏的影响。
Some people believe that such huge concerts have a bad influence on teenagers.

2、人口的增长给中国造成了很大的压力。
Population growth caused great pressures in China.

八、对……（的）理解 (a rational understanding of...)

> 理解, along with 懂 and 了解, is translated into English as "to understand, to comprehend", but there are differences in nuance among these three Chinese words. 懂 is understanding at a basic level, 理解 focuses on an understanding based on rational thinking, and 了解 is based more on one's sensibility or intuition; e.g. 大亮完全不懂礼貌。(Daliang has absolutely no understanding of courtesy.) 中国人和美国人对人权的理解很不一样。(The Chinese have a very different understanding of "human rights" from Americans.) 青少年经常认为他们的父母不了解他们。(Youth often feel that their parents don't understand them.) All three can function as verbs, and may or may not take an Object. In addition, 理解 and 了解 also function as nouns.

☞ 现在我也很高兴，可以很理性地看我的过去，而对未来的理解比过去更客观。

1、 他对这些问题的理解是非常正确的。

His understanding of these problems is totally correct.

2、 那时候我刚开始学中文，对中国文化不太了解，所以对中国人为什么这样做也不理解。

At that time I had just started to learn Chinese. I wasn't familiar with the culture, therefore I didn't understand why the Chinese would do things in certain ways.

九、为了……而…… ((to do something) in order to/that...)

> As discussed in Lesson 9, Sentence Pattern 3, 而 is a classical Chinese word used in modern Chinese as a conjunction to indicate a variety of relationships. Here, it links up a 为了…… phrase indicating a purpose with a Verb Phrase indicating the action taken to achieve this purpose. This pattern is used mostly in written Chinese.

☞ 比如有些人为了阻止我演出而编造了一些谎言，……

1、 电话公司为了方便更多人上网而增添了这项服务。

In order to make it convenient for more people to go on line, the telephone company added this service.

2、 他为了表示自己的愤怒而写了这首歌。

He wrote this song in order to express his rage.

十、与其……（倒）不如…… (rather than..., it would be better to...)

> ✍ This pattern is rather literary, and it is used to express a choice or comparison between two options after weighing their pros and cons. 与其, literally "(compared) with it", introduces the inferior option; and 不如, literally "not as good as...", introduces the preferred option.

☞ 因为与其听他说谎，倒不如大骂一顿最让我舒服。

1、与其打国际长途电话，倒不如给她发电子邮件。
Instead of calling her international long distance, it would be better to e-mail her.

2、不少人觉得与其在国营单位工作，不如自己下海去做生意。
Many people would rather go into businesses on their own than work in government-owned units.

十一、于是 (so, hence, thereupon)

> ✍ 于是 is a conjunction that occurs in the middle of an extended discourse to introduce a situation or event that is both *subsequent* and *consequential to* the event or situation stated in the preceding sentence. It encompasses the functions of two other conjunctions 然后 and 所以 which occupy the same grammatical position. 然后 introduces the action or event that *follows chronologically* the preceding action or event, and 所以 introduces the action or event that *results from* the pre-stated cause. The meanings of 然后 and 所以 are subsumed under 于是. Moreover, unlike 然后 and 所以, which usually occur in tandem with another conjunction in the preceding clause (i.e. 先……然后……; 因为…… 所以……), 于是 usually functions independently.

☞ 我和他针锋相对地争论，最后彻底激怒了他。于是他就给文化部写信，破坏我们本来就很少的演出机会。

1、她们下岗以后，找了很久都没找到合适的工作，后来看到开饭馆可以赚钱，于是就把下岗费凑在一起，合伙开了这个小饭馆。
After being laid off from work, they tried for a long time to find suitable jobs, but to no avail. Later, when they saw that one can make money by running a restaurant, they pooled their unemployment compensation and opened this little restaurant.

2、老徐本来想买一台大彩电，后来听说电脑对孩子的学习很有帮助，于是就买了电脑，不买彩电了。
Lao Xu originally wanted to buy a big-screen colored TV, but later he heard that computers

are very helpful to children in their studies, so he bought a computer instead of a TV.

十二、首先 (first of all)

> ✍ 首先 is a movable Adverb, which means it can precede either the subject or the verb in the sentence. It is used to introduce the first action, event, or condition/prerequisite in a given context.

☞ 首先一个人关心自己的生存环境是天经地义的事。

1、如果你希望别人尊重你，首先你得尊重别人。

If you expect others to respect you, you have to respect others first.

2、有人说要当一个好的音乐家，首先要热爱生活，你觉得对吗？

Some people say that if one wants to be a good musician, one must first love life with passion. Do you agree?

崔健说：我最喜欢纽约，它是疯狂的城市

练习

一、读课文回答问题

1、为什么崔健说他的摇滚乐比较个人化？

2、为什么崔健认为中国的摇滚乐仍处于萌发阶段？

3、为什么崔健认为一九九二年是他最愉快的一年？

4、崔健以前看到人睁眼说谎的时候，他做什么？现在他有什么样的理解？

5、为什么崔健的一个朋友的父亲给文化部写信，破坏崔健的演出机会？

6、崔健认为他的创作和政治有关联吗？为什么？

7、崔健对中国的未来有什么看法？

二、听录音回答问题

1、对很多中国人来说，为什么邓丽君会有这么大的影响？

2、邓丽君是什么时候出生的？

3、邓丽君的歌在哪些地方流行过？

4、老邓、小邓指的是谁？

5、邓丽君想用歌声来表现什么？

6、邓丽君最后死在什么地方？

三、完成对话

1、A：美国人对 Steven Spielberg 的电影有什么看法？

　　B：（对……有……的评价；称为）

2、A：我觉得咱们每个星期都考试实在有点紧张。

B：（从……来讲，造成）

3、A：徐慧在孩子还没出生以前就跟她的丈夫离婚了，这是怎么一回事啊？

B：（为……而……；于是）

4、A：我有个朋友想去日本学习摇滚乐，你觉得怎么样？

B：（与其……倒不如……；对……理解）

5、A：请你谈谈这个暑期中文班的特点。

B：（跟……结合；处于……阶段）

四、阅读短文回答问题

　　崔健于1961年出生在一个朝鲜族的音乐家庭，他的母亲是一名舞蹈演员，父亲是一位专业小号(trumpet)演奏者。由于受到家庭和父亲的影响，崔健从14岁时起就开始学习吹小号，并且在20岁那年成了一名专业小号演奏者。但是崔健很快就对西方流行音乐产生了强烈的兴趣，他开始学习弹吉他(guitar)，并且在北京的酒吧里演唱自己创作的歌曲。1987年，崔健发行了他第一张的专辑(album)，其中包括他的成名作《一无所有》。歌中唱道："我要给你我的追求，还有我的自由，可你却总是笑我，一无所有。"崔健成长在六十年代和七十年代，那一代的年轻人受到的是正统的共产主义教育，而八十年代的新政策不但改革了中国的政治体制，也打开了中国的大门，西方的影响一下子进入中国，旧的体制正被打破，新的还没有建立，人们在不安地发现原来自己在内心深处真的是"一无所有"。所以这首歌一问世就受到了极大的欢迎，无论在哪儿都可以听见人们在弹唱这首歌。崔健在创作的早期就已经形成了自己独特的风格，与当时流行的校园歌曲相比，崔健的作品表现出一种清新、自然、追求个性、独立发展和自由的特色，在歌词方面，这一点体现得更为明显，崔健也把东方和西方的乐器和不同的摇滚乐演奏技巧结合在一起。由于他的努力，中国人开始体会到摇滚乐的魅力，因此很多人称崔健为"中国摇滚第一人"。

回答问题:

1、崔健出生在一个什么样的家庭？他受到了父母的什么影响？

2、《一无所有》这首歌的时代背景是怎么样的？为什么受到大家的欢迎？

3、崔健的创作有什么特点？

4、为什么崔健被称为"中国摇滚第一人"？

5、请你听一首崔健早期创作的歌曲和一首近期创作的歌曲，比较一下它们在歌词、乐器演奏和音乐风格方面的不同。

五、翻译

1. What do you think about the book "Privacy"?

2. From the perspective of social development, I think the book represents a kind of social progress, but many people could not understand the content of this book.

3. Is it because the book is relatively commercialized and goes against (not in accord with) Chinese tradition?

4. It is possible. Many people criticize this book because it describes the relationship between men and women in a straightforward fashion. It is a product of the merger between Chinese and western culture.

他用一首自己写的 "一无所有" 唱红了全国

六、段落练习

摇滚音乐和西方文化

第一段: 介绍摇滚音乐的历史，摇滚音乐有一些什么特点
……被称为……; 从……起; ……开始出现; 最开始
……, 后来……, 到现在……; ……是……一种现
象; ……是……的产物; 从……上讲, ……表现……
感情; ……反映了……

第二段: 摇滚音乐和西方文化的关系

1、西方文化的特点
……的特点是……; 首先, ……看重……; 比方说,
……; 第二、……; 除了……以外, 还有……;

2、摇滚乐所表现的文化和精神
从……来讲……; 为了……; 把……与……结合起
来; 以便, ……; 比如……; ……表现……感情; 于
是, 产生了……; ……受到……

第三段: 对摇滚音乐的评价
总之……; 通过……表现了……; ……反映了……;
……对……有……影响; ……在……阶段, ……就象
……一样; ……是一种……的方式

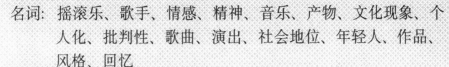

有用的词:

名词: 摇滚乐、歌手、情感、精神、音乐、产物、文化现象、个人化、批判性、歌曲、演出、社会地位、年轻人、作品、风格、回忆

动词: 创作、表现、批判、唱歌、写歌、唱红、评价、表演、处于、吸引、受到、欢迎、带来、创造、结合

形容词: 直接、彻底、简单、强烈、愤怒、愉快、很理性、客观、美好

七、作文

《我最喜欢的一个美国摇滚乐队或摇滚歌手》

八、讨论

1、为什么摇滚乐在中国也会流行?

2、崔健说摇滚乐是音乐与商业结合的产物, 你有什么看法?

3、崔健用音乐表示自己的愤怒和情感, 你觉得这是不是一个好办法? 为什么? 你通常是怎样表示自己的愤怒的?

4、你喜欢不喜欢摇滚乐? 为什么?

九、语言实践 🚴

1、去卖音乐CD、录音带的商店或地方采访那里的售货员:

(1) 了解现在哪些音乐CD或录音带卖得最好?

(2) 摇滚乐的CD或录音带卖得怎么样?

2、采访喜欢摇滚乐的大学生:

(1) 最喜欢的摇滚乐队是哪个?

(2) 为什么喜欢这样的乐队?

(3) 对崔健有什么看法？崔健代表现代年青人的思想和情感吗？为什么？

(4) 除了崔健以外，还有谁的歌声最能表现现在中国年青人的情感？

新长征路上的摇滚

词曲: 崔健

问问天, 问问地, 还有多少里？

求求风, 求求雨, 快离我远去。

山也多, 水也多, 分不清东西,

人也多, 嘴也多, 讲不清道理。

怎样说, 怎样做, 才真正是自己？

怎样歌, 怎样唱, 这心中才得意？

一边走, 一边想, 雪山和草地,

一边走, 一边唱, 领袖毛主席。

噢， 1234567

ROCK'N'ROLL ON THE NEW LONG MARCH

Ask heaven, ask earth
"How many more miles to go?"
Beg the wind, beg the rain
"Please leave me alone."
Many mountains, many rivers
But can't get my bearings.
Many people, many mouths
But can't make any sense of them.

What to say? What to do?
To find the real me?
What song? How to sing it?
To finally be satisfied?
Walking along and thinking about
Snowy mountains and green pastures.
Walking along and singing about
Our great leader Chairman Mao.

Oh! 1234567....

An Intermediate Chinese Course

第十一课 中国的住房改革

国家的住房政策也发生了相应的变化

课文

一、简介

这几年，中国人有几件最关心的大事，其中[1]之一就是买房。过去，中国实行的是低收入、低消费的社会主义制度，所以对中国的老百姓来说住房是一种福利。也就是说，只要你有单位，就不必[2]为买房子发愁，因为单位一般都给自己的职工提供住房。过去，两间一套的房子，每月房租个人只负担几块，最多十几块钱，占个人月工资收入的百分之五左右，其它的都由国家或者单位负担。由于国家和单位的建房资金十分有限，满足不了单位职工住房的需求，所以住房越来越紧张，无房户和缺房户越来越多。

九十年代以来，经济政策改变了，人们的收入增加了。国家的住房政策也发生了相应的变化。这个变化的最大特点就是住房商品化，

Notes [1]其中, meaning "among which..., in the midst of...", brings the focus to a particular case within the group or set stated in the preceding clause or sentence. Thus, the 其中 clause never occurs in isolation, but rather in the middle of an extended discourse. 其中 often occurs at the beginning of a clause, as in the text, but not necessarily so; e.g. 这三个说法都对，你选其中最简单的就行了。(All three ways of saying it are correct. You can just choose the simplest way.)

[2]The adverb 不必 is synonymous with 不用. It can modify a verb phrase (i.e. no need to do something), an adjective (including those referring to emotional states, like 难过 and 着急), and even a clause. When 不必 is used to modify a monosyllabic adjective, there is a tendency to add another modifier in order to maintain a smooth rhythm. Examples:

不必写信了，我已经给他打电话了。　　　　　(modifying a verb phrase)
You don't need to write to him any more. I have called him already.
不必紧张。　　　　(modifying an adjective)
No need to be nervous.
不必你自己来。(modifying a clause)
No need for you to come yourself.

即政府大力发展经济商品房，并⁽³⁾用单位补贴或是银行贷款的办法鼓励普通群众购买住房，最终⁽⁴⁾用商品房制度取代福利分房的制度。一些专家指出，住房改革的根本问题是要调整好人们的工资收入，单位补贴和房价的合理比例，使大多数靠工资收入的人买得起房子。下面一则新闻就是一家电台报道的有关住房改革的基本原则。看完这则新闻以后，请你跟中国的老百姓谈谈，了解一下他们的住房情况和买房的烦恼。

--- 生词 ---

1. ……之一	zhī yī	NP.	one of...
2. 实行	shí xíng	V.	to implement, to put into practice
3. 低收入	dī shōu rù	NP.	low income
4. 消费	xiāo fèi	V/N.	to consume; consumption
5. 社会主义	shè huì zhǔ yì	N.	socialism
6. 制度	zhì dù	N.	system
7. 福利	fú lì	N.	welfare
8. 发愁	fā chóu	VO.	to worry, to be anxious
9. 一般	yī bān	Adv/Adj.	generally; ordinary, typical
10. 职工	zhí gōng	N.	staff, employee
11. 提供	tí gōng	V.	to provide
12. 套	tào	Classifier.	set (of clothing, books, housing,

Notes ⁽³⁾并 is usually used in written Chinese. It links up two parallel disyllabic Verbs, indicating further action following the first one. Functionally speaking, it is similar to "and" in English that links up two verbs. When 并 connects two clauses, the Subject of the second clause is identical to the one in the first clause, and is often omitted.

她创作并自己演唱了这首歌。
She composed and personally performed singing this song.

⁽⁴⁾The 终 in 最终 is a rather formal word, so 最终 too is used mostly in written form. It functions both as an adjective (e.g. 最终目的 "the ultimate goal") and as an adverb (e.g. 最终解决了问题 "the problem was finally resolved"). The less formal synonym for 最终 is 最后. Aside from a difference in the level of formality, 最后 has a usage not shared by 最终. 最后 (not最终) can be used to indicate the last one in a sequence of actions, as in 先……再/然后……最后……, 最终 cannot.

ideas, etc.)

13. 房租	fáng zū	N.	rent (for housing)
14. 月工资	yuè gōng zī	NP.	monthly salary
15. 收入	shōu rù	N.	income
16. ……左右	zuǒ yòu	Adj.	...more or less, approximately...
17. 其他	qí tā	Adj.	the rest
18. 由	yóu	Prep.	by
19. 建房	jiàn fáng	VP.	to build houses
20. 十分	shí fēn	Adv.	very, extremely
21. 有限	yǒu xiàn	Adj.	limited
22. 严重	yán zhòng	Adj.	serious, grave
23. 满足	mǎn zú	V./Adj.	to satisfy; satisfied, content
24. 需求	xū qiú	N.	need, demand (vs. supply)
25. 紧张	jǐn zhāng	Adj.	tight, tense, in short supply
26. 无房户	wú fáng hù	NP.	household with no housing
27. 缺房户	quē fáng hù	NP.	households short on housing
28. 增加	zēng jiā	V.	to increase
29. 相应	xiāng yìng	Adj.	corresponding
30. 特点	tè diǎn	N.	(distinctive) characteristic, feature
31. 商品化	shāng pǐn huà	V./Adj.	to commoditize; commoditized
32. 即	jì	Adv.	namely, that is
33. 大力	dà lì	Adv.	energetically, vigorously
34. 补贴	bǔ tiē	V./N.	to subsidize; subsidy
35. 银行	yín háng	N.	bank
36. 贷款	dài kuǎn	VO./N.	to grant or to get a loan; loan
37. 群众	qún zhòng	N.	the masses
38. 购买	gòu mǎi	V.	to purchase
39. 最终	zuì zhōng	Adv.	finally, in the end
40. 取代	qǔ dài	V.	to replace
41. 分房	fēn fáng	VO.	to allocate or assign housing
42. 专家	zhuān jiā	N.	expert
43. 指出	zhǐ chū	V.	to point out
44. 调整	tiáo zhěng	V.	to adjust
45. 比例	bǐ lì	N.	proportion, scale

46. 则	zé	*Classifer.*	classifier for news items
47. 新闻	xīn wén	*N.*	news
48. 电台	diàn tái	*N.*	TV Station
49. 有关	yǒu guān	*V/Adj.*	to be related (to...); relevant (to...)
50. 原则	yuán zé	*N.*	principle

你会用下面的词吗？

之一、实行、低收入、消费、社会主义制度、福利、发愁、一般来说、职工、提供、套、房租、月工资、收入、左右、其它部分、由、合理、分房、十分严重、年代、政策、增加、发生、变化、特点、商品化、银行贷款、鼓励、普通群众、购买、最终、取代、专家指出、根本、调整、比例、大多数、有关、基本原则、烦恼

过去，单位一般都给自己的职工提供住房

二、电视节选

新闻一则：中国的住房改革

（根据电视原文改编）

　　住房制度的改革是老百姓最关心的问题之一。作为向住房制度改革目标过渡的重大一年，今年即将[5]出台的房改措施将使中国的普通群众最终告别已经实行了几十年的福利分房（制度）。

　　新的房改政策的基本原则之一就是国家、单位和个人三方面合理负担。而个人负担多少，如何负担是其中最敏感的问题。据建设部有关部门透露，买房时个人负担的合理额度将是家庭年均收入的四倍。

　　国家、单位、个人三方面合理负担的基本含义是国家对商品房行价格调控和政策扶持，主要是大力发展经济适用房。单位则主要是对无房户和缺房户发放住房补贴，而个人负担的合理额度则平均为家庭收入的四倍。比如，一个月平均收入一千六百元的家庭在购买住房时负担的费用应该是七万六千八百元。当然了，这只是个理论上[6]的推算。根据各地、各单位的不同情况，各个家庭需要承担的具体费用会有相应[7]的变化，但是不会跟这个标准差得太远。

Notes [5]The adverb 即将, meaning "to be about to", is the literary equivalent to the colloquial 就要 or 快要。 As such, it is used mostly in written Chinese. Since formal written Chinese tends to maintain a disyllabic rhythm, the verb that follows 即将 is typically a disyllabic word, whereas 就要 or 快要 does not have this restriction; e.g. 新年 就要/快要 到了。(New Year's will be here soon.) becomes 新年即将到来。(not 新年即将到（了）) in formal written style.

　　[6]When 上 is suffixed to an Abstract Noun such as 理论、实际、技术、内容、艺术、价格, etc., it means "in terms of...", indicating that the statement is from the perspective of that Noun. The noun "XX" may have the preposition 在 added in front with no difference in meaning, e.g. （在）技术上没有问题。(There are no problems from the technological point of view.) "XX 上" may also be incorporated into the structure "从XX上来看/说/考虑" meaning "to...from the point of view of XX".

—◆— 生词 —◆—

51. 目标	mù biāo	N.	goal, target
52. 过渡	guò dù	V/Adj.	to transition; transitional
53. 重大	zhòng dà	Adj.	important, great, major, significant
54. 即将	jí jiāng	Aux.	about to, on the point of
55. 出台	chū tái	VP.	(lit. "to go on stage") to appear, to emerge (after having been in a planning or preparatory phase), to be unveiled
56. 措施	cuò shī	N.	(refer to dealing with a problem or issue) measure
57. 将	jiāng	Aux.	about to, will soon
58. 告别	gào bié	VP.	to say good-bye to, to leave (behind)
59. 敏感	mǐn gǎn	Adj.	sensitive
60. 建设部	jiàn shè bù	NP.	Department of Construction
61. 有关部门	yǒu guān bù mén	NP.	related departments or sectors
62. 透露	tòu lù	V.	to reveal
63. 额度	é dù	N.	specified amount or ratio
64. 年均	nián jūn	Adj.	annual average
65. 倍	bèi	N.	noun/number of times/multiples
66. 含义	hán yì	N.	meaning, implication
67. 价格	jià gé	N.	price
68. 调控	tiáo kòng	Abbrev.	to adjust and control
69. 扶持	fú chí	V.	to help sustain, to support, to give aid to
70. 适用	shì yòng	Adj.	suitable, applicable
71. 发放	fā fàng	V.	to provide, to grant

Notes (7)相应 is basically a verb meaning "to mutually respond", as in 政府与老百姓应该互相相应。(The government and the people should respond to each other.) But this word has come to be used mostly as an adjective, e.g. 收入与消费是相应的。(There is a corresponding relationship between income and consumption.) 住房商品化给家庭生活带来了一些相应的变化。(The commoditization of housing has brought some corresponding changes in family life.) 相应 with 地 suffixed to it may also function as an adverb, e.g. 老师们的工资涨了，学费也相应地增加了。(Teachers' salaries have gone up, and tuition has also increased correspondingly.)

72. 平均	píng jūn	*N/Adj.*	average
73. 为	wéi	*V.*	to be
74. 当然	dāng rán	*Adv.*	of course
75. 理论上	lǐ lùn shàng	*PrepP.*	in theory, theoretical, theoretically
76. 推算	tuī suàn	*V/N.*	to calculate; calculation
77. 各	gè	*Adj.*	each
78. 承担	chéng dān	*V.*	to bear (responsibility), to take responsibility for
79. 具体	jù tǐ	*Adj.*	concrete (vs. abstract)
80. 费用	fèi yòng	*N.*	expenses
81. 标准	biāo zhǔn	*N/Adj.*	standard
82. 差	chà	*V/Adj.*	to differ, to be short; inferior

你会用下面的词吗？
目标、过渡、重大、即将、措施、告别、敏感、有关部门、
透露、年均、倍、含义、价格、适用、发放、平均、为、当
然、理论上、推算、各、承担、具体、费用、标准、差

有的中国人已经告别了实行了几十年的福利分房制度

句型

一、实行 (to implement, to carry out, to put into practice)

> ✍ 实行 is a Transitive Verb used mostly in official contexts. It typically takes such Objects as 政策、制度、措施、计划、改革, etc.

☞ 过去，中国实行的是低收入、低消费的社会主义制度，所以对中国的老百姓来说住房是一种福利。

1、那时候中国还没实行独生子女政策，所以他们家有三个孩子。

China had not yet implemented the one-child policy at that time, so they have three kids.

2、学分制是什么时候在中国的大学实行的？

When did China put the credit system into effect in universities?

二、给（／为）……提供 (to provide so-and-so with such-and-such, to provide such-and-such to so-and-so)

> ✍ 提供, "to provide", is a transitive verb, and its object is the thing being provided. In this structure, the object of the preposition 给 or 为 is the beneficiary of the things provided. An alternative way to express the same idea is "提供……给……", but 为 cannot be used in this latter structure.

☞ 也就是说，只要你有单位，就不必为买房子发愁，因为单位一般都会给自己的职工提供住房。

1、如果要提高教育质量，政府就必须每年给学校提供大量的资金。

The government must provide a large amount of funding to schools annually if it wants to improve the quality of education.

2、经济的发展为很多人提供了新的就业机会。

The development of the economy has provided new occupational opportunities for many people.

三、由······VP ((something) to be up to/ done by somebody)

> 由 is a preposition used to introduce the agent who is in a position or has the power or prerogative to do something. It typically occurs with such verbs as 负责、介绍、创作、导演、主持、办理、承担、促成、翻译、解决、提供, etc. 由 and 被 are both translated into the passive voice in English, but the two are not interchangeable in Chinese. 被 usually carries a negative connotation, as though something is inflicted upon the recipient, whereas 由 never carries such a connotation. 由 is always followed by its object (the agent of action), whereas the object of 被 may be omitted.

☞ 过去，两间一套的房子，每月房租个人只负担几块，最多十几块钱，……其它的都由国家或者单位负担。

1、这个电视节目由小陈主持，老谢导演，你看怎么样？
This television program should be hosted by Xiao Chen and directed by Lao Xie, what do you think?

2、这首歌是她创作的，还是由她自己来介绍吧。
This song was created by her, so let her introduce it herself.

四、即 (that is, namely)

> 即 is another Classical Chinese word still used in modern written Chinese. It is synonymous with the colloquial phrase 也就是, meaning "that is, namely". Both 即 and 也就是 are used to introduce an explanation or paraphrases of the term just mentioned.

☞ 这个变化的最大特点就是住房商品化，即政府大力发展经济商品房，

1、电脑，即电子计算机，已经逐渐进入普通老百姓的家庭了。
Computers i.e., electronic calculators, have gradually entered the homes of ordinary people.

2、下岗，即失业，从社会发展上来讲，是体制改革的产物。
Being laid off, in other words, being unemployed, from the point of view of social development, is a product of reform of the system.

五、　用A取代B (to replace B with A)

> ✍ This structure literally means "use A to substitute for B". There is nothing mysterious about this structure, except that the English equivalent reverses the order of the two components.

☞ 这个变化的最大特点就是住房商品化，即政府大力发展经济商品房，…… 最终用商品房制度取代福利分房制度。

1、我们很快就会用电脑来取代人做这样的工作了。
We will soon be replacing humans with computers in doing this type of work.

2、老板为了省钱，到了第三个月，就又去雇了一批新工人取代这些已经工作了两个月的工人。
When the third month came around, the boss replaced workers who had been working for two months with new workers in order to save money.

六、　使 (to make, to cause)

> ✍ In Northern colloquial Chinese, 使 is used as a verb in the sense of 用 (cf. Lesson 4, 借你的梳子使使). This usage of 使 is rather limited. The broader usage of 使 in standard Mandarin is as a causative verb in sentences wherein the subject is the cause, and the object of 使 is a complete clause (i.e. subj.+VP) indicating the result. 叫 and 让 are synonymous with 使 in this usage, but 使 is rather formal, whereas 叫 and 让 are colloquial.

☞ 一些专家指出，住房改革的根本问题是要调整好人们的工资收入、单位补贴和房价的合理比例，使大多数靠工资收入的人买得起房子。

1、一首"一无所有"使崔健成为中国有名的摇滚乐手。
The song "There's Nothing" made Cui Jian a famous rock star in China.

2、愤怒使他写了很多有批判性的、比较有政治性的摇滚歌曲。
Rage has led him to write many critical and political rock songs.

七、(从……)向……过渡 (to transition (from...) to...)

> ✍ The Verb 过渡 originally meant "to cross (a river)", but now it is used figuratively to mean "to transition (from one stage to another)". It can also be used as an adjective, as in 过渡时期 (transitional period).

☞ 作为向住房制度改革目标过渡的一年，今年将出台的房改措施将使中国的普通群众最终告别已经实行了几十年的福利分房（制度）。

1、中国正在逐渐从计划经济向市场经济过渡。

China is gradually transitioning from a planned economy to a market economy.

2、从一种制度向另一种制度过渡需要相当长的时间，不能太急。

A transition from one system to another takes a rather long time. It can't be rushed.

八、A 是 B 的……倍 (A is ...times as much as B)

> ✍ The word 倍 indicates "times, -fold", and the expression "A 是 B 的……倍" means "A is ...times/fold of B".

☞ 据建设部有关部门透露，买房时个人负担的合理额度将是家庭平均收入的四倍。

1、中国的人口是美国的六倍，可是美国人的平均收入差不多是中国人的二十倍。

China's population is 6 times that of U.S., but the average income of Americans is almost 20 times that of the Chinese.

2、摇滚乐歌手的收入如果不是普通人的一百倍，起码也是几十倍。

The income of a rock star is at least 30 or 40 times that of an ordinary person – if it is in fact not 100 times.

九、……，则……(adverb used to indicate a contrast with the previous sentence/clause)

> 则, an adverb from Classical Chinese, is used today only in formal writing. It is a non-movable Adverb, which means it must be placed after the subject and before the verb phrase. It is used in the second clause in a complex sentence to signal a contrast with the situation in the preceding clause. It is somewhat similar to 却 in meaning, but 却 conveys contrariness to expectations or the norm, whereas 则 contrasts the situations in the two contiguous clauses.

☞ 国家、单位、个人三方面合理负担的基本含义是国家对商品房进行价格调控和政策扶持，主要是大力发展经济适用房，单位则主要是对无房户发放住房补贴……

1、年青人比较喜欢摇滚乐，老年人则觉得它太吵，太疯狂。

Young people prefer rock music, but old people think rock music is too noisy and crazy.

2、过去，离婚的人都会觉得有很大的社会压力，现在则好象没有什么问题了。

In the past, divorced people felt a great deal of pressure from society, but this doesn't seem to be a problem anymore.

十、根据……(的情况)(in line with, according to)

> 根据 (according to) is a preposition. It is most commonly used to lead off an independent prepositional phrase in the beginning of a sentence to "set the stage" for the event in the main clause, as in the example from the text. A second way in which a 根据 phrase is used is as a modifier for a verb, e.g. 学生们根据考试成绩分班。(The students are assigned to classes according to their placement test results.) In both of these usages, 根据 may be replaced by 据. However, 根据 is preferred in longer phrases and phrases that have a disyllabic rhythm (e.g. 根据情况/法律/政策/统计/事实, etc.) whereas 据 is preferred with monosyllabic objects, e.g. 据我看. Moreover, when the logical object of "according to" is unstated, only 据 may be used, e.g. 据说 (not根据说). 根据 has one other usage, which is not shared by 据, and that is as the verb in a sentence, meaning "to be based on...", e.g. 你的消费应该根据你的收入。(Your consumption must be based on your income.)

☞ 根据各地、各单位的不同情况，各个家庭需要承担的具体费用会有相应的变化，但是不会跟这个标准差得太远。

1、买什么样的房子，买多大的房子，都必须根据自己的工资收入情况，不能
光喜欢就买。

In deciding what kind of house and how big a house to buy, one must take one's income
situation into consideration. One can't just buy whatever house one fancies.

2、有的家长既不考虑孩子的兴趣，也不根据孩子的具体情况，强迫孩子去当
画家、音乐家，这其实对孩子一点好处也没有。

Some parents force their children to be artists and musicians, never taking into consideration
their children's interests nor paying attention to their children's real situations. Actually,
this is not good at all for the children.

十一、跟……差得很远／差得不远 (to differ from/to be short of...by far/not far)

> One of the functions of 差 is as a verb, meaning "to be short, to differ"; e.g. 还差五分钟。 (It's still
> five minutes until the time.) 我们还差一毛钱。 (We're still short by a dime.) Even the idiomatic
> adverbs 差不多 and 差一点 originated from this verbal usage of 差. As a verb, 差 can take a
> complement, e.g. 差得很远/差得不远. In the above construction, "差得很远/差得不远" is
> preceded by the prepositional phrase "跟……" to indicating the object or target against which
> the subject is being compared or measured. 差 can also function as an adjective meaning "inferior,
> of poor quality", e.g. 我的汉语原来很差！(My Chinese was originally quite bad!)

☞ 根据各地、各单位的不同情况，各个家庭需要承担的具体费用会有相
应的变化，但是不会跟这个标准差得太远。

1、中国生产的电脑跟美国的差得不太远。

The computers produced in China are quite comparable to those produced in America.

2、有时候孩子能做到的跟父母希望的差得很远。

Oftentimes there is a huge gap between what children are capable of and what their parents
hope for them.

练习

一、读课文回答问题 📖

1、在九九年以前中国的住房制度是什么？为什么有单位的人不必为买房子发愁？
2、以前房租由谁负担？占个人月工资的多少？
3、为什么这几年住房越来越紧张、无房户和缺房户越来越多？
4、什么叫住房商品化？
5、住房改革的目的是什么？
6、根据新的房改政策，住房由哪三方面合理负担？个人负担的合理额度将是多少？
7、根据新的房改政策，单位的合理负担是什么？

听录音回答问题

1、大陆住房改革的目标是什么？
2、什么是空置房？
3、有哪些原因造成空置率很高？
4、政府推行了什么政策来鼓励百姓买房？
5、为什么北京人说只有傻瓜才买房？
6、公有住房租金该占双职工家庭工资的百分之几才合理？
7、怎样才能解决空置率过高的问题？

三、完成对话 👫

1、A：这些下岗工人领到的下岗费够用吗？
   B：（对……来说；由）

2、A：听说这几年中国的离婚率也高了。
　　B：（据……；占百分之……）

3、A：你来中国以后学了多少生词？跟在美国的学习比起来怎么样？
　　B：（是……倍；跟……差得很远）

4、A：你们来北京才几个星期，中文就已经有这么大的进步了！
　　B：（给……提供；使）

5、A：美国的父母都很尊重孩子，中国的父母呢？这种情况会不会发生变化？
　　B：（则；向……过渡）

6、A：现在大学生毕业以后，好象都得自己找工作，学校不再管工作分配了，是吗？
　　B：（用……取代；即）

7、A：为什么经济发展了，国家和单位反而会让这么多工人下岗呢？
　　B：（根据……的情况；实行）

商品房越来越多

四、阅读短文回答问题

　　中国人常用"衣食住行"来概括生活中的各个层面，也常常把"安居乐业"开玩笑地说成"安居才能乐业"，由此可以看出住房在人们生活中的重要地位。中国是一个人口众多的国家，尤其在人口密集的城市，住房问题向来是很难顺利解决的大问题。另外，由于中国长期以来实行政府盖房、单位分配住房的制度，所以存在着分房不平等的现象，一方面是"有人没房住"，普通老百姓一家三代挤在一间房里，刚结婚的人也没有新房；另一方面是"有房没人住"，一些领导利用手里的权力拿到好多房子，有的房子根本就是空着没人住。

　　住房改革政策实行以后，人们都得用钱买房了，所以很多空着没人住的房子也被退了回来，出售给没房住或者住房紧张的居民，在一定程度上解决了一些人的住房问题。但是目前，除了经济适用房以外，商品房的价格还是太高，离老百姓的平均收入还是差得太远，一套商品房的价钱往往是一个家庭年收入的8倍到15倍，老百姓根本就买不起。但是现在由于分期付款制度已经在大多数地区实行，而且人们也逐渐改变了传统的"不借钱、不欠债"的观念，通过向银行贷款，分期付款购买住房的做法已经越来越普遍。再加上城市的公共交通也发达起来，就算住在郊区，也可以坐车、做地铁、甚至开着私人汽车到市内上班，所以越来越多的人也接受了购买位于郊区的低价房。

回答问题:

1、请你解释一下"有人没房住"和"有房没人住"的现象及其原因。

2、住房改革政策带来了什么变化？

3、为什么普通老百姓购买商品房还有困难？

4、分期付款制度为什么能解决一部分人的住房问题？

5、为什么郊区的低价房越来越受到人们的欢迎？

6、你觉得应该从哪些方面来解决中国的住房问题？

五、 翻译

1. There are three people in Old Wang's family, and they all live in one room.
2. According to relevant sources, family situations like Old Wang's make up 50% of the population in the big cities.
3. Although China has now implemented a policy for housing reform, it is not easy for Old Wang and his family to escape (to part from) the problem of housing shortage.
4. As for their situation now, they still cannot afford to buy a (commercial) house. But Old Wang hopes that his housing situation will become better in the future.
5. Because the government now encourages people to buy their own homes, work units also subsidize some of the housing expense for their employees. People can also take out a loan from the bank.

六、 段落练习

我怎么实现我的 "美国梦"： 汽车和房子

第一段： 什么是美国梦？
……就是……； ……的中文翻译是……； ……是指……； ……代表……； ……反映了……

第二段： 一般的美国人对美国梦的看法
要是……， 一般的人都会说……； ……其中之一就是……； 给……提供……； 由于……， 所以……

第三段： 我怎么实现我的美国梦
首先……； 也就是说……； 只要……就……； 然后， ………用的办法……； 最终， ……； ……的根本问题是……； 为了……， 就要……

七、作文

《中国人的住房情况和买房的烦恼》

八、讨论

1、由国家或者单位提供住房有什么好处和坏处？中国为什么要用商品房制度取代分房制度？

2、美国大多数人靠什么买房子？怎样才能使中国大多数靠工资收入的人买得起房子？

3、房改政策的基本原则之一是国家、单位、个人三方面合理负担，可是房子买了以后就属于个人的了，为什么还要国家和单位负担呢？

九、语言实践

1、采访你们的老师：了解一下老师家里的住房情况，向他们了解住房改革政策的内容。并请他们谈谈对住房改革政策的看法。

2、请首都经贸大学总务处房管科的有关人员和大家座谈。谈一谈：

(1)学校的分房制度和房租制度

(2)学校的卖房政策和住房管理制度

(3)学校怎么解决无房和缺房的问题

新旧住房有很大的不同

第十二课　环境污染问题

现代的科技文明为人们的生活增添了很多的方便，然而也给生活带来了许多
严重的问题，比如说，空气、噪音等环境污染。

课文

一、简介

> 　　这几年，随着中国经济的快速发展，人们的生活水平也在不断提高，拥有⁽¹⁾电话、彩电、录像机、影碟机、洗衣机、电脑、甚至汽车的家庭也越来越多了。现代的科技文明为人们的生活增添了很多的方便，然而也给生活带来了许多严重的问题，比如说，空气、噪音等环境污染。下面的电视采访就反映了北京市现在面临的一个严重的问题：空气质量差，污染程度高。看完这个报道后，请你去了解一下北京市最近几年采取了什么措施解决这个问题。如果你是北京环境保护局局长，你对改善空气的污染有些什么措施？如果你是一个北京市民，你有什么建议⁽²⁾给北京市政府？

---------- 生词 ----------

1. 污染	wū rǎn	*V/N.*	to pollute; pollution
✓ 2. 随着	suí zhe	*Prep.*	along with, in the wake of
3. 快速	kuài sù	Adj.	rapid

Notes ⁽¹⁾拥有 (to possess) is much more formal than its colloquial counterpart 有, and it is associated with objects of substantial proportions, such as 土地 (land), 人口 (population), 财产 (property), 博士学位 (Ph.D. degree), etc., and not with mundane objects such as household goods.

⁽²⁾建议 functions as either a Transitive Verb or a Noun. As a Transitive Verb, its object is usually a clause (subj. + VP). For example, 我建议你们先了解一下北京的污染问题 (I suggest that you first learn about the problem of pollution in Beijing.). When 建议 is a Noun, it often serves as the Object of the Verbs 提 (to bring up, to raise) or 有. The Measure Word for 建议 is 条、个、or 点.

4. 水平	shuǐ píng	N.	standard, level
5. 不断	bú duàn	Adv.	unceasingly, continuously
6. 拥有	yōng yǒu	V.	to own, to possess
7. 彩电	cǎi diàn	NP.	color TV set
8. 影碟机	yǐng dié jī	N.	video compact disc (VCD) player
9. 洗衣机	xǐ yī jī	N.	washing machine
10. 现代	xiàn dài	N/Adj.	present era, modern times; modern
11. 文明	wén míng	N.	civilization
12. 增添	zēng tiān	V.	to add, to increase
13. 方便	fāng biàn	Adj/N.	convenient; convenience
14. 然而	rán ér	Conj.	and yet, but
15. 空气	kōng qì	N.	air
16. 噪音	zào yīn	N.	noise
17. 质量	zhì liàng	N.	quality
✓18. 采取	cǎi qǔ	V.	to adopt (policy, method, measure, etc.)
19. 解决	jiě jué	V.	to solve
20. 保护	bǎo hù	V/N.	to protect; protection
21. 局长	jú zhǎng	N.	director of a bureau
✓22. 改善	gǎi shàn	V/N.	to improve; improvement
23. 建议	jiàn yì	V/N.	to suggest; suggestions

你会用下面的词吗？
污染、随着、快速、水平、不断、拥有、彩电、影碟机、洗衣机、现代、文明、增添、方便、然而、空气、噪音、质量、采取、解决、保护、局长、改善、建议

二、电视节选

还北京蓝天
根据电视原文改编

为了了解北京市空气质量的现状（zhuàng）以及对人们生活、健康的影响，记者在街头随机采访了一些行人。

————————————————

记者：　　　"你对北京市的空气质量满意吗？"

行人一：　　"哎呀，这可[3]是不满意。我们就住在二环边上。危害太大了。几乎每天我们上班的时候打开窗户，味儿（就）特大。所以白天都不敢打开窗户。夏天最热的时候还不敢打开窗户"。

行人二：　　"反正北京这天，不就这灰蒙蒙（huī mēng）的样子"。

行人三：　　"以前是蓝天白云。那孩子还问'妈妈，怎么蓝天看不见，老看见白云？'"

记者（问孩子）："那你妈妈怎么回答的？"

行人三的孩子：　　"妈妈说，都污染了"。

————————————————

的确[4]如这个孩子所说，正是污染夺走了北京的蓝天。从空中俯（fǔ）

Notes [3]The 可是 in 可是不满意 should not be misconstrued as "but". It is actually a very colloquial way to emphasize a statement. 可 alone – before a verb phrase or a stative verb - is an adverb meaning "certainly, indeed" - the same as 的确 or 确实, except that it is used only in colloquial speech. 是 is used to further affirm the statement, meaning something like "it is SO that..." So 可是不满意 is an emphatic way to say "indeed (we are) certainly NOT satisfied"!

[4]的确 (indeed) is a movable adverb. It may be placed directly before a Verb or an Adjective in the Predicate of the sentence, or at the very beginning of the sentence to modify the entire sentence. For example, 她的确没学过这个语法。 (She really hasn't learned this grammar point before.) 下岗以后的生活的确不容易。 (Life after being laid off is really tough.) 的确中国这二十年的变化非常大。 (Indeed, China has gone through tremendous changes in the last 20 years.)

瞰北京就会发现在蓝天和城市之间（是）一个巨大的烟尘层。象一个锅盖一样常年笼罩在北京市上空。这个烟尘锅盖阻挡了北京人看见蓝天，看见明亮的太阳，而生活在这个锅盖下面的人们自然也很难呼吸到清洁的空气。

而⁽⁵⁾这个常年笼罩在北京头上的锅盖又是如何形成的呢？每年二千八百万吨燃烟从大大小小的烟囱中直接排向天空。五千多个建筑工地的扬尘、宵尘直接升向天空，一百四十万辆机动车排放的尾气直接冲向天空，街头巷尾的露天烧烤烟雾直接扩散在天空。这些就是形成锅盖的主要原料。再加上北京的地理结构，三面环山，又是一个簸箕，污染物很难扩散，因此锅盖就很少有揭开的时候了。

————◆————

赵以忻（北京环境保护局局长）："世界卫生组织有一个监测网络，北京就参加了这个网络，在五十多个的城市里边，有十个污染最严重的城市，那么北京是在这十个之一的。世界十个污染最严重的城市之一，这顶帽子不光彩啊"。

———◆——— 生词 ———◆———

24. 还	huán	V.	to return
25. 蓝天	lán tiān	NP.	blue sky
26. 现状	xiàn zhuàng	NP.	current condition
27. 健康	jiàn kāng	N/Adj.	health; healthy
28. 记者	jì zhě	N.	reporter, journalist

Notes ⁽⁵⁾而 is sometimes called the "generic conjunction" because it can be used to indicate either an analogous or contrasting relationship, and it can appear at the beginning of a clause, a sentence, or even a paragraph to connect it with the preceding segment. It serves the same function as these conjunctions in English: and, and then, and yet, moreover, furthermore, but, however.

29. 街头	jiē tóu	N.	street corner, street
30. 随机	suí jī	Adj/Adv.	random; randomly
31. 行人	xíng rén	N.	pedestrian
32. 满意	mǎn yì	Adj/N.	to be satisfied; satisfaction
33. 二环	èr huán	Place N.	Second Ring Road
34. 危害	wēi hài	V/N.	to endanger; danger
35. 味儿	wèir	N.	odor, smell,
36. 特	tè	Adv.	especially
37. 白天	bái tiān	N.	day time
38. 不敢	bù gǎn	VP.	dare not to
39. 夏天	xià tiān	N.	summer
40. 反正	fǎn zhèng	Adv.	anyway, anyhow, in any case
41. 灰蒙蒙	huī méng méng	Adj.	gray, overcast, smoggy
42. 白云	bái yún	NP.	white cloud
43. 的确	dí què	Adv.	indeed, really
44. 夺走	duó zǒu	VP.	to snatch away
45. 空中	kōng zhōng	N.	in the sky, in the air
46. 俯瞰	fǔ kàn	VP.	to look down at, to overlook
47. 巨大	jù dà	Adj.	huge, tremendous, enormous
48. 烟尘层	yān chén céng	NP.	layer of smoke and dust
49. 锅盖	guō gài	N.	lid of a pot
50. 常年	cháng nián	Adv.	throughout the year, year-round
51. 笼罩	lǒng zhào	V.	to cover, to shroud over
52. 上空	shàng kōng	N.	the sky above
53. 阻挡	zǔ dǎng	V.	to block
54. 明亮	míng liàng	Adj.	bright
55. 太阳	tài yáng	N.	sun
56. 自然	zì rán	N/Adj.	nature; natural
57. 呼吸	hū xī	V/N.	to breathe; breathing
58. 清洁	qīng jié	Adj.	clean
59. 形成	xíng chéng	VP.	to form
60. 千	qiān	Number.	thousand

61. 万	wàn	*Number.*	ten thousand
62. 吨	dūn	*N/Classifier.*	ton
63. 燃烟	rán yān	*NP.*	the smoke caused by burning something
64. 烟囱	yān cōng	*N.*	chimney, smokestack
65. 排	pái	*V.*	to eject, to discharge, to line up
66. 向	xiàng	*Prep.*	toward
67. 建筑工地	jiàn zhù gōng dì	*NP.*	construction site (工地: work site)
68. 扬尘	yáng chén	*NP.*	rising dust
69. 宵尘	xiāo chén	*NP.*	night dust
70. 升	shēng	*V.*	to rise, to go up
71. 辆	liàng	*Classifier.*	classifier for vehicles
72. 机动车	jī dòng chē	*N.*	motor vehicle
73. 排放	pái fàng	*VP.*	to eject, to discharge
74. 尾气	wěi qì	*NP.*	exhaust fumes
75. 冲	chōng	*V.*	to surge, to rush, to dash
76. 街头巷尾	jiē tóu xiàng wěi	*N.*	streets and lanes, everywhere (in the city)
77. 露天	lù tiān	*Adj.*	in open air
78. 烧烤	shāo kǎo	*VP.*	to barbecue
79. 烟雾	yān wù	*N.*	smoke, smog
80. 扩散	kuò sàn	*V.*	to spread, to diffuse
81. 主要	zhǔ yào	*Adj.*	main, primary
82. 原料	yuán liào	*N.*	raw material
83. 地理结构	dì lǐ jié gòu	*N.*	geographical structure, topography
84. 环山	huán shān	*Adj.*	surrounded by mountains
85. 簸箕	bò ji	*N.*	dust pan (horseshoe-shaped basket originally made of bamboo)
86. 揭开	jiē kāi	*VP.*	to uncover, to reveal
87. 赵以忻	zhào yǐ xīn	*Personal N.*	Zhao Yixin

89.	世界卫生组织	shì jiè wèi shēng zǔ zhī	*NP.*	World Health Organization
90.	监测网络	jiān cè wǎng luò	*NP.*	monitoring network
91.	顶	dǐng	*Classifier.*	classifier for hats
92.	帽子	mào zi	*N.*	hat, label
93.	光彩	guāng cǎi	*N/Adj.*	radiance, splendor; honorable, glorious

你会用下面的词吗？

还、蓝天、现状、健康、记者、街头、随机、行人、满意、二环、危害、几乎、味儿、特白天、不敢、夏天、反正、灰蒙蒙、样子、白云、的确、夺走、空中、城市、巨大、烟尘层、锅盖、常年、阻挡、明亮、太阳、自然、呼吸、清洁、形成、千、万、吨、烟囱、排、向、建筑工地、升、辆、机动车、排放、尾气、冲、街头巷尾、露天、烧烤、烟雾、扩散、主要、原料、地理结构、环山、簸箕、揭开、世界卫生组织、网络、顶、帽子、光彩

这上面写着什么？

句型

一、随着…… (along with, in pace with)

> ✍ "随着+obj." is a Prepositional phrase indicating an event or situation which is followed closely by the event or situation stated in the main clause of the sentence. This pattern is usually used in formal contexts only.

☞ 这几年，随着中国经济的快速发展，人们的生活水平也在不断提高。

1、随着住房政策的改革，越来越多的中国老百姓买了房子。

Since the housing policy reform, more and more Chinese have bought their own homes.

2、她对中国文化的了解也随着她的中文水平的提高加深了。

Her understanding of Chinese culture has deepened as her Chinese language proficiency improves.

二、为（/给）……增添 (to add/to increase...to/for...)

> ✍ 增添 and 增加 both mean "to increase", but 增添 tends to be used with things that are not numerically quantifiable, as in the examples below, and 增加 tends to be used with things that are quantifiable, and in fact sometimes focuses on the amount of increase. 增添 is always followed by an object, whereas 增加 may be used without an object. For example, 近年来，北京增加了几十万辆机动车。 (In recent years, Beijing has added hundreds of thousands of motor vehicles.) 机动车增加了，空气的质量就差了。 (As the number of motor vehicles increases, the quality of the air is getting worse.) Both 增添 and 增加 may be preceded by a prepositional phrase "为/给..." to indicate the recipient of the increase.

☞ 现代科技文明为人们的生活增添了很多的方便，然而也给生活带来了许多严重的问题，

1、学校这几年为语言实验室增添了很多新设备。

In the last few years, the college has added a great deal of new equipment to the language lab.

2、我希望这不会给你增添什么麻烦。

I hope this will not add too much trouble for you.

三、 然而 (yet, but, however)

> ✍ The Conjunction 然而 is used at the beginning of a sentence to indicate a contrary relationship with the preceding segment in the discourse. It differs slightly from 而 alone in that the word 然 affirms the preceding statement, so the gist is "yes, but..." or "granted that this is so, and yet..." Both 然 and 而 are from classical Chinese, so 然而 is used today only in formal written Chinese. Semantically, it is similar to 可是 and 但是, but 可是 and 但是 are often used in tandem with 虽然 in a two-clause sentence, while 然而 is used independently, and the relationship with the preceding sentence is only implied.

☞ 现代科技文明为人们的生活增添了很多的方便，然而也给生活带来了许多严重的问题。

1、很多人觉得独生子女都是"小皇帝"，然而却不知道他们的烦恼。
   Many people think that single children are all "little emperors". What they do not know, however, is that single children also have worries.

2、中国近十几年经济有了很大的发展，然而不少地区还是相当落后。
   For the past ten years or more, China's economy has developed rapidly. There are, however, many places which are still quite backward.

四、 采取 (to adopt/take (policy/attitude/measure, etc.)

> ✍ 采取 is a Transitive Verb, and its Objects are typically such abstract nouns as: 方针、政策、策略、形式、措施、态度、手段、方法, etc.

☞ 看完这个报道以后，请你去了解一下北京市最近几年采取了什么措施解决这个问题。

1、老师采取了各种不同的方法来提高大家的学习兴趣。
   The teacher adopted different methods to raise students' interest in learning.

2、他们打算采取新的政策，希望能改善两国的关系。
   They plan to adopt new policies in hopes of improving the relationship between the two

countries.

五、对……满意／不满意 (to be satisfied/ dissatisfied with...)

> ✍ 满意 is a stative verb meaning "to be satisfied". To indicate the object of one's satisfaction, a prepositional phrase "对..." is used before it, as in the examples below. However, in colloquial speech, sometimes 满意 is used as though it is a transitive verb meaning "to be satisfied with", e.g. 我不满意这次考试的成绩。 (I'm not satisfied with my performance on this test.) This type of irregularity sometimes pops up in the contemporary language, perhaps due to influence from English. The proper way to express this idea is 我对这次考试的成绩不满意。

☞ 你对北京市的空气质量满意吗？

1、同学们对学校的生活环境都比较满意。

The students are quite satisfied with their living environment at school.

2、那个饭馆的饭非常贵，可是大家对他们的服务却不太满意。

Although that restaurant is quite expensive, people are not satisfied with their service.

六、几乎 (almost, nearly)

> ✍ 几乎 means "almost, (but not quite)", "nearly", and is synonymous with 差不多 in this sense. For example, 他几乎找了半个北京才找到这家书店。 (He searched almost half of Beijing before finding this bookstore.) However, 几乎 does not share the meaning of "approximately" with 差不多; e.g. 我等了差不多一个小时 means "I waited for approximately an hour (more or less)", whereas 我等了几乎一个小时 means "I waited for nearly an hour". 几乎 can also mean 差一点, indicating that something unpleasant or undesirable almost happened (but luckily it did not happen). For example, 他几乎弄湿了裤子。 (He almost got his pants wet, but luckily he didn't.)

☞ 几乎每天我们上班的时候打开窗户，味儿（就）特大。

1、她说的中文几乎（＝差不多）跟中国人说的一样了。

Her Chinese is almost as good as that of native Chinese speakers.

2、圆圆的爸爸妈妈越吵越厉害，几乎（＝差一点）就打起来了。

Yuanyuan's parents' argument got so bad that they almost began to hit each other.

七、 反正 (anyway, anyhow, in any case, after all)

> ✍ The Adverb 反正 indicates that the situation described in that sentence is unalterable regardless of other variable circumstances. 反正 usually occurs before the subject of the sentence or clause, but it may also occur just before the verb, so it is a movable adverb. The other variable circumstances in the background are often implicit, but sometimes they are stated explicitly; e.g. 无论/不管他们去不去，反正我去。(I'll go regardless of whether they go or not.) 你说什么都没用，反正他不会听你的。(Anything you say is useless, in any case he won't listen to you.)

☞ 反正北京这天，不就这灰蒙蒙的样子。

1、 徐慧觉得，反正她的前夫是不会回来了，还找他干什么呢？

Xu Hui felt that her husband wouldn't be coming back in any case, so why should she bother to look for him?

2、 不少中国人认为，反正孩子是自己的，他们的事家长都有权过问。

Quite a few Chinese believe that children belong to their parents after all, so parents have the right to know everything about their children.

八、 如……所说 (as...put (s) it, as is said by...)

> ✍ The prepositional phrase 如...所说 (as is said by...) is equivalent to 像...说的 (那样), but it is rather formal and therefore used mostly in written form only. Its function is to support the main statement by citing a source – often an authoritative source – for that view. This prepositional phrase is a movable adverbial phrase, which means that it may be located in front of a sentence (as in the example from the text and Example 2), or after the subject and before the verb phrase (as in example 1).

☞ 的确如这个孩子所说，正是污染夺走了北京的蓝天。

1、 中国的摇滚乐，如崔健所说，还是处于萌发阶段。

As Cui Jian put it, rock music in China is still in its budding stage.

2、 正如徐慧所说的那样，一个只顾自己的男人是留不住的。

Just as Xu Hui said, a man who cares only about himself is not worth keeping.

九、正是 (It is precisely...)

> ✍ One way to indicate that a statement is unequivocal is to add 正是 (It is precisely...) in front of it. Another context in which 正是 occurs is when 是 is the main verb of the sentence, and 正 (precisely) is used to modify it. E.g., 她选的正是我最喜欢的那个。(The one she chose was precisely the one I liked best.)

☞ 的确如这个孩子所说，正是污染夺走了北京的蓝天。

1、正是因为过去的那种不合理的、福利性的分房制度，才使住房问题越来越大，国家的负担也越来越重。

The unreasonable welfare housing distribution system of the past is precisely the reason why the housing problem got worse and worse and the government's burden became heavier and heavier.

2、正是因为李大亮自己不尊重别人，不注意别人对他的一举一动的反应，才使大家都讨厌他。

Everyone dislikes Li Daliang precisely because he is disrespectful to others and pays no attention to others' reaction to his behavior.

建文明城市
做文明市民
保护城市环境
造福首都人民
广告招商电话
67718566

"保护城市环境，造福首都人民"是什么意思？

练习

一、读课文回答问题

1、记者为什么在街头随机采访行人？

2、行人一为什么连夏天最热的时候都不敢打开窗户？

3、为什么北京的天都是灰蒙蒙的样子？

4、常年笼罩在北京市上空的是什么？它形成的原因是什么？

5、北京大概有多少辆机动车？

6、为什么北京的污染空气很难扩散？

7、在参加世界卫生组织监测网络的五十多个城市里边，北京有一顶什么"帽子"？

二、听录音回答问题

1、解振华是谁？

2、北京市的空气污染有哪两种？

3、造成空气污染的原因除了民众烧煤及开机动车外，还有什么？

4、为了解决空气污染问题，北京市计划以什么来取代燃煤？

5、无煤区会在哪儿实施？

6、为什么有一万四千辆的面的被淘汰？

7、在2000年北京市计划花多少钱来做环境保护的工作？

三、完成对话

1、A：圆圆的父母这样吵架对孩子的影响实在不好，圆圆对自己的父母有什么看法？

  B：（给……增添；对……不满意）

2、　A：北京的污染这么严重，北京市政府也该做些什么了吧？

　　　B：（随着；采取）

3、　A：老张说没有什么人跟他们办公室的李大亮合得来。

　　　B：（如……所说；几乎）

4、　A：不少人都认为正是这些疯狂的电影和音乐使美国越来越多的青少年犯罪。

　　　B：（对……有影响；然而）

5、　A：我今天头疼，不想去上课了。

　　　B：（反正；再加上）

四、阅读短文回答问题

　　2001年夏天，在北京努力申办2008年奥运会时，北京的环境问题是一个引人关注的问题。北京的环境污染严重有它的自然原因：北京位于内陆地区，气候干燥，降雨较少，再加上北京的北边就是蒙古高原，这十几年来，草原的生态环境恶化，造成北京风沙天气的增多，因此北京的上空多半的时候看起来都是灰蒙蒙的，难得看得见蓝天白云。北京的环境问题也有其它人为的原因：一个是北京市内有很多污染严重的工厂，每天排出大量工业废水、废气、废料；一个是北京的人口越来越多，每天都产生出无数的生活垃圾；另外随着汽车的增多，汽车废气的排放也严重起来。北京的冬天气候寒冷，屋子里需要暖气，就得烧煤，因此北京的冬天空气污染的问题就更严重了。

　　为了解决环境污染的问题，北京市政府作出了很多努力，比方说在北京的周围地区种树、种草，让重污染的工厂搬离北京，采取措施来限制小汽车而发展公共交通等等。通过这些办法，北京的环境问题有了一定的好转，但是离完全解决污染问题的目标还很远。希望在2008年，奥运会在北京举办的时候，我们每天都能看见蓝天，看见明亮的太阳，呼吸到清洁的空气。

回答问题：

1、根据你的了解，为什么说北京的环境问题是北京申办奥运会的一个弱项？

2、请你描述一下，你住在北京的这段时间内北京的空气、环境的情况。

3、北京的环境污染问题有什么自然原因？

4、还有什么也造成了北京的环境污染越来越严重？

5、北京市政府采取了什么措施？你认为哪些措施有效？哪些措施还应该采取或者做得还不够？

6、有的人认为，发展经济和保护环境是不可能同时做到的，你对这有什么看法？

五、翻译

1. The newspaper says that the Chinese government will adopt a new set of measures to solve the problems of environmental pollution. Is it really true?

2. Yes, it is true. Because of the development of modern science and technology, people are now paying more and more attention to environmental protection.

3. Then are you satisfied with the present situation? Do you have any suggestions for the city government?

4. I am not completely satisfied. Although the city government has taken some measures, it takes time to solve the problems of air and noise pollution.

空气污染不能算是中国特色

六、段落练习

我对解决北京城市污染问题的一些建议

第一段：问题的严重性
根据……，……情况已经……；作为……，我认为……；……必须……；不然，……将会造成……

第二段：我的几条建议
随着……；为了……，……提出下面几条……建议；首先，……采取……措施；第二，……；……对……实行……政策；第三，……；用……取代……；为……提供

第三段：我认为我的建议会有什么效果
如果……的话；……实行……的措施；……得到……改善；不但……而且……；……越来越……；从……向……过渡；最后……；……使……

七、作文

《给北京市政府有关环境保护的建议》

八、讨论

1、经济发展就一定带来污染吗？为什么？
2、既然知道笼罩在北京头上的锅盖是如何形成的了，为什么北京政府这些年还不能解决这个问题呢？
3、你来北京以后觉得什么污染问题最严重？对你的身体和学习有什么影响？

九、语言实践

1、采访几位40岁以上的中老年人，请他们谈谈五、六十年代环境跟现在的有什么不同？在他们看来这种不同是由什么造成的？跟什么有关系？

2、采访一位交通（民）警，请他谈谈他的工作对他的身体有什么影响？他采取了什么措施？

空气质量差，污染程度高是北京面临的一个严重的问题

句型索引

D

当（着）……的面 +VP (to VP to one's face, to VP in the presence of), *L4* （十一）

对……（不）管用 (to be of (no) use, to be (in) effective), *L6* （十一）

对……的态度 (attitude toward...), *L9* （六）

对……进行+ Obj. (to carry out, to conduct, to implement), *L3* （八）

对……（的）理解 (a rational understanding of...), *L10* （八）

对……满意／不满意 (to be satisfied/dissatisfied with...), *L12* （五）

（对……有……的）评价 (to have a...(qualitative) evaluation of...), *L10* （二）

对……有影响 (to have influence/impact on...), *L2* （五）

F

反正 (anyway, anyhow, in any case, after all), *L12* （七）

G

各 V 各的 (each V his/her own...), *L7* （九）

给（／为）……提供 (to provide so-and-so with such-and-such, to provide such-and-such to so-and-so), *L11* （二）

根据+ Obj. (according to, on the basis of), *L3* （七）

根据……（的情况）(in line with, according to), *L11* （十）

跟……差得很远／差得不远 (to differ from/to be short of...by far/not far), *L11* （十一）

跟……结婚／离婚 (to be married to/to divorce somebody), *L7* （一）

跟……似的 (to be like...), *L5* （九）

跟/和/与……相处 (get along with...), *L4* （一）

跟（／给）……打招呼 (to greet, to touch base with), *L1* （七）

（跟）……合（谈／处）得来／不来 (can/cannot get along with), *L4* （七）

够……V 的 (sufficient to V, plenty enough for someone to V), *L5* （八）

关于…… (with regard to, about, concerning), *L1* （三）

光……就…… (merely, just), *L6* （七）

H

互相 (mutually, each other), *L4* （二）

还……呢 (used to convey ridicule or disdain), *L5* （十）

J

即 (that is, namely), *L11* （四）

几乎 (almost, nearly), *L12* （六）

甚至…… (even to the extent that...), *L2* （四）

实行 (to implement, to carry out, to put into practice), *L11* （一）

实在 (indeed, really), *L7* （八）

使 (to make, to cause), *L11* （六）

是指…… （的意思） (to refer to, to designate), *L6* （二）

首先 (first of all), *L10* （十二）

受到+ V (receive, enjoy, endure, suffer, to be... V-ed), *L2* （二）

数 N + Adj. (to reckoned/count N as...), *L7* （二）

随时随地 (at all times and all places), *L8* （七）

随着 (along with, in the pace with), *L12* （一）

V

V+ Adj.-1+ V+ Adj.-2+ 一个样／不一样 (it is [not] the same whether... or...), *L3* （三）

V 得起／V 不起 (can/cannot afford to), *L2* （八）

W

（唯一的）前提是…… (the only prerequisite/premise is...), *L7* （七）

为（／给）……增添 (to add/to increase...to/for...), *L12* （二）

为了…… (in order to, for the purpose of), *L1* （二）

为了……而…… ((to do something) in order to/that...), *L10* （九）

无论……都／也…… (no matter what/who/where/when), *L1* （一）

X

想（／记）起来…… (to recall, to remember), *L1* （六）

象……这样的人 (a person such as....), *L4* （八）

Y

也就是说 (that is to say, in other words), *L4* （三）

一 V 就是 (+period of time/amount) (it will be... whenever V), *L2* （六）

（一个）偶然（的机会） (coincidentally, by chance), *L8* （三）

因（为）……而…… (due to, owing to, because), *L6* （三）

用 A 取代 B (to replace B with A), *L11* （五）

由 ……VP ((something) to be up to/ done by somebody), *L11* （三）

由于 (due to, as a result of), *L5* （二）

有（／无）权 +V (have the right/no right to V), *L9* （五）

又不／没 +V (used in negation for emphasis), *L5* （七）

于是 (so, hence, thereupon), *L10* （十一）

与（/跟）……结合 (to combine/integrate...with...), *L10* （三）

与其……（倒）不如…… (rather than..., it would be better to...), *L10* （十）

Z

（再）加上 (in addition, moreover), *L5* （三）

在……环境下 (under... condition, under... circumstances), *L2* （一）

造成（压力/后果/影响） (to cause pressure/ consequence/ influence...), *L10* （七）

……，则…… (adverb used to indicate a contrast with the previous sentence/clause), *L11* （九）

怎么就这么/那么…… (how come it is/was so/that), *L7* （四）

占……（百分之……） (to constitute, to account for...(per cent)), *L8* （二）

正是 (It is precisely...), *L12* （九）

……之一 (one of the...), *L9* （七）

只好 (to have no alternative but...), *L6* （八）

自从……（以来/以后） (since, from), *L3* （一）

总之 (in sum, in short), *L3* （四）

足足V了(+period of time/amount) (fully, as much as..., not a bit less than...), *L5* （五）

作为 (as, being...), *L4* （十）

生词索引

A

B

比例	bǐ lì	N.	proportion, scale, L11
笔	bǐ	Classifier.	a sum (of money), L6
毕业	bì yè	V.	to graduate, L7
必需品	bì xū pǐn	N.	necessity, necessary item , L8
编辑	biān jí	N/V.	editor; to edit, L1
编造	biān zào	V.	to fabricate, L10
便	biàn	Adv.	therefore, L8
便于	biàn yú	Adv.	easy to, convenient for, L8
标准	biāo zhǔn	N/Adj.	standard, L11
表达	biǎo dá	V.	to express, to convey, L9
表现	biǎo xiàn	V/N.	to display, to express; manifestation, L10
别出心裁	bié chū xīn cái	Idiom.	to adopt an original approach, to take a different tack, L8
簸箕	bò ji	N.	dust pan (horseshoe-shaped basket originally made of bamboo), L12
补贴	bǔ tiē	V/N.	to subsidize; subsidy, L11
不断	bú duàn	Adv.	unceasingly, continuously, L12
不敢	bù gǎn	VP.	dare not to, L12
不顾	bú gù	V.	not care about, not attend to , L3
不管	bù guǎn	Prep.	regardless of, L1
不管用	bù guǎn yòng	Idiom.	of no use, useless, L6
不好意思	bù hǎo yì si	Adj.	embarrassed, L4
不合理	bù hé lǐ	Adj.	unreasonable, L5
不近人情	bú jìn rén qíng	Idiom.	lit. "not in line with human feelings," unreasonable, L5
不拘小节	bù jū xiǎo jié	Idiom.	to not be bothered about small matters, L4
不耐烦	bú nài fán	Adj.	impatient, irritated, annoyed, L9
不是滋味	bú shì zī wèi	Idiom.	to be left with a bad taste in one's mouth, to be dismayed, to feel bad, L6
不同程度	bù tóng chéng dù	Adv.	to various degrees, L5
不以为然	bù yǐ wéi rán	Idiom.	do not think so, to take exception to , L4
布置	bù zhì	V.	to assign, to arrange, L8

C

采访	cǎi fǎng	V.	to interview, L1
采取	cǎi qǔ	V.	to adopt (policy, method, measure, etc.), L12
彩电	cǎi diàn	NP.	color TV set, L12
参加	cān jiā	V.	to participate, to join in, L6

藏起来	cáng qǐ lái	VP.	to hide, L9
操心	cāo xīn	V.	to worry about, to take pains with , L5
差	chà	V/Adj.	to differ, to be short; inferior, L11
拆信	chāi xìn	VO.	to open a letter, L9
产生	chǎn shēng	V.	to emerge, to produce, L9
产物	chǎn wù	N.	product, L10
常年	cháng nián	Adv.	throughout the year, year-round, L12
厂长	chǎng zhǎng	N.	factory chief, L5
唱歌	chàng gē	VO.	to sing (a song), L4
唱红	chàng hóng	VP.	to make a song popular by singing, L10
潮起潮落	cháo qǐ cháo luò	Idiom.	the flowing and ebbing of the tide, natural rhythm, L10
吵	chǎo	V/Adj.	to quarrel (often followed by object 架), to make a lot of noise; noisy, L5
车厢	chē xiāng	N.	train car, L1
车站	chē zhàn	N.	bus station, bus stop, train station, L1
彻底	chè dǐ	Adv.	completely, thoroughly, L10
陈明	chén míng	Personal N.	Chen Ming, L1
称为	chēng wéi	VP.	to be called as , L10
成长	chéng zhǎng	N.	growth, maturation, L2
成为	chéng wéi	VP.	to become/to be (in a role or profession), L2
承担	chéng dān	V.	to bear (responsibility), to take responsibility for, L11
秤	chèng	N.	scale, steelyard, L3
秤砣	chèng tuó	N.	the weight of a steelyard or scale, L3
冲	chōng	V.	to surge, to rush, to dash, L12
冲昏了头	chōng hūn le tóu	Idiom.	dizzy (with excitement or joy), L7
重新	chóng xīn	Adv.	again, anew, afresh, L6
抽屉	chōu tì	N.	drawer, L4
臭脚	chòu jiǎo	NP.	stinky foot/feet, L4
初级	chū jí	Adj.	beginning level, elementary, L8
出	chū	V.	to produce, L10
出版社	chū bǎn shè	N.	publisher, L7
出国	chū guó	VO.	to go abroad, L7
出路	chū lù	N.	outlet, a way out, opportunity, L3
出台	chū tái	VP.	(lit. "to go on stage") to appear, to emerge (after having been in a planning or preparatory phase), to be unveiled, L11
出现	chū xiàn	V.	to appear, to emerge, L6
出远门	chū yuǎn mén	VP.	to go far away from home, L1
出众	chū zhòng	Adj.	"stand out in a crowd," outstanding,

			L7
厨房	chú fáng	*N.*	kitchen, *L7*
储存	chǔ cún	*V.*	to store, to stock, *L8*
处罚	chǔ fá	*V/N.*	to exact penalty, to punish; penalty, punishment, *L3*
处于	chǔ yú	*VP.*	(literary) to be situated (in a certain stage or circumstance), *L10*
穿衣	chuān yī	*VO.*	to wear clothes, apparel, *L4*
传统	chuán tǒng	*N.*	tradition, *L5*
窗户	chuāng hù	*N.*	window, *L7*
创造	chuàng zào	*V.*	to create, *L10*
创作	chuàng zuò	*V/N.*	to create; creative work, *L10*
从山	cóng shān	*Personal N.*	Cong Shan, *L8*
从小	cóng xiǎo	*PrepP.*	since childhood, *L2*
促成	cù chéng	*V.*	to help bring about, to make possible , *L8*
崔健	cuī jiàn	*Personal N.*	Cui Jian, *L10*
存在	cún zài	*V/N.*	to exist; existence, *L9*
措施	cuò shī	*N.*	(refer to dealing with a problem or issue) measure, *L11*

D

答应	dā yìng	*V/N.*	to consent; consent, *L7*
打工	dǎ gōng	*VP.*	to work (at menial or odd jobs), *L6*
打扫	dǎ sǎo	*V.*	to sweep, to clean, *L5*
打听	dǎ tīng	*V.*	to inquire about , *L9*
打印	dǎ yìn	*V.*	to type and print out, *L8*
打招呼	dǎ zhāo hu	*VO.*	to greet, to let (someone) know, to touch base (with someone), *L1*
大多数	dà duō shù	*N.*	great majority, vast majority, *L4*
大姐	dà jiě	*N.*	"elder sister," a polite form of address for a woman about one's own age, *L3*
大力	dà lì	*Adv.*	energetically, vigorously, *L11*
带	dài	*V.*	(refer to children) to look after, to raise, *L7*
带来	dài lái	*VP.*	to bring, to lead to, *L5*
代表	dài biǎo	*V/N.*	to represent; representative, *L6*
代名词	dài míng cí	*N.*	pronoun, substitute word, *L6*
贷款	dài kuǎn	*VO/N.*	to grant or to get a loan; loan, *L11*
单位	dān wèi	*N.*	work unit, *L3*
当	dāng	*V.*	to become, *L2*
当……的面	dāng...de miàn	*PrepP.*	to somebody's face, in somebody's presence, *L4*

当年	dāng nián	N.	in that year (当...: on/in/at that particular...), L7
当然	dāng rán	Adv.	of course, L11
当中	dāng zhōng	Prep.	among, in the midst, L6
导购	dǎo gòu	N.	"purchase advisor," merchandise pusher , L6
到处	dào chù	Adv.	everywhere, L6
到底	dào dǐ	Adv.	after all, in the final analysis (conveys emphasis in questions), L4
道德	dào dé	N.	morals, morality, L3
的确	dí què	Adv.	indeed, really, L12
等	děng	N.	etc., and so on, L6
低收入	dī shōu rù	NP.	low income, L11
地理结构	dì lǐ jié gòu	N.	geographical structure, topography, L12
地面	dì miàn	N.	ground, L1
地毯	dì tǎn	N.	carpet, L6
地位	dì wèi	N.	status, L10
点儿	diǎnr	Quan.	(=一点儿) some, L3
电话铃	diàn huà líng	NP.	telephone ring , L9
电话员	diàn huà yuán	N.	telephone operator, L6
电脑	diàn nǎo	N.	computer, L8
电台	diàn tái	N.	TV Station, L11
电子邮件	diàn zǐ yóu jiàn	N.	e-mail, L8
调控	tiáo kòng	Abbrev.	to adjust and control, L11
调整	tiáo zhěng	V.	to adjust, L11
盯盯	dīng ding	V.	to fix one's eyes on, to persevere in a difficult/tedious task , L5
顶	dǐng	Classifier.	classifier for hats, L12
丢	diū	V.	to lose, to (academic) specialty, to abandon, L7
东城区	dōng chéng qū	Place N.	East City District, L6
动摇	dòng yáo	V.	to waver, to shift, to loosen up, L9
肚子	dù zi	N.	belly, stomach, L7
段	duàn	Classifier.	a period (of time), section, segment, L6
对待	duì dài	V.	to treat (people), L1
对应	duì yìng	Adj.	equivalent, corresponding, L9
吨	dūn	N/Classifier.	ton, L12
顿	dùn	Classifier.	(for a meal, a round of scolding, etc.), L5
多少	duō shǎo	Adv.	more or less, L10
夺走	duó zǒu	VP.	to snatch away , L12

E

额度	é dù	N.	specified amount or ratio, L11
恶心	ě xīn	Adj.	disgusting, nauseating, L4
饿坏	è huài	VP.	starving, extremely hungry, L5
二环	èr huán	Place N.	Second Ring Road, L12

F

发愁	fā chóu	VO.	to worry, to be anxious, L11
发放	fā fàng	V.	to provide, to grant, L11
发火	fā huǒ	VO.	to get angry, to lose one's temper, L5
发展	fā zhǎn	V/N.	to develop; development, L2
罚款	fá kuǎn	VO/N.	to exact a fine; fine, L3
翻	fān	V.	to rummage through, to toss around, L4
翻译	fān yì	V/N.	to translate; translation, L9
烦恼	fán nǎo	N.	worry, vexation, L2
反而	fǎn ér	Adv.	on the contrary, contrary to norm, L9
反应	fǎn yìng	N.	reaction, response, L4
反映	fǎn yìng	V.	to reflect, L2
反正	fǎn zhèng	Adv.	anyway, anyhow, in any case, L12
方便	fāng biàn	Adj/N.	convenient; convenience, L12
方面	fāng miàn	N.	aspect, L2
方式	fāng shì	N.	way, pattern, L5
房改	fáng gǎi	NP.	housing reform, L6
房租	fáng zū	N.	rent (for housing), L11
放心	fàng xīn	V/Adj.	to be at ease; feel relieved, L1
放学	fàng xué	VO.	to be let out of school , L9
非正式	fēi zhèng shì	Adj.	informal, unofficial, casual, L10
费	fèi	N.	fee, expense, L6
费用	fèi yòng	N.	expenses, L11
分房	fēn fáng	VO.	to allocate or assign housing, L11
分工	fēn gōng	VP/N.	to divide the work; division of labor, L5
分量	fèn liàng	N.	weight, L3
愤怒	fèn nù	N.	anger, wrath, L10
疯狂	fēng kuáng	Adj.	crazy, wild, L10
夫妻	fū qī	N.	husband and wife, L5
扶持	fú chí	V.	to help sustain, to support, to give aid to, L11
符合	fú hé	V.	to correspond with, to match, to meet (requirements), L6

服务中心	fú wù zhōng xīn	NP.	service center, *L6*
福利	fú lì	N.	welfare, *L11*
辅助	fǔ zhù	V.	to assist, *L8*
俯瞰	fǔ kàn	VP.	to look down at, to overlook, *L12*
复习	fù xí	V/N.	to review; review, *L8*
付荃荃	fù quán quán	Personal N.	Fu Quanquan, *L1*
负担	fù dān	V/N.	to bear (a burden); burden, *L5*

G

改编	gǎi biān	V/N.	to adapt; adaptation, *L6*
改革	gǎi gé	N/V.	reform; to reform, *L5*
改善	gǎi shàn	V/N.	to improve; improvement, *L12*
干扰	gān rǎo	V/N.	to disturb, to interfere; interference, *L9*
甘心	gān xīn	Adj.	willingly, *L7*
赶快	gǎn kuài	Adv.	at once, quickly, *L4*
感觉	gǎn jué	V/N.	to feel; feeling, sense perception, to be acquainted with, *L4*
感情	gǎn qíng	N.	feelings, emotion, *L1*
钢琴	gāng qín	N.	piano, *L2*
钢琴家	gāng qín jiā	N.	pianist, *L2*
岗位	gǎng wèi	N.	post, position , *L6*
高	gāo	Adj.	high, advanced, *L8*
高高的	gāo gāo de	Adj.	on the high side, a bit more than full measure, *L3*
高级	gāo jí	Adj.	senior, high-ranking, high class, *L1*
搞	gǎo	V.	(colloquial) to do, to be engaged in, *L10*
告别	gào bié	VP.	to say good-bye to, to leave (behind), *L11*
歌曲	gē qǔ	N.	song , *L10*
歌手	gē shǒu	N.	singer, *L10*
隔	gé	V.	to separate (by a partition), to be apart by (an interval or distance), *L7*
个人化	gè rén huà	V/Adj.	to individualize/personalize; individualized, *L10*
个体户	gè tǐ hù	N.	self-employed people, entrepreneur, *L3*
个子	gè zi	N.	(refer to a person) height, build, *L7*
各	gè	Adj.	each, *L11*
根本	gēn běn	Adv.	simply, (not) ... at all, *L6*
根据	gēn jù	Prep.	according to, *L3*
工具	gōng jù	N.	tool, *L8*
工种	gōng zhǒng	NP.	kind of job, *L6*

工资	gōng zī	N.	wages, L6
工作人员	gōng zuò rén yuán	NP.	staff, employee, L3
公开	gōng kāi	Adj/V.	public, open (vs. confidential); to make public, L9
公平秤	gōng píng chèng	NP.	"fair scale" (standard scale placed in markets for checking weight), L3
共同	gòng tóng	Adj/Adv.	common, shared, mutual; together, jointly L8
购买	gòu mǎi	V.	to purchase, L11
够呛	gòu qiàng	Adj.	(colloquial) lit. "enough to make one choke," unbearable, terrible, L5
鼓励	gǔ lì	V/N.	to encourage; encouragement, L8
骨头	gǔ tou	N.	bone, L5
故事	gù shi	N.	story, L1
故意	gù yì	Adv.	intentionally, L4
雇用	gù yòng	V.	to hire, L6
刮风	guā fēng	VO.	(wind) blows, windy, L1
关联	guān lián	V/N.	to be inter-related; connection, relevance , L10
关系	guān xì	N.	relation, relationship, connection, L4
关心	guān xīn	V/N.	to be concerned with, to care about; concern, L10
关于	guān yú	Prep.	regarding, L1
观念	guān niàn	N.	concept, L5
光	guāng	Adv.	only, just, L6
光彩	guāng cǎi	N/Adj.	radiance, splendor; honorable, glorious, L12
广告	guǎng gào	N.	advertisement, L7
规定	guī dìng	V/N.	to stipuulate; regulation, stipulation, L3
规律	guī lǜ	N.	regular pattern, regularity, L10
锅盖	guō gài	N.	lid of a pot, L12
国家	guó jiā	N.	country, L6
国内	guó nèi	NP/Adj.	in one's own country; domestic, L7
国营	guó yíng	Adj.	state-operated, L3
过渡	guò dù	V/Adj.	to transition; transitional, L11
过多	guò duō	Adj.	excessive, in surplus, L6
过去	guò qù	Adv/N.	in the past; past, L5
过问	guò wèn	V.	to concern oneself with, to take an interest in, L9

H

| 含义 | hán yì | N. | meaning, implication, L11 |

寒假	hán jià	N.	winter break, L8
喊声	hǎn shēng	NP.	the sound of shouting, L5
好合好散	hǎo hé hǎo sàn	Idiom.	(refer to a couple) to part friends after having gotten along well together , L7
好景不长	hǎo jǐng bù cháng	Idiom.	good times don't last long, L7
好像	hǎo xiàng	Aux/V.	to seem; to be like, L4
和和	huò huo	VP.	(colloquial) to mix, to make a mess, L5
合得来	hé de lái	VP.	to get along well, L4
合伙	hé huǒ	VP.	to pool resources, to partner up, L7
合适	hé shì	Adj.	appropriate, suitable, qualified, L6
后辈	hòu bèi	N.	the younger generation, L10
呼吸	hū xī	V/N.	to breathe; breathing, L12
互相	hù xiāng	Adv.	mutually, L4
花	huā	V.	to spend, L2
华声日（月）报	huá shēng rì (yuè) bào	NP.	Hua Sheng Daily (Monthly) (cf. Lesson 10), L6
滑	huá	Adj.	slippery, L1
画画	huà huà	VO.	to paint, to draw a picture, L1
画家	huà jiā	N.	painter, artist, L2
怀孕	huái yùn	VO.	to become pregnant, L7
欢迎	huān yíng	V.	to welcome, L3
环境	huán jìng	N.	environment, L2
环山	huán shān	Adj.	surrounded by mountains, L12
还	huán	V.	to return, L12
黄瓜	huáng gua	N.	cucumber, L3
晃晃	huàng huang	VP.	to wander aimlessly, L6
谎言	huǎng yán	N.	lie, L10
灰蒙蒙	huī méng méng	Adj.	gray, overcast, smoggy, L12
回答	huí dá	V/N.	to answer; answer, L9
回见	huí jiàn	Idiom	good-bye, L3
回忆	huí yì	V/N.	to recall; memories, L10
会说话	huì shuō huà	VP.	to be a good talker, L1
婚姻	hūn yīn	N.	marriage, L5
活	huó	Adj.	flexible, lively, active, L3
活动	huó dòng	V/N/Adj.	to move about, to exercise; activity; active, L9
活儿	huór	N.	(colloquial) work, L5

J

基本	jī běn	Adj.	basic, L8
机动车	jī dòng chē	N.	motor vehicle, L12
机制	jī zhì	N.	mechanism, L10

激烈	jī liè	Adj.	fierce, intense, L5
激怒	jī nù	V.	to enrage, to infuriate, L10
急	jí	Adj.	urgent, L6
即	jì	Adv.	namely, that is, L11
即将	jí jiāng	Aux.	about to, on the point of, L11
挤	jǐ	V/Adj.	to squeeze; crowded, L5
技术	jì shù	N.	skill, technology, L6
寄钱	jì qián	VO.	to send money (寄: to mail), L7
计量法	jì liàng fǎ	NP.	measurement regulations, L3
计算机	jì suàn jī	N.	(=电脑) computer, L8
记者	jì zhě	N.	reporter, journalist, L12
家长	jiā zhǎng	N.	parents, the head of a family, L5
家务	jiā wù	N.	housework, L5
加	jiā	V.	to add, L4
加拿大	jiā ná dà	N.	Canada, L7
假如	jiǎ rú	Conj.	if, L7
价格	jià gé	N.	price, L11
嫁	jià	V.	(of a woman) to marry, L7
监测网络	jiān cè wǎng luò	NP.	monitoring network, L12
坚持	jiān chí	V/N.	to insist, to persist; insistence, persistence, L7
检查	jiǎn chá	V.	to check, to inspect, L3
简单	jiǎn dān	Adj.	simple, L10
简介	jiǎn jiè	N.	a brief introduction, L1
健康	jiàn kāng	N/Adj.	health; healthy, L12
建房	jiàn fáng	VP.	to build houses, L11
建立	jiàn lì	V.	to establish, L10
建设部	jiàn shè bù	NP.	Department of Construction, L11
建议	jiàn yì	V/N.	to suggest; suggestions, L12
建筑工地	jiàn zhù gōng dì	NP.	construction site (工地: work site), L12
将	jiāng	Aux.	about to, will soon, L11
讲究	jiǎng jiu	V.	to be particular about, to pay attention to, L4
讲述	jiǎng shù	V.	to tell about, to give an account of, L1
讲台	jiǎng tái	N.	classroom or lecture platform, L5
交	jiāo	V.	to turn in (assignment), L8
交朋友	jiāo péng you	VO.	to make friends, L9
教子不可强按头	jiào zǐ bù kě qiáng àn tóu	Idiom.	when you teach your children, you shouldn't force them to learn things in which they are not interested, L2
揭开	jiē kāi	VP.	to uncover, to reveal, L12
接电话	jiē diàn huà	VO.	to answer the phone, L6
街道	jiē dào	N.	street (social service agency in urban

bedroll," to pack up (and leave) (cf. Note 9), *L5*

K

开放	kāi fàng	*V/Adj.*	to open (vs. to restrict); open, liberal, *L3*
开始	kāi shǐ	*V/N.*	to start; beginning, *L5*
看……的脸子	kàn...liǎn zi	*N.*	lit. "to look at so-and-so's (ugly) face," to bear so-and-so's temper/mood (cf. Note 5), *L5*
看情况	kàn qíng kuàng	*Idiom.*	"to look at the situation," depending on the situation, *L7*
看重	kàn zhòng	*V.*	to regard as important, to value, *L5*
靠	kào	*V.*	to rely on, to lean on, *L9*
科技	kē jì	*Abbrev.*	(=科学技术) science and technology, *L8*
科学	kē xué	*N.*	science, *L8*
可能	kě néng	*Adj/N/Adv.*	possible; possibility; possibly, *L3*
可惜	kě xī	*Adv/Adj.*	it's a pity that..., too bad..., *L7*
可笑	kě xiào	*Adj.*	ridiculous, laughable, *L7*
客观	kè guān	*N/Adj.*	objectivity; objective, *L10*
课堂教学	kè táng jiào xué	*NP.*	classroom teaching, *L8*
空间	kōng jiān	*N.*	space, *L9*
空气	kōng qì	*N.*	air, *L12*
空中	kōng zhōng	*N.*	in the sky, in the air, *L12*
口	kǒu	*Classifier.*	(=一口) a mouthful of..., *L5*
哭	kū	*V.*	to cry, *L7*
苦恼	kǔ nǎo	*Adj.*	vexed, worried, *L6*
裤子	kù zi	*N.*	trousers, pants, *L1*
跨世纪	kuà shì jì	*VO.*	to straddle two centuries, to cross over to a new century, *L8*
快速	kuài sù	*Adj.*	rapid, *L12*
困惑	kùn huò	*N/V.*	perplexity; to feel perturbed, *L5*
扩散	kuò sàn	*V.*	to spread, to diffuse, *L12*

L

拉	lā	*V.*	to pull, to grab, *L2*
拉不下脸	lā bù xià liǎn	*Idiom.*	cannot lower one's "face," unable to forego one's dignity, *L6*
拉开	lā kāi	*VP.*	to pull out, to open, *L4*
来	lái	*V.*	(colloquial) to buy/have, *L3*
来劲儿	lái jìnr	*VO/Adj.*	(colloquial) to surge in

路口	lù kǒu	N.	intersection,, L7
路上	lù shang	PrepP.	on the way, during the journey, L1
率	lǜ	N.	rate, ratio, L5
乱	luàn	Adj.	messy, L4
乱得慌	luàn de huāng	VP.	awfully jumbled, extremely upset, L5
乱七八糟	luàn qī bā zāo	Idiom.	at sixes and sevens, in a mess, L4

M

骂	mà	V.	to scold, to curse, L10
卖菜	mài cài	VO.	to sell vegetables, L3
满不在乎	mǎn bú zài hu	Idiom.	not be bothered at all, not care in the least, L4
满意	mǎn yì	Adj/N.	to be satisfied; satisfaction, L12
满足	mǎn zú	V/Adj.	to satisfy; satisfied, content, L11
毛病	máo bìng	N.	shortcoming, defect, L4
帽子	mào zi	N.	hat, label, L12
没收	mò shōu	V.	to confiscate, L3
没想到	méi xiǎng dào	Idiom.	unexpected, by surprise, L7
没治	méi zhì	VP.	beyond remedy, no cure, L5
美好	měi hǎo	Adj.	beautiful, L10
门	mén	Classifier.	item, subject , L1
萌发阶段	méng fā jiē duàn	NP.	budding stage, L10
秘密	mì mì	N.	secret, L9
秘书	mì shū	N.	secretary, L7
面临	miàn lín	V.	to face (an impending crisis/dilemma), L6
敏感	mǐn gǎn	Adj.	sensitive, L11
明白	míng bai	V/Adj.	to understand; clear, L7
明亮	míng liàng	Adj.	bright, L12
明显	míng xiǎn	Adj.	obvious, evident, L8
磨	mó	V.	to rub, to grind , L3
某种	mǒu zhǒng	NP.	certain kind (某: a certain...), L9
母爱	mǔ ài	NP.	motherly love, L1
目标	mù biāo	N.	goal, target, L11

N

奶奶	nǎi nai	N.	(parental) grandmother, L2
南京	nán jīng	Place N.	Nanjing, L7
男友	nán péng yǒu	NP.	boyfriend, L7
难过	nán guò	Adj.	to feel bad, to have a hard time, L7
挠头	náo tóu	VO/Adj.	to scratch one's head; vexing, brain-racking , L5

脑子	nǎo zi	N.	brain, *L3*
内容	nèi róng	N.	content, *L8*
嗯	ng	*Intj.*	mm..., hm... (indicating one heard what the other person said), *L5*
溺爱	nì ài	V.	to spoil (a child), *L2*
年代	nián dài	N.	era, decade, *L3*
年均	nián jūn	*Adj.*	annual average, *L11*
年龄	nián líng	N.	age, *L6*
年龄段	nián líng duàn	NP.	age group, *L6*
弄湿	nòng shī	VP.	to get wet, *L1*
努力	nǔ lì	V.	to make great efforts, to try hard, *L10*
女工	nǚ gōng	NP.	female worker, *L6*
女性	nǚ xìng	N.	female, women, *L5*

O

| 偶然 | ǒu rán | *Adj.* | coincidental, accidental, fortuitous, *L8* |

P

趴	pā	V.	to lean over on (a ledge), to bend over, to lie prone, *L7*
排	pái	V.	to eject, to discharge, to line up , *L12*
排放	pái fàng	VP.	to eject, to discharge, *L12*
培训	péi xùn	V/N.	to train; training, *L6*
培养	péi yǎng	V.	to cultivate, to nurture, *L1*
碰运气	pèng yùn qì	VO.	to try one's luck, *L6*
批判	pī pàn	V/N.	to criticize; criticism, *L10*
批判性	pī pàn xìng	N.	critical character, *L10*
篇	piān	*Classifier.*	measure word for articles, *L9*
偏见	piān jiàn	N.	bias, prejudice, *L10*
拼命	pīn mìng	*Adv.*	with all one's might, exerting one's utmost, *L7*
平均	píng jūn	N/Adj.	average, *L11*
评价	píng jià	V/N.	to evaluate, to appraise; evaluation, *L8*
评评	píng ping	V.	to judge, to evaluate, *L5*
婆婆	pó po	N.	mother-in-law, *L7*
破坏	pò huài	V.	to destroy, to sabotage, *L10*
普遍	pǔ biàn	*Adj.*	common, widespread, *L8*
普通	pǔ tōng	*Adj.*	common, ordinary, *L1*

Q

| 嘁 | qī | *Intj.* | Geez! (expressing exasperation), *L5* |

期望	qī wàng	N/V.	expectation; to expect, L2
其他	qí tā	Adj.	the rest, L11
其中	qí zhōng	Prep.	among (which, them, etc.), in (which, it, etc.), L6
起码	qǐ mǎ	Adv.	at least, L6
器具	qì jù	N.	implement, utensil, L3
千	qiān	Number.	thousand, L12
千千万万	qiān qiān wàn wàn	Adj.	"thousands and ten thousands", multitudes , L6
前辈	qián bèi	N.	the older generation, L10
前夫	qián fū	NP.	former husband, L7
前提	qián tí	N.	premise, prerequisite, L7
墙	qiáng	N.	wall, L2
强烈	qiáng liè	Adj.	strong, intense, fierce, L10
敲门	qiāo mén	VO.	to knock on the door, L5
亲近	qīn jìn	Adj.	close, intimate, L9
轻点儿	qīng diǎnr	Adv.	gently, softly, L2
清洁	qīng jié	Adj.	clean, L12
清洁工	qīng jié gōng	N.	sanitation worker, L6
情感	qíng gǎn	N.	feeling, L10
穷	qióng	Adj.	poor, L2
趋势	qū shì	N.	trend, tendency, L8
取代	qǔ dài	V.	to replace, L11
权利	quán lì	N.	right, L9
全部	quán bù	Adj.	all, L6
全方位	quán fāng wèi	N/Adj.	all directions; comprehensive, L8
全国	quán guó	NP.	the whole country, L10
缺	quē	V.	to be short of, to lack, L6
缺房户	quē fáng hù	NP.	households short on housing, L11
却	què	Adv.	on the contrary, however, L3
群众	qún zhòng	N.	the masses, L11

R

然而	rán ér	Conj.	and yet, but, L12
燃烟	rán yān	NP.	the smoke caused by burning something , L12
人才	rén cái	N.	qualified and/or trained personnel, talented person, L8
人员	rén yuán	N.	personnel, staff, L6
人种	rén zhǒng	N.	racial or ethnic group, L1
忍不住	rěn bú zhù	VP.	to be unable to bear, cannot help but..., L4
认错	rèn cuò	VO.	to acknowledge a mistake, to admit a

			fault, *L3*
认罚	rèn fá	*VO.*	to accept punishment, *L3*
认识	rèn shi	*V.*	to know (someone), *L4*
认为	rèn wéi	*V.*	to deem, to construe, *L4*
仍	réng	*Adv.*	(literary) still, *L10*
日子	rì zi	*N.*	life, livelihood (过日子: to get by from day to day, *L6*
如何	rú hé	*Adv.*	(literary) how, *L10*

S

嗓子	sǎng zi	*N.*	throat, voice, *L4*
扫地	sǎo dì	*VO.*	to sweep the floor, *L5*
沙发	shā fā	*N.*	sofa, *L2*
商品化	shāng pǐn huà	*V/Adj.*	to commoditize; commoditized , *L11*
商业	shāng yè	*N.*	commerce, business, *L3*
上对下	shàng duì xià	*Idiom.*	superior to subordinate, *L9*
上空	shàng kōng	*N.*	the sky above, *L12*
上网	shàng wǎng	*VO.*	to get on the web, *L8*
烧烤	shāo kǎo	*VP.*	to barbecue, *L12*
少年宫	shào nián gōng	*NP.*	youth palace, *L1*
舍得下	shě de xià	*VP.*	to be willing to part with, not to begrudge (舍不得: can't bear to part with), *L7*
摄像机	shè xiàng jī	*N.*	video recorder, *L4*
社会主义	shè huì zhǔ yì	*N.*	socialism, *L11*
深	shēn	*Adj.*	deep, *L1*
甚至	shèn zhì	*Adv.*	even to the point of..., *L3*
声	shēng	*N.*	sound, *L2*
生存环境	shēng cún huán jìng	*NP.*	environment for existence or survival, *L10*
生活	shēng huó	*N.*	life; living, *L5*
生气	shēng qì	*VP/Adj.*	to get angry; angry, *L4*
生物	shēng wù	*N.*	biology, *L8*
升	shēng	*V.*	to rise, to go up, *L12*
省吃俭用	shěng chī jiǎn yòng	*Idiom.*	to live frugally (lit. "to economize on food and utility items"), *L2*
失去	shī qù	*V.*	to lose, *L6*
失业	shī yè	*VP.*	to lose one's job, to be unemployed, *L6*
湿	shī	*Adj.*	wet, *L4*
十分	shí fēn	*Adv.*	very, extremely, *L11*
时代	shí dài	*N.*	times, era, *L9*
实施	shí shī	*V/N.*	to implement; implementation, *L3*
实现	shí xiàn	*V.*	to realize, to become reality, *L2*

实行	shí xíng	V.	to implement, to put into practice, L11
实在	shí zài	Adv.	really, truly, L7
使使	shǐ shi	V.	to use briefly (cf. Note 6), L4
使用	shǐ yòng	V/N.	to use, to utilize; usage, L8
式	shì	N.	type, style, L2
世界	shì jiè	N.	world, L8
世界卫生组织	shì jiè wèi shēng zǔ zhī	NP.	World Health Organization, L12
适用	shì yòng	Adj.	suitable, applicable, L11
试用期	shì yòng qī	N.	"trial use" period, probation period, L6
收发	shōu fā	V.	to receive and send, L8
收据	shōu jù	N.	receipt, L3
收入	shōu rù	N.	income, L11
首	shǒu	Classifier.	classifier for song or poem, L10
首先	shǒu xiān	Adv.	first, first of all, L10
受到	shòu dào	VP.	to receive, L2
梳头	shū tóu	VO.	to comb the hair, L4
梳子	shū zi	N.	comb, L4
舒服	shū fu	Adj.	comfortable, L10
属于	shǔ yú	VP.	to belong to, L9
数	shǔ	V.	to count, to reckon...as...(cf. Sentence Pattern 2), L7
数学	shù xué	N.	mathematics, L8
帅	shuài	Adj.	handsome, L7
双手	shuāng shǒu	NP.	both hands, L7
谁也别跑	shéi yě bié bǎo	idiom	don't anybody run away, L10
水平	shuǐ píng	N.	standard, level, L12
顺便	shùn biàn	Adv.	conveniently, in passing, along the way, L5
顺利	shùn lì	Adv/Adj.	smoothly; smooth, L1
顺应	shùn yìng	V.	to adapt to, to conform to, L8
顺着	shùn zhe	VP.	to follow, to obey, L2
说白了	shuō bái le	Idiom.	to speak frankly, to be perfectly candid , L10
说法	shuō fǎ	N.	way of saying something, explanation, view, L2
说谎	shuō huǎng	VO.	to tell a lie, L10
……似的	shì de	Prep.	as if..., just like...as (cf. Sentence Pattern 9), L5
四季	sì jì	N.	four seasons, all seasons, L5
算	suàn	V.	to count, L6
随机	suí jī	Adj/Adv.	random; randomly, L12
随时随地	suí shí suí dì	Adv.	at any time and any place, L8
随着	suí zhe	Prep.	along with, in the wake of, L12
岁	suì	N.	years of age, L6

孙子	sūn zi	N.	grandson, *L6*

T

太阳	tài yáng	N.	sun, *L12*
态度	tài du	N.	attitude, *L8*
弹	tán	V.	to play (the piano or a plucked string instruments like guitar), *L2*
谈	tán	V.	to talk about, *L1*
谈心	tán xīn	VO.	to have heart-to-heart talk, *L9*
趟	tàng	Classifier.	classifier (for a trip), *L6*
讨厌	tǎo yàn	Adj/V.	disgusting, annoying; to dislike, *L4*
套	tào	Classifier.	set (of clothing, books, housing, ideas, etc.), *L11*
特	tè	Adv.	especially, *L12*
特点	tè diǎn	N.	(distinctive) characteristic, feature, *L11*
特色	tè sè	N.	characteristics, distinguishing features, *L1*
特殊	tè shū	Adj.	special, *L2*
提出	tí chū	V.	to put forward (a proposal), to bring up (an issue) , *L7*
提供	tí gōng	V.	to provide, *L11*
题库	tí kù	N.	a pool of questions, *L8*
体制	tǐ zhì	N.	system, *L6*
天经地义	tiān jīng dì yì	Idiom.	principles of heaven and earth, law of nature, *L10*
天生的	tiān shēng de	Adj.	inherent, innate, god-given, *L9*
添乱	tiān luàn	VO.	to add to a mess, *L5*
条	tiáo	Classifier.	item, article, *L3*
贴	tiē	V.	to paste, to glue, *L2*
挺	tǐng	Adv.	very, rather, quite, *L1*
挺	tǐng	V.	to hold up/out (a part of one's body) straight, to endure stoically, *L7*
通常	tōng cháng	Adv.	usually, generally, *L6*
通过	tōng guò	V/Prep.	to go through, to pass; by means of, through, *L8*
同志	tóng zhì	N.	comrade, *L1*
投资	tóu zī	VO.	to invest, *L6*
头	tóu	Adj.	first (in the sense of "initial, earliest"), *L6*
头发	tóu fa	N.	hair , *L4*
透露	tòu lù	V.	to reveal, *L11*
突然间	tū rán jiān	Adv.	suddenly, unexpectedly, *L1*

团委	tuán wěi	N.	committee of the Communist Youth League (short for 共青团委员会), L7
推	tuī	V.	to push, L1
推算	tuī suàn	V/N.	to calculate; calculation, L11

W

外边	wài biān	N.	outside, L5
外地	wài dì	NP.	other locations (within the country), non-local , L6
玩	wán	V.	to play, L5
完全	wán quán	Adj/Adv.	complete; completely, L2
万	wàn	Number.	ten thousand, L12
万儿八千	wànr bā qiān	Idiom.	(colloquial) eight thousand or ten thousand dollars, a lot of money, L5
往……吐痰	wǎng...tǔ tán	VP.	to spit toward, L4
危害	wēi hài	V/N.	to endanger; danger, L12
唯一	wéi yī	Adj.	only, sole , L7
为	wéi	V.	to be, L11
为人师表	wéi rén shī biǎo	Idiom.	to serve as a teacher, to act as an example for others (师表: an exemplary teacher, a role model), L5
尾气	wěi qì	NP.	exhaust fumes, L12
未来	wèi lái	N/Adj.	future, L10
味儿	wèir	N.	odor, smell,, L12
温暖	wēn nuǎn	Adj.	warm, L5
文化部	wén huà bù	N.	Ministry of Culture, L10
文明	wén míng	N.	civilization, L12
稳定	wěn dìng	Adj.	stable, L5
污染	wū rǎn	V/N.	to pollute; pollution, L12
无房户	wú fáng hù	NP.	household with no housing, L11
无论	wú lùn	Conj.	no matter (what), L1
无梦	wú mèng	VP.	to have no dream (无: 没有), L7
无人不知	wú rén bù zhī	Idiom.	没有人不知道, well known, L10
无私	wú sī	Adj.	selfless, unselfish, L1
无所谓	wú suǒ wèi	Idiom.	to be indifferent, it doesn't matter, L7
捂住	wǔ zhù	VP.	to cover (with one's hands), L7

X

希望	xī wàng	N/V.	hope; to hope, L2
洗衣机	xǐ yī jī	N.	washing machine, L12
系统	xì tǒng	N.	system, L8
系统化	xì tǒng huà	V/Adj.	to systematize; systematic, L10

细则	xì zé	NP.	detailed clause, L3
下班	xià bān	VO.	to go off work, L7
下岗	xià gǎng	VO.	to be laid off, to leave one's post, L6
下海	xià hǎi	VO.	lit. "to plunge into the sea," to leave government employment and go into the private sector , L3
下面	xià mian	Loc.	the following, L1
下雨	xià yǔ	VO.	to rain, L1
夏天	xià tiān	N.	summer, L12
显然	xiǎn rán	Adv.	apparently, obviously, L9
现代	xiàn dài	N/Adj.	present era, modern times; modern, L12
现象	xiàn xiàng	N.	phenomenon, L2
现状	xiàn zhuàng	NP.	current condition, L12
羡慕	xiàn mù	V.	to envy, L2
相处	xiāng chǔ	V.	to get along (with one another), L4
相应	xiāng yìng	Adj.	corresponding, L11
想通	xiǎng tōng	VP.	to straighten out one's thinking, to be reconciled/resigned to a reality, L7
响	xiǎng	V/Adj.	to ring, to sound off; loud, L9
项	xiàng	Classifier.	item, L1
像……似的	xiàng...shì de	Prep.	as if, L6
向	xiàng	Prep.	toward, L12
向钱看	xiàng qián kàn	Idiom.	"look toward money," to be obsessed with money, L3
消费	xiāo fèi	V/N.	to consume; consumption, L11
宵尘	xiāo chén	NP.	night dust, L12
小皇帝	xiǎo huáng dì	NP.	Little Emperor, L2
小穆	xiǎo mù	Personal N.	Little Mu, L3
小声点儿	xiǎo shēng diǎnr	Adv.	quieter, keep one's voice down, L2
小型	xǐao xíng	Adj.	small scale, L10
小子	xiǎo zi	N.	fellow, rascal, rogue, L3
新词	xīn cí	NP.	new term, L6
新闻	xīn wén	N.	news, L11
新鲜	xīn xiān	Adj.	fresh, L3
信封	xìn fēng	N.	envelope, L9
信箱	xìn xiāng	N.	mailbox, L9
形成	xíng chéng	VP.	to form, L12
行人	xíng rén	N.	pedestrian, L12
幸福	xìnq fú	Adj/N.	happy, content, to enjoy good fortune; happiness, L7
休息	xiū xi	V.	to rest, to take a break, L3
需求	xū qiú	N.	need, demand (vs. supply), L11
需要	xū yào	V/N.	to need; need, L5

徐慧	xú huì	Personal N.	Xu Hui, L7
学费	xué fèi	N.	tuition, L6
学历	xué lì	N.	educational background, L6
巡回	xún huí	V.	to go on tour (for performance), to make a circuit , L10

Y

压力	yā lì	N.	pressure, L2
烟尘层	yān chén céng	NP.	layer of smoke and dust, L12
烟囱	yān cōng	N.	chimney, smokestack, L12
烟雾	yān wù	N.	smoke, smog, L12
严肃	yán sù	Adj.	serious, earnest, L7
严重	yán zhòng	Adj.	serious, grave, L11
颜色	yán sè	N.	color, L10
演出	yǎn chū	V.	to perform, L10
扬尘	yáng chén	NP.	rising dust, L12
养活	yǎng huó	VP.	to support, to provide a living (for someone), L6
样子	yàng zi	N.	manner, demeanor, appearance, shape, L7
摇滚乐	yáo gǔn yuè	NP.	rock and roll, L10
要人条件	yào rén tiáo jiàn	NP.	hiring requirements , L6
爷爷	yé ye	N.	(parental) grandfather, L2
也许	yě xǔ	Adv.	perhaps, L7
页	yè	Classifier.	page, L9
一般	yī bān	Adv/Adj.	generally; ordinary, typical, L11
一辈子	yí bèi zi	N.	all one's life, L7
一边……一边	yì biān...yì biān	Adv.	at the same time, simultaneously, L4
一部分	yí bù fèn	NP.	one segment, L6
一定的	yí dìng de	Adj.	a certain (amount, time, etc.), fixed, L6
一个样	yí ge yàng	Adj.	the same, L3
一无所有	yī wú suǒ yǒu	Idiom.	have nothing, the title of one of Cui Jian's songs, L10
一下子	yí xià zi	Adv.	all of a sudden, L6
一一	yī yī	Adv.	one by one, L8
一直	yì zhí	Adv.	all along, continuously, L1
衣裳	yī shang	N/V.	clothes; clothing, L5
以便	yǐ biàn	PrepP.	so that, in order to, L6
以及	yǐ jí	Prep.	and, as well as..., L10
以来	yǐ lái	Conj.	since..., L3
艺术	yì shù	N.	arts, L10
意思	yì si	N.	meaning, L4

议论	yì lùn	V./N.	to discuss (at length); to gossip about, L9
因素	yīn sù	N.	factor, L5
因特网	yīn tè wǎng	N.	internet, L8
音乐	yīn yuè	N.	music, L10
银行	yín háng	N.	bank, L11
隐私	yǐn sī	N.	one's secrets, confidential private matters , L9
印象	yìn xiàng	N.	impression, L1
应付	yìng fu	V.	to deal with, to cope with, L6
赢得	yíng dé	VP.	to win, to obtain (through struggles), L10
影碟机	yǐng dié jī	N.	video compact disc (VCD) player, L12
影响	yǐng xiǎng	N./V.	influence; to influence, L2
拥有	yōng yǒu	V.	to own, to possess, L12
优越	yōu yuè	Adj.	superior; advantageous, L2
由	yóu	Prep.	by, L11
有关	yǒu guān	V./Adj.	to be related (to...); relevant (to...), L11
有关部门	yǒu guān bù mén	NP.	related departments or sectors, L11
有权	yǒu quán	VO.	to have the right, L9
有限	yǒu xiàn	Adj.	limited, L11
于是	yú shì	Conj.	therefore, thereupon, L10
于思远	yú sī yuǎn	Personal N.	Yu Si Yuan, L8
愉快	yú kuài	Adj.	happy; pleasant, L10
与	yǔ	Conj.	(formal) and, with (used with noun or NP only), L4
与其A倒不如B	yǔ qí...dào bù rú	Conj.	(literary) A is not as good as B, L10
语文	yǔ wén	N.	language and literature, L8
预习	yù xí	V./N.	to preview; preview, L8
原创	yuán chuàng	NP.	original creation, L10
原料	yuán liào	N.	raw material, L12
原意	yuán yì	NP.	original meaning/intention, L9
原因	yuán yīn	N.	reason, L6
原则	yuán zé	N.	principle, L11
圆圆	yuán yuan	Personal N.	Yuanyuan, L5
远大公司	yuǎn dà gōng sī	NP.	Yuan Da Company, L6
月工资	yuè gōng zī	NP.	monthly salary, L11

Z

再加上	zài jiā shàng	VP.	furthermore, L5
早点	zǎo diǎn	N.	breakfast, L6
早市	zǎo shì	NP.	morning market, L6

澡堂	zǎo táng	N.	public baths, bathhouse, L4
噪音	zào yīn	N.	noise, L12
造成	zào chéng	VP.	to cause, to result in, L10
则	zé	Classifer.	classifier for news items , L11
怎么着	zěn me zhe	Q.	"what's going on?", L3
增加	zēng jiā	V.	to increase, L11
增添	zēng tiān	V.	to add, to increase, L12
占	zhàn	V.	to occupy, L8
长大	zhǎng dà	VP.	to grow up, L2
长得……	zhǎng de	VP.	to be physically...(describing a person's physical attributes), L7
掌握	zhǎng wò	V.	to grasp, to master, L8
涨到	zhǎng dào	VP.	to go up to, to rise to, L6
丈夫	zhàng fu	N.	husband, L7
招工	zhāo gōng	VO.	to recruit workers, L6
找碴儿	zhǎo chár	VO.	(colloquial) to find fault, to pick a quarrel, L5
找门路	zhǎo mén lù	VO/Idiom.	(门路: channel, connections) to look for ways, to solicit help from potential backers, L7
赵以忻	zhào yǐ xīn	Personal N.	Zhao Yixin, L12
照顾	zhào gù	V.	to take care of, L1
照相	zhào xiàng	VO.	to take pictures, L5
折	shé	V.	to break, to snap, L5
真正	zhēn zhèng	Ad/Advj.	real, really, L10
针锋相对	zhēn fēng xiāng duì	Idiom.	to give tit for tat, to be diametrically opposed , L10
挣	zhèng	V.	to earn, L5
睁眼	zhēng yǎn	VO.	to open one's eyes, with eyes wide open, L10
征服	zhēng fú	V.	to overcome, to conquer, L10
争论	zhēng lùn	V/N.	to debate, to argue; debate, argument, L10
政策	zhèng cè	N.	policy, L3
政府	zhèng fǔ	N.	government, L3
政治	zhèng zhì	N.	politics, L10
证件	zhèng jiàn	N.	credentials, documents (e.g. I.D., permit, license, etc.), L3
支持	zhī chí	V/N.	to support; support, L8
知己	zhī jǐ	N.	(lit. "to know self") bosom friend, L8
知足	zhī zú	V/Adj.	to be content; content, L2
之父	zhī fù	NP.	……的父亲，father of..., L10
之间	zhī jiān	Prep.	among..., between..., L9
……之一	zhī yī	NP.	one of... , L11

248

职工	zhí gōng	N.	staff, employee , L11
直接	zhí jiē	Adv/Adj.	directly; direct, L10
指	zhǐ	V.	to designate, to signify , L6
指出	zhǐ chū	V.	to point out, L11
制度	zhì dù	N.	system, L11
质量	zhì liàng	N.	quality, L12
中年	zhōng nián	N.	middle age, L6
中心	zhōng xīn	N.	center, L5
重大	zhòng dà	Adj.	important, great, major, significant, L11
重要	zhòng yào	Adj.	important, L4
主持人	zhǔ chí rén	N.	(program) host/hostess, moderator, L1
主要	zhǔ yào	Adj.	main, primary, L12
注意	zhù yì	V.	to pay attention, L4
专家	zhuān jiā	N.	expert, L11
专业	zhuān yè	N.	(academic) specialty, major, L7
赚钱	zhuàn qián	VO.	to earn money, L3
追赶	zhuī gǎn	V.	to chase and catch up with, L8
准确	zhǔn què	Adj/Adv.	accurate; accurately, L9
着凉	zháo liáng	VO.	to catch a cold, L1
资金	zī jīn	N.	resources, capital, L6
仔细	zǐ xì	Adj/Adv.	careful; carefully, L9
自然	zì rán	N/Adj.	nature; natural, L12
自身	zì shēn	N.	oneself, L10
总之	zǒng zhī	Adv.	in short, in a word, L3
足	zú	Adj.	full, sufficient, L3
足足	zú zú	Adv.	fully, as much as, L5
阻挡	zǔ dǎng	V.	to block, L12
阻止	zǔ zhǐ	V.	to block, to obstruct, L10
最后	zuì hòu	Adv.	finally, L7
最终	zuì zhōng	Adv.	finally, in the end, L11
尊重	zūn zhòng	V.	to respect, L4
……左右	zuǒ yòu	Adj.	...more or less, approximately..., L11
作法	zuò fǎ	N.	way of doing something, L2
作为	zuò wéi	V/Prep.	being, in the role of; as, L4

缩略语表

Abbrev.	Abbreviation
Adj.	Adjective
AdjP.	Adjectival phrase
Adv.	Adverb
Aux.	Auxiliary verb
Classifier.	Classifier/measure word
Conj.	Conjunction
Idiom.	Idiomatic expression
Intj.	Interjection
Loc.	Localizer
N.	Noun
NP.	Noun phrase
Number.	Number word
Personal N.	Personal name
Place N.	Place name
Prep.	Preposition
PrepP.	Prepositional phrase
Pro.	Pronoun
Quan.	Quantifier
V.	Verb
VO.	Verb object construction
VP.	Verb phrase

ALSO BY HONG GANG JIN & DE BAO XU

Crossing Paths: Living and Learning in China
An Intermediate Chinese Course
By Hong Gang Jin and De Bao Xu
with Delin Chao, Yea-fen Chen, Min Chen
Photography by Laurie A. Wittlinger
Crossing Paths is designed to help advanced beginners establish a solid foundation for interaction and communication with Chinese people. The topics and settings that are included here are drawn from the actual experiences of hundreds of students who studied abroad in China, and from professors who taught and lived with students in China. Texts for each lesson are based on real life conversations that foreign students are likely to engage in throughout their stay. Each text is accompanied by language notes that clearly explain how to incorporate new vocabulary, idioms, and grammar patterns into students' everyday speech. In simplified characters.
Paperback, 0-88727-370-X

China Scene: An Advanced Chinese Multimedia Course
By Hong Gang Jin, De Bao Xu and James Hargett
This course provides third and fourth year students with a rigorous but engaging presentation of modern Chinese based on new instructional theories and methods. Subjects are contemporary and diverse, with topics such as single-parent households, film and theater personalities, baby adoptions, China's gymnasts, and the market economy. In the text, students are introduced to new vocabulary and structures through original television texts. The accompanying audio and video materials provide authentic broadcast media reports from mainland China, allowing students to hear and see for themselves how the texts they are reading and translating appear in life. The text includes both traditional and simplified characters, and workbook sections.
Textbook & Workbook, Paperback, 0-88727-330-0
2 Audiocassettes, 0-88727-332-7
VHS Videocassette, 0-88727-333-5

Chinese Breakthrough: Learning Chinese through TV and Newspapers
By Hong Gang Jin, De Bao Xu and John Berninghausen
This audio-visual program targets students who are at the intermediate-to-advanced level, and emphasizes the comprehension of Mandarin Chinese television programs. In addition, the fully annotated ensemble (videotapes, audiotapes, textbook, workbook, and CD-ROM) provides authentic journalistic Chinese in printed form and in the rapidly spoken form of radio and TV news broadcasters. In traditional and simplified characters.
Textbook, Paperback, 0-88727-194-4
Workbook, Paperback, 0-88727-210-X
Mac CD-ROM, 0-88727-248-7
VHS Videocassette, 0-88727-195-2
4 Audiocassettes, 0-88727-211-8

Please visit our website at **www.cheng-tsui.com** for information
on these and many other books.

CHENG & TSUI PUBLICATIONS OF RELATED INTEREST

Cheng & Tsui Chinese-Pinyin-English Dictionary for Learners
Wang Huan, Editor-in-Chief
"What makes this dictionary stand out from most others is that it combines…learner features…with [the] sophistication of some of the better pinyin-English dictionaries."
—Journal of the Chinese Language Teachers Association
Paperback, 0-88727-316-5

Across the Straits: 22 Miniscripts for Developing Advanced Listening Skills
By Jianhua Bai, Juyu Sung and Hesheng Zhang
This thoughtfully developed Chinese language program aims to improve the listening skills of intermediate and advanced students. It utilizes recordings of unscripted conversations on a variety of topics, introducing students to social and cultural issues in Taiwan, mainland China, and the U.S. These engaging dialogues are designed specifically to facilitate learning and provoke discussion.
Student's Book (T), Paperback, 0-88727-305-X
Student's Book (S), Paperback, 0-88727-309-2
Transcript of audio portion (T & S), Paperback, 0-88727-307-6
3 Audiocassettes, 0-88727-306-8

Making Connections: Enhance Your Listening Comprehension in Chinese
By Madeline K. Spring
Listening comprehension is a vital part of language learning—but one that is frequently underemphasized in Chinese textbooks except at the advanced levels (see *Across the Straits*, above). *Making Connections* helps fill that gap for beginning and intermediate students. It offers students an early start to develop strategies that will improve their listening comprehension. This set includes 2 audio CDs, containing natural and unrehearsed conversations by native Mandarin Chinese speakers; the book includes extensive written exercises that guide students through the conversations, and focus on particular aspects of the language that surface in each dialogue.
Paperback with 2 Audio CDs (Traditional Char. Ed.), 0-88727-365-3
Paperback with 2 Audio CDs (Simplified Char. Ed.), 0-88727-366-1

Taiwan Today: An Intermediate Course—Revised Second Edition
By Shou-hsin Teng and Lo Sun Perry
This highly regarded intermediate level text brings the customs, traditions, and manners of present-day Taiwan to life. Interactive student participation is encouraged through the use of role-playing techniques, puzzles, and the presentation of stimulating topics for further discussion. In traditional and simplified characters, with pinyin.
Paperback, 0-88727-342-4
3 Audiocassettes, 0-88727-261-4

Please visit our website at **www.cheng-tsui.com** for information
on these and many other books.